Magical Quest
Six Steps to Career Success

Also by Tarin Frances

It's Never Too Late!
The New American

Magical Quest

Six Steps to Career Success

_____

_____

_____

Tarin Frances

Sirene Impressions
Long Beach, CA

Cover photo from ArtToday.com, Inc., 3420 N. Dodge Blvd., Suite F, Tucson, AZ 85716.

Published by Sirene Impressions. Copies of this book are available from: Sirene Impressions, 3712 East First, Long Beach, CA 90803.

ISBN 0-9674449-2-6

The plans you make, your path to choose.
Which road will you take?
You try not to lose, but how will you know?
And who's to judge?
You want the answer, something to show.
No one will tell, 'cause no one can know.

CONTENTS

Magical Quest
Six Steps to Career Success

Introduction

Creating A Life Worth Living

Everyone who asks, receives.
Anyone who seeks, finds.
If only you will knock, the door will open.

Matthew 7:8

Life is a journey, a trip to places, feelings, and experiences unknown. Within this mystery lies the beauty of life. Still we yearn to know which path to take on our journey. "What do I want to do with my life?" teenagers and adults of all ages ask. Your journey can be glorious and grand or miserable and mundane. The choice depends on you. Explore with curiosity the possibilities for your life, embarking on a personal discovery into your soul, and you will see a magnificent selection of options unfold. Your world expands while your frustrations diminish. Together we'll make your experience exciting, worthwhile, productive.

I have selected only the ingredients essential for effective planning. Woven throughout this book are words of encouragement and support combined with simple specific action steps. Finding your niche doesn't have to be difficult. If you follow these steps with enthusiasm and an open mind, you will find valuable assistance in selecting your path. If you commit to completing your goals, you will experience a rewarding career and life. Using the clear, concise steps, you will learn about yourself, discover new ideas, and clarify your goals. We work together: I provide the information on the *how to*; you agree to complete the suggestions offered. It's truly that simple. This process works for people of all ages, educational levels, and ethnic backgrounds. It works for you in any stage of your life:

- student
- recent graduate
- career changer
- satisfied employee
- laid-off employee
- homemaker
- frustrated employee
- short & long-term unemployed
- retiree

Even if you just seek a new challenge in your work life, this guide is for you.

Know however, that career planning, like life, is a process with no definite answers. *The magical answer* doesn't exist. You must uncover your path for yourself. Anticipation, change, and surprise bring vitality to life. Being able to discover your exact future by looking into a crystal ball might take the fun and excitement out of life.

After viewing the title of this book, a colleague said, "Career planning isn't magical; it requires lots of planning and hard work."

It's true that experiencing a worthwhile career does take a lot of effort. It requires time and commitment. Still the journey *can be* magical! Unfortunately, many people don't know how to *create* this magic. Further, many don't even believe it's possible.

Magic is simply the art of creating illusions, orchestrating ordinary moves in an extraordinary manner. Understood this way, magic can produce outstanding results. First, begin to look forward to taking action. Finding a career doesn't have to be arduous and stressful; instead it can be an exciting journey of discovery. Second, shift your mind to expect positive outcomes. Begin to believe that your dreams will come true. With a heightened magical perception, a perception of belief, or a positive self-fulfilling prophecy, our dreams become our reality. Life *appears* as if it were magical. When you believe in your essence and the possibility of things to come, transcending a completely rational state of being, the most amazing results develop. The *magic* is created by our expectations combined with our commitment to complete our goals.

Occasionally, some of my students wish for a fairy godmother to wave her magic wand and make the selection. Others hope for a computer that can receive their career criteria and then print out the perfect choice. Obviously, this is unrealistic and possibly undesirable. Do we really want to be told what to do and exactly how the future will unfold? I think not. Exploring new terrain yields a colorful, fruitful life: the magical quest is creating your special career success.

We all posses the ability to dream and create our ideal career; thus, the *computer* lies inside each of us. Designing the ultimate life is a wonderful lifelong pursuit. For what does our life become if we do not aspire to our true passions? Only we can choose to take some daily action, large or small, towards living the life we desire, toward realizing our dreams.

Some people postpone making a decision by aimlessly working or going to school, avoiding the career issue. These folks plan to choose a career later — hoping it will eventually *hit* them. Usually this approach isn't a good idea, as the choice is left to chance. If you're a student, you may need time to explore before selecting a major by taking a variety of classes, interviewing key individuals, and perhaps volunteering in a field of interest. This allows for personal growth and discovery. You don't need to choose a major right away: instead focus on completing general education courses. If you're re-entering the job market or going through a major life

change, you may also need at least a year or so to search and find yourself again. Trust your instincts as to how much time you need; but, set a realistic date as to when you'll make a selection. You know when you're truly exploring or just procrastinating! Be honest with yourself.

Unfortunately, many people use the default decision-making strategies instead of creating their optimal scenario. By not deciding, they wait for circumstances to direct their lives. This, of course, is making the decision not to decide. Many *wait-until-later* people end up just *falling* into a job, taking whatever comes their way and not really *creating* the life they desire. It's easy to get into a decent job and then settle in. Time passes quickly and soon you've been there for five years while you intended to stay only a year. Staying in a dead-end job or accepting a job solely because it's easy to obtain are examples of default decision-making. Avoid this type of planning at all costs and assist in the creation of your destiny by making a conscious choice to contribute positively to your future. Do not let your circumstances control you.

You will feel power over, and autonomy in, your life when you play an active role in shaping your future. You participate in creating your destiny.

Too often people feel frustrated in their working life because they are out of balance, focusing solely on the facts and figures, the practical aspects, while ignoring their feelings. Others melt so far into their dreams, loosing sight of reality, that they neglect to follow a plan designed to produce results. A balance of the rational and intuitive works best: apply specific plans to dreams. This process is not mystical. Completing a nuts-and-bolts plan and expecting positive outcomes creates a life you cherish. What are some of your desires? Somewhere deep inside your soul, the knowledge of your future waits to be uncovered. Some people know their reasons for living, yet more go through life casually, uncertain of their direction. Their purpose stays buried within.

This guide is designed to provide you with a variety of suggestions that you can use to end the cycle of uncertainty. You will uncover your destiny. Spending time planning your career is a worthwhile investment in your future. You will muster the courage to live passionately in the moment by moving towards the fulfillment of your purpose, making your life heroic.

I have seen thousands of people blossom by creating the path they desire. I, too, went through my own career frustrations, feeling exhausted from trying different college majors and then numerous jobs, until I finally followed the strategies revealed in this book. Ultimately I found my direction, my vocation, my purpose.

Unfortunately, most of us are not taught *how* to find our direction. As children, our fresh, alive, intuitive nature naturally leads us to our passions, but quite often our desires become buried by negative input, and lack of support. This experience leads to self-doubt, stifling of our creativity, and eventually fear. Soon we lose our way. When we reach adulthood, many of us our unsure of our direction. Often many career ideas appeal to us, but we are not sure where to begin. Further, some of us do not want to put effort into creating and committing to our future. Some students, for example, decide to wait until they graduate to *figure it out*. Others begin working without much of a plan, postponing the decision. *I'll figure it out later*, the undecided say. Later becomes a year, then two or three, and soon five years or more pass by. Others believe they don't have time to devote to career and life planning. This is an unfortunate misconception since career planning actually saves time, money, *and* disappointment. Preparing and exploring yourself and possible options greatly reduces feelings of dissatisfaction. Address yourself, your fears and concerns, your desires, and your world flows much more effectively, blossoming sweetly.

In spite of my promise of positive outcomes, many people choose not to explore their career and life-style options. Fear keeps many individuals from defining their goals. Others feel overwhelmed at the idea of selecting one or two or even three careers from hundreds of possibilities. Still others are too comfortable in their current position, although not completely happy. There's no pressure to change. Lack of motivation, low self-esteem, absence of loving support, and insecurity also inhibit people from following their hearts.

Other individuals choose the hit-or-miss career search, trying job after job or major after major, *hoping* to fall into something they like. These people believe it is easier to accept the first option that comes their way than to spend time exploring other careers that might suit them better. Sometimes this strategy works. Usually the hit-or-miss tactic is not effective, and individuals become dissatisfied with their selection. Some begin to look for something different while others stay stuck in mediocre, dissatisfying positions. The frustration cycle begins again.

In many workshops I repeatedly hear conflict from the participants: *What am I going to do with my life? I don't have time to waste. I don't know what I should do!* Perhaps you have heard your own similar inner dialogue droning endlessly, zapping your energy, and diminishing your enthusiasm. Soon you become immobile. Next you're stuck!

Avoid these questions, and instead, commit to the process of exploring. The information in this book will assist you in reducing possible frustrations. You will begin to turn your career and life aspirations into reality by exploring yourself and determining what you want to accomplish.

Making your dreams come true calls for passion, belief, and commitment. Embrace your task! The journey of creating and developing your life is thrilling, invigorating, and enjoyable! At times during your quest, you may feel frustrated and defeated, as self-exploration and career investigation stir up a myriad of feelings. But, if you make a high emotional, intellectual, and physical investment, this process will spur you to increased enthusiasm for your future. Savor and enjoy the results from the career and life choices you make.

You have the power to select a fulfilling, realistic direction bringing joy and happiness. You may face your fears or overcome inhibiting negative emotions and beliefs. Planning calls for courage because you are asked to reveal your true desires and expose your inner self.

Your set of circumstances are unique, yet the process of discovery is similar regardless of your age, education, background, and work history. You might be a college or high school student seeking a college major. Possibly you've achieved a career goal and now desire a new direction. Perhaps you feel very unfocused and seek a clearer path. Or you may have a ho-hum job and seek a new direction. Maybe you have some kind of vision, but feel reluctant to express your interests. You may even know what you want, yet would like to confirm your choice. You may feel tired and worn-out, although with a glimmer of hope. Perhaps you enjoy your current work, but seek alternatives for possible change. Exploring yourself and your options will be beneficial in any of these scenarios, whether you're younger or older, educated or uneducated, skilled or unskilled, positive or negative.

Fear often taints our desires because we worry about failure and possible ridicule from others. If you failed in the past, divulged your passions to someone close and were not supported, you may feel reluctant to begin again. Or, if confusion surrounds your thoughts and feelings about making decisions for your future, you may feel uptight about moving forward. Drop these worries now — or at least while you're contemplating and exploring! Remember the ingredients for success or failure lies in every person. At this moment you posses special talents; and with the right attitude, knowledge, commitment, courage, and love, you can expand your splendid self. Know, however, that you are enough.

Make a pledge to create excellence in your life and you will feel wonderful. Together we'll travel along your path, first fuzzy and confused, then later clear and focused. Clarity and definition about you and your future emerge when you complete the short exercises and assimilate the information given. Have fun with your discoveries! As you learn and grow, your goals may expand or change. Studies show the average person will have from three to five careers within a lifetime. Thus, career planning is a lifelong adventure, so use this book during the various transitions you experience on your journey.

Without direction we wander aimlessly.
Without purpose we question daily.
Without love we yearn for connection.

Searching provides direction.
Uncovering offers purpose.
Discovery brings a connection.
With these we find peace.

THE THREE IMPORTANT QUESTIONS

To advance forward during your discoveries, keep the three questions in the forefront of your concerns. Try on pieces of the answer as we move along.

◆ Who am I?

Of course, you already know on some level who you are. You play many roles, such as: student, employee, manager, daughter, son, parent, dancer, athlete, artist, etc. Yet, you are more than just roles. You encompass hundreds of fine-cut facets; each one representing an adjective or attribute that describes you, shimmering and glowing. See yourself as a beautifully-cut diamond, not an old broken piece of glass. You reflect hundreds of glimmering points of light. Are you creative and original or more matter-of-fact and logical? How do you look at life? Are you good with numbers, math, and science? Perhaps you are compassionate and like to help people. Are you confident and self-assured or more passive and unsure about yourself? Later we will explore your attitude, values, interests, skills, and personality. When you know yourself, you then begin to know what you want. Making a plan becomes easier.

You also have your soul. Your soul is different than your personality or your skills. It is your deep inner self, the part of you that wants to be noticed and nurtured. Your soul speaks to you indirectly through your intuition and your longings. Sometimes our souls act with chaotic, unexpected action. When you listen to the desires of your soul your life feels right.

◆ What's my purpose?

Why will you work? Of course, most of us work for money so we can live; however, there are other reasons to work. What purpose will motivate you to get out of bed and go to work? Do you want to reduce crime, create new ideas, invent technical products, help people, be famous? Each person has a contribution to make to society. The world calls you to give your personal best, making your life meaningful. You will eventually discover your compelling reasons for working — spurring you to get up daily and give the world your gifts, however humble or grand.

♦ How will I get there?

Finally you will create a specific plan leading you to your destination. The more specific your plan, the greater likelihood that you will eventually experience your plan. Goals are ongoing as you adapt and create, manifesting your purpose your goals may change. In the third part of this book we will cover goal-setting, resumé and cover letter writing, job search, and follow-up.

CAREER PLANNER

The step-by-step ideas in this book will assist you in uncovering your thoughts and feelings about you and your career path, ultimately providing you with answers to these three important questions. The *Creative Career Planner* indirectly incorporates the three important questions, illustrating the process. To sculpt a specific path for yourself use, the model below:

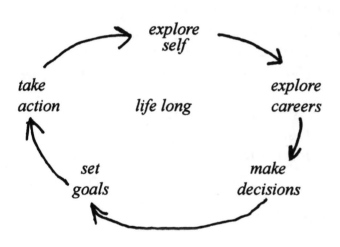

Following these steps provides you with a guide, keeping you on target. Sometimes individuals think they are at a particular step in their planning when actually they have jumped ahead, skipping steps. A student of mine, Janice, came to see me because she was not sure if she should become a nurse or teacher (*make decisions*). I asked her to state ten qualities she wanted in her work (*explore self*). At first Janice did not know what was important to her. Through discussion, however, she discovered her key work values: money and creativity. Then Janice realized neither teaching nor nursing would fit her monetary desires and that nursing would not meet her passion for creativity. She originally selected nurs-

ing and teaching because she traditionally believed they would always be needed in our society, not because they fit with her purpose. Janice had not thoroughly completed the first step, *explore self*; therefore she was not ready for the third step, *make decisions*.

The first chapter in this book, *Belief*, covers attitude, self-esteem, and support systems. The second chapter, *You*, addresses values, interests, skills, and personality, focusing on the question, *Who am I?* The third chapter, *Careers*, includes ideas on how to learn about your career options. The fourth chapter, *Decisions*, discusses integrating choices, making decisions, and addressing the question, *What's my purpose?* The fifth chapter, *Goals*, uncovers ways to sketch your plan and overcome possible road blocks, covering the question, *How will I get there?* The sixth chapter, *Action*, includes employment information, networking, overcoming fears, and motivation.

Career planning is a thrilling adventure of self-discovery. Each chapter provides the necessary pieces for a beautiful journey of surprise, contentment, and success. You may run excitedly at first, then stumble, even crawl, determined to increase the speed of your travels. Ultimately you will soar to a peaceful place in your heart, clear and calm, bright and sparkling. You will create a life worth living.

Commit to completing the exercises and activities in this book. Commit to exploring the possibilities. Commit to you!

Little does one know what lies beneath their exterior until they meet one who is true to their soul.

It is only then that they can discover life's true meaning ... for turning outwardly to find love and nurturing is merely a personal affirmation that it has yet to be discovered within one's self.

Truly then ... the process of learning how to love and nurture self before all else cannot be selfish ... for it must be a daily process ... a process of living life in such a way that the end result is ... you are doing everything you love to do.

How sad it is ... that this lesson has not been learned ... since doing everything I love to do still eludes me, therefore, I have yet to discover how to love and nurture others.

Perhaps this is my greatest lesson to learn.

Your Total Health
Dr. James Masen

Chapter One

BELIEF - Know Your Magical Power

For those who believe, no proof is necessary.
For those who don't believe, no proof is possible.

John & Lyn St. Clair Thomas

Daily, thousands of people talk themselves out of living their dreams, deciding even before attempting them to negate and criticize their ideas. They allow their *internal critic* to dominate their personal conversations. Hope, triumph, and creativity die back immediately to fault, limitations, and proof. In this chapter, I will encourage and urge you to fantasize and believe that your dreams can come true. I will address attitude, belief, self-talk, self-esteem, and support systems, setting the foundation for positive, productive career planning. Without the right attitude and mind-set, planning becomes worthless. Your innocent, open, loving aspects must appear for exciting planning to prevail. Put a smile on your face and dream with enthusiasm.

DEVELOP A POSITIVE ATTITUDE

Do you bounce out of bed, happy, ready to start your day? Or, do you listen to your alarm for the third time and think of reasons why you don't want to get up? Developing a positive attitude is crucial for success in your career. It is a skill you cultivate and practice.

A close friend of mine had a negative attitude and complained about his job, yet he was not willing to change his situation. I said to him, "Why don't you at least change your attitude and be more optimistic for just one month and see what happens?" He accepted my challenge, and during that month, I saw him smile and laugh more. He seemed full of joy. He began to wear suits to work and applied for a new position within his company, eventually being promoted to a job with more responsibility and a higher salary! By seeing the positive in his experiences and surroundings, he noticed the possibilities in his environment that eventually brought him greater happiness. He began to expect success.

Even problems may provide opportunities. In the Chinese culture, the character for *chaos* means *opportunity*. Every situation you encounter gives you the opportunity to improve your skills and add to your life experiences. So-called negative experiences provide the best circumstances for personal growth and increased knowledge. Remember, it is all in your perspective, so look for the good in situations and see the opportunities to learn. Enjoy life. Put zest and spunk into your personality, walk with your head high, radiate vitality and élan. Make an outstanding investment in yourself and cultivate a positive attitude. Being energetic and persevering is an acquired skill, one you can practice. You learn how to create your own party.

Developing a positive attitude simply involves making a slight shift in your perspective. One way, for example, to improve your disposition is to consciously will yourself to focus on something positive. As trite as it sounds, tell yourself to think of the things you're thankful for instead of criticizing your life. This technique reminds me of a reoccurring scenario my father and I used to play out when I was a small girl. I would come into his room late at night after a bad dream and tell him I couldn't sleep because I was scared. He would tell me to think of something good, like ice cream. After some coaxing, I would head back to my room and fall asleep thinking of a huge sundae, with six scoops of strawberry ice-cream, tons of chocolate sauce, mounds of whipped cream, chocolate sprinkles, and a cherry. The scary stuff vanished.

Another technique for clearing the mind of negativity is to write in a journal. Writing, free-flow, with no set topic allows you to release the *garbage thoughts* from your mind. Negative thoughts take up space in your mind without benefiting you. Critical thoughts and worries no longer have power when you bring them out in the open. Julia Cameron suggests in *The Artist's Way* to write for 30 minutes every day. Stating the benefits of journal writing, Ms. Cameron says, "The pages lead us out of despair and into undreamed-of solutions." Clearing out the unwanted makes room for the wanted.

Finally, you might consider keeping a detailed log of your complaints, criticisms, and worries for one week. At the end of the week review your list and evaluate. You may decide that some of your negative mantra thoughts serve no purpose and deserve to be thrown out!

BELIEVE IN YOURSELF

In addition to exuding a positive attitude for productive planning, also believe in your ability to create the results you desire. Could you imagine an Olympic runner stepping up to the start line of a race and saying, "Oh, geeez, I hope I don't trip"? A runner will not win if he or she is worrying about falling instead of focusing on running fast and winning the race. Our minds can focus clearly on only one thought at a time; thus the runner must think of the specific desired goal in order to win. An Olympic winner has undoubtedly practiced a positive internal dialogue with action statements that sup-

port the goal. The winner has decided to win *before* the race begins. Likewise you must decide to have success in your life.

> *Set your sights high, the higher the better.*
> *Expect the most wonderful things to happen, not in the future but right now.*
> *Realize that nothing is too good.*
> *Allow absolutely nothing to hamper you or hold you up in any way.*
>
> Eileen Caddy
> *Footprints on the Path*

Expect to win. Realize your power in the self-fulfilling prophecy and practice creating the expectations you desire.

See yourself achieving the results you want. Believe that you can make worthwhile changes in your life. Envision your fantasy coming true and imagine that it already exists in reality. Consciously putting your desires into your subconscious mind creates a catalyst for change. Your rational mind knows your visualization is not true; however, the new message is so strong it begins to influence your behavior. You will act in the new way because your mind wants to change the contradiction between reality and your new desires.

Remember a time when you felt confident and achieved the results you wanted. For example, maybe you had a successful job interview, planned a special event, completed a large project, spoke assertively to someone, played on a winning team, or made a large purchase. In your experience, you knew without doubt how to act and what to say. You exuded confidence and your attitude correlated directly with your outcome. Whatever you believe to be true will eventually become reality. As Richard Bach in his book *Illusions* wrote, "Know your limitations and they are yours." Therefore, expect the best and you will achieve the results you want as long as you are willing to put forth the effort necessary to complete your goals.

Believe that you are capable and worthy of living your dreams. Why have a doubting belief system? What good does doubt bring you? Faith in your ability to succeed, at the very least, brings you hope and hope keeps you alive. As the Apostle Paul said, "Faith is the substance of things hoped for, the evidence of things not seen." Believe in yourself and surround yourself with positive, motivated people.

CREATE DESIRE

Your expectations for success must be connected with a deep desire for your specific goal. The task of turning your dreams into reality requires energy, commitment, and desire. A profound passion for your vision equates to just love for your vision. However, your aspirations — whatever you decide upon — must be supported with intent; otherwise, they will never take physical form. Be willing to designate time and effort toward completing your goals. If you want to earn a college degree, for instance, you must register for classes, attend regularly, complete your assignments, and study for tests, committing to the process for at least four years. If you want to be a photographer, you must be willing to learn the skills of photography, take thousands of pictures, and endure lots of rejection as you seek a clientele, buyers, and jobs. You take the necessary steps to achieve your goals not because you *have to* but because you *want to.*

Success will be yours if you have enough passion for your goals and are willing to take the steps necessary to make them become reality. You must want your vision with all your heart and soul. You must choose to continue towards your goals, even in the face of rejection and setbacks, even when you feel you can go no further. Often, when we feel like giving up, victory is only a step away. As the saying goes, *It's often the darkest before the dawn.* With the two ingredients *desire* and *willingness,* you will accomplish your goals.

ENJOY THE PROCESS

Next, decide to relish your career search. It is not only the outcome that brings you happiness, but also the experience and the lessons you learn while on your path. In pursuing your goals, focus on exploring and savoring what happens each moment. Experiencing your travels is similar to experiencing the development of a child. Once a child is born, the excitement is not for him or her to hurry and grow up. Instead enjoyment comes from watching, feeling, and loving the baby while he or she grows and develops throughout life. Your reward in achieving goals occurs continuously from your encounters while you travel, not solely from arriving at your destination.

I said to a friend of mine who had played professional football, "What was it like to catch the ball and score a touchdown?" He said, "It was short, all over in an instant." The real rewards for him were in the whole sport: playing the game, practicing, knowing his teammates, traveling, growing, and learning about life. Yes, it was exciting for him to win; still, the touchdown was only a flash, not the full picture. In short, the journey was his reward. So above all, enjoy the experience of learning about yourself and your options. Once you do make a decision, focus on the beauty of learning while on your path. It's easy to become frustrated about not having an answer, yet for the time being you must allow yourself to feel O.K. about not knowing. During the middle phase of this exploratory process, you may begin to feel even more confused and unsure than you do this moment. Relax. This is precisely how discovery unfolds — you expand, examine, and ponder yourself and options and that may seem confusing. But through the process you begin to feel confident about eliminating possibilities because you're now clear about who you are and what you want. (Remember, *Who am I?* and *What's my purpose?*) Many old choices may be thrown out as new ones emerge. During this shuffle, the possibilities grow and you may feel more uncertain. Hang on when this happens. It's natural, appropriate. Use this discomfort as a way to practice accepting uncertainty, especially since it's a part of life!

CREATE HARMONIOUS THOUGHTS

What you think of yourself affects your actions and your career path. Your power lies in your internal dialogue. Sometimes we criticize ourselves without reason, causing us to not take action. Studies have shown that the person we talk to the most is ourself and that for most people at least 75% of our self-talk is negative. Thoughts like, "Oh, I couldn't do that!" "I'm so fat," "I can't learn that," or "I'm so bad at..." erode our self-confidence. Begin to replace your negative internal dialogue with positive thoughts. Increase the probability of experiencing success by increasing your positive self-talk.

Your mind continuously puts ideas into your psyche. In some areas of your life you may feel very confident and assured, while self-doubt may dominate other areas. Remember that what you believe to be true often in fact happens. For example, if you tell yourself it is time to leave an inadequate job and work in a more rewarding career, and you fully believe in the idea, you will take steps towards achieving your goal. Conversely, if you are afraid of being trapped and not able to change, you will make choices that support your fearful beliefs. Fill your subconscious with images you want in your life.

In addition to negative thoughts, we often experience conflicting or opposing thoughts. For example, I might say, "I hate my job, and I need a change!" Then in the next instant I say, "I can't change because I can't afford to re-train!" Other conflicting thoughts might occur in your relationships. You might say, "I'm so sick of my relationship and the way my partner treats me! I want to leave it now." In the next breath you might say, "But I can't leave because my kids will suffer and it will devastate me financially!" Again, conflicting beliefs. Aside from being contradictory, both of these examples give only two outcomes, stay or go, when actually a multitude of solutions exist. Developing compatible thoughts allows for an abundance of ideas to unfold naturally.

If you have opposing thoughts, reduce your internal struggle by formulating harmonious perceptions. Challenge yourself to adapt a more open belief system. First, examine your thoughts and beliefs and determine if conflicts occur in your internal script. If there are contradictions, then generate new resolutions about your career and life style. Your resolution statement then becomes an *affirmation*. A statement of behaviors or things you would like to experience or have in your life. Below are some examples of changed thought patterns with new affirmations:

Conflicting Thoughts

"I can't work at this job anymore; I hate it!"
"I can't leave my job because I have don't have experience in anything else and I don't have time to retrain!"

Anxiety

Resolution

New Thought

"I have a positive work situation that fits naturally with my lifestyle and financial needs."

Conflicting Thoughts

"I want to stay in school, but I don't have a major and enough money to pay for it!"
"I'm so confused!"

Anxiety

Resolution

New Thought

"I am a successful student with enough resources to pay for college."
"I am in the process of exploring my options and on my way to knowing my destiny."
"My future unfolds easily and naturally."

Conflicting Thoughts

"I finally have a college degree, but no job."
"All the jobs are low paying and I don't even like the few jobs that are available."

Anxiety

Resolution

New Thought

"I am exploring exciting career options that will satisfy me personally and monetarily."

Conflicting Thoughts

"I'm sick of my relationship; I can't be in it any more."
"I can't leave my relationship because I won't be able to support myself and I'll be lonely."

Anxiety

Resolution

New Thoughts

"I am in a healthy loving relationship."
"I have a career that is financially and emotionally satisfying."

.

Conflicting Thoughts

"I like my job but my salary is too low!"
"I'm at the top of the pay scale and won't make anymore money. I can't leave the company because I'll retire soon and then lose all my retirement money."

Anxiety

Resolution

New Thought

"I have work that is satisfying and meets my monetary and security needs."

Conflicting Thoughts

"I want a career where I can be creative."
"I can't work in a creative field because there are no jobs and no money. It's too competitive, I'll never be hired!"

Anxiety

Resolution

New Thoughts

"I work in an exciting, creative career that meets my monetary and security needs."
"I have a career that is financially and emotionally satisfying."

Clashing inner expressions immobilize productive action. Ask yourself if you have inharmonious thoughts. Explore these feelings. Next you'll write some new ideas.

COMMIT TO YOURSELF

Create new affirmations. The suggestions in this section will assist you in forming congruent affirmations designed to reduce your anxiety level. Use the previous examples as guidelines when creating your new thoughts. Write your affirmations in the present as if they were already happening in your life. Your rational mind knows that your new goal statement isn't true, yet your subconscious mind begins to believe the new idea. This causes anxiety because of the disparity between your thoughts and reality, so your subconscious mind begins to coax you into taking action to relieve the tension and incongruent feelings. Your action moves in the direction of the new thoughts that you've programmed your mind to believe. Your behavioral changes fit with your new affirmations.

To assist you in identifying and recreating your inner dialogue complete the following steps listed below:

1. Write on a piece of paper your current inner dialogue.
2. Identify any opposing or negative thoughts.
3. Explore what you would really like.
4. Brainstorm for new ideas that feel right and do not antagonize each other.
Make your affirmations positive and in the present tense, as if they have already occurred. Avoid statements such as, "I am going to ..." or "I hope to ..." instead write "I choose to ...," "I am ...," "I have ..." or "I will ..."
5. Use the above examples as guidelines to help you generate new thoughts for yourself.

6. Write each new thought on an index card and tuck in your purse or wallet.
7. Consciously replace your old thoughts with these new thoughts.
8. Read the cards daily until they become a part of you and your inner dialogue.

This process takes practice and time because you are developing new skills, new thought processes for yourself. You may feel anxious or out of control while you change — this is a normal feeling! Initially, your behaviors may not match your thoughts. Yet with a commitment to change, you will begin to act differently. You will feel more balanced and calm once you adopt these fresh concepts into your belief system. Trust in the process and know that changes can occur smoothly and naturally. Your life will begin to form congruently with your new thoughts. Solidification of your changes occurs gradually and requires time. Be patient with yourself. As your life progresses naturally and positively in the manner you desire, repeat the steps above and elaborate with additional positive principles.

While exploring yourself and forming your career plans, remember that your inner thinking influences your life. If you feel blocked during your planning, re-examine your belief system and your internal dialogue.

CHALLENGE NEGATIVE MESSAGES

Believe you are capable and worthy of experiencing the career and life you want. Often we hear discouragement rather than encouragement. Programming from our surroundings greatly affects our level of self-esteem, so notice the input you receive and have received from others. The notion that *birds of a feather flock* together is true. Notice the people in your life and how they influence you. We tend to become like the people around us. Determine if the people you associate with most are good for you, and, if not, begin to select new friends who share your similar positive outlook on life.

Continuously we are programmed by outside forces that we often internalize as our own. Statements from parents are sometimes negative. Messages from society teach us to conform to certain behaviors and beliefs. For example, a man is sometimes considered strange or assumed to be gay if he sells cosmetics. Stereotypes and prejudices are taught overtly, as well as in subtle ways with words, silence, gestures, and facial expressions. Various forms of media, such as movies, television, newspapers, and magazines reinforce stereotypes. Below are some prejudicial beliefs you may have learned, but are usually inaccurate:

- Women should not be engineers or police officers.
- People in charge of a company should be white, not black.
- Men are better leaders than women.
- Being an artist is not a real job.

- You're nothing without a college degree.
- Power and money are the reasons why we work.
- It's too risky to start a business.
- Blacks are the only good singers and dancers.
- You'll never be hired if you go into a creative field.
- Asians are always good in math and engineering.
- All minorities take advantage of affirmative action.
- Women are too emotional.
- Whites are smarter than blacks.
- Men who cry are wimps.
- You're only a little fish in a big pond.
- If you have a tattoo, you are irresponsible.
- Gays should stay with their own kind.

Avoid buying into negative conditioning and stereotyping. If you accept any of the statements listed above or any other limiting beliefs, open your mind and look at the topic from a fresh vantage point. Imagine your life with different circumstances. Through this process perhaps a new perspective unfolds, bringing you greater insight into yourself and those individuals different from you. The shackles of prejudice have caused timid, repressed human growth. Seeds for human growth are stifled by the imagined block of prejudice covering the light of truth. Narrow viewpoints limit your outcomes.

Allow yourself to see unlimited potential for yourself *and* others. Examine your self-concept and stereotypical beliefs and determine if you restrict yourself in any way. Do your beliefs hold you back? Have beliefs from others kept you from following your own unique path? Do society's standards influence the choices you make? Feel capable of accomplishing anything you can imagine. Powerfully shape your image in the direction *you* desire.

Unfortunately, many people have limited thinking. Individuals sometimes believe they are not from the *right* gender, ethnic group, or economic class. Or they think they do not posses certain qualities, such as high intelligence or good organizational skills, which are often necessary for a particular career. If a woman wants to own and manage a business, for example, but believes she is not independent and skilled enough or the right gender, she may sabotage her idea even before beginning. Think of the person who wants to go to college but views this goal as one for smarter people. Maybe you long to be well known and admired, yet cannot imagine yourself in this role. Determine if you hold yourself back. If you have negative ideas, *why* do you think in this fashion? Expand your thinking to be congruent with your dreams. Create positive affirmations to play in your mind, using techniques offered in the previous section. Journal writing also offers assistance for changing biased thoughts. Explore your perceptions through free-flow writing, commenting on yourself and your actions. Respect yourself and your particular strengths and talents. Being able to disregard stereotypes and negative messages is a sign of high self-esteem. If necessary, begin to build a more open-minded belief system.

If your feel overwhelmed with this section, consider seeking counseling. These suggestions are not a panacea for pain or unresolved childhood issues, but merely one way to strengthen your motivation and desire for achieving goals.

DEVELOP A HIGH SELF-ESTEEM

Only you can measure your level of self-love. Most of us at one time or another feel insecure about our capabilities and talents. Usually, however, a person with high self-esteem feels good about him or herself the majority of the time. Your ultimate goal is to love yourself unconditionally (and hopefully others as well). Self-love is contagious and allows you the freedom to love others without judgment and expectations. Your level of self-esteem greatly affects your career choices, your ability to transform and live your dreams. For instance, if you do not value yourself, you may select a low-paying career that is not challenging; and then perhaps feel disgruntled, treating others poorly because you are not treating yourself with respect. Your frustration mounts.

Conversely, a healthy self-esteem gives you the necessary confidence to select a field that fulfills you and meets most of your desires. We are only capable of giving out that which we have inside; therefore, you want positive, loving feelings inside of you. Achieving goals in life requires risk, combined with continuous effort. When you feel good about yourself, you have the courage to plunge enthusiastically with full force into this game called life. Your ability to risk is directly related to how you feel. Increase your self-love by implementing the following suggestions:

1. Take pride in your appearance. Groom and dress with care to look your best; make every day special in its own way.
2. Live healthy: exercise regularly, get sufficient rest, and eat proper foods. Don't abuse your body with drugs or alcohol.
3. Observe your own *self-talk*. Speak optimistically and encouragingly to yourself. Do not be unnecessarily hard on yourself. Be gentle with yourself.
4. Surround yourself with positive people. *Avoid*, like the plague, critical and unmotivated people. Leave negative environments.
5. Be honest, yet tactful, with yourself and others. Express yourself without excuses.
6. Create relationships with people who support you, giving and receiving respect.
7. Adopt a role model. Emulate this person's positive qualities and actions.
8. Be assertive. Say how you feel, *when worthwhile*. (Use *I* statements, instead of *you* blaming statements. For instance say, "I feel frustrated when..." instead of "You make me angry when...") Remember, your *feelings* are worthy of being heard.
9. Read inspirational messages, quotes, stories, and books.
10. Visualize yourself having the kind of lifestyle you desire. (Tip — cut pictures from magazines of things you want to experience or own and put around your home.)
11. Give freely to yourself and others. For example, give a gift for no reason or help with a special need or project.
12. Develop a sense of humor. Be able to laugh at yourself!
13. Be curious.
14. Be a learner and an explorer: read, attend seminars and classes, take lessons, visit new places, join community groups, anything!
15. Work towards achieving your goals on a regular basis. Complete the commitments you make to yourself and to others.

Quite possibly suggestion #15 may be the most important item on the list. Caroline Myss, an intuitive healer, states that we "build our self-esteem by doing things." Cultivating our will may be the number one self-esteem builder. Completing productive tasks makes us stronger. Doing what we were called to do also makes us stronger. Working towards achieving a goal step-by-step increases our stamina and skill level, which in turn increases our confidence. By completing small goals, we begin to see results; we have proof that we can do it. This builds our commitment *muscle*. Committing to and actually doing something consistently, such as working out three times a week or studying two hours a day, increases this muscle. As a best friend of mine says, "Just keep moving!" By accomplishing, we begin a positive cycle of achievement — the *snowball effect* in action. Focus on the baby steps, lay a brick a day, and soon your house will be built — almost appearing magically! You become the person you imagined, fully living your potential.

Remember, however, that you are glorious right now. Change is only necessary if you deem it so. In addition love from others benefits your self-esteem, providing fuel to move you into action. Your main desire for success must come from you. The following quote summarizes the benefits of self acceptance.

> *One has just to be oneself. That's my*
> *basic message.*
> *The moment you accept yourself as*
> *you are, all burdens,*
> *all mountainous burdens simply*
> *disappear.*
> *Then life is a sheer joy, a festival of*
> *lights.*
>
> Bhagwan Shree Rajneesh
> *The Sound of One Hand Clapping*

Cultivate a belief in you. Your passion and desire to create a better life provides the drive to stay committed to your goals, even when you feel like giving up.

LISTEN TO YOUR INTUITION

While you shape your career, listen to your inner voice. This voice is the knowledge inside of you that gives you direction. It truly is your internal compass. When a woman acts on her inner voice, she may say, "I followed my intuition." A man, however, may say, "I followed my gut." Your intuition is something you know without knowing how you know it. *The American College Dictionary* defines intuition as, "direct perceptions of truths, fact, etc., independently of any reasoning process; pure untaught knowledge." Another way I heard intuition described was by a darling four-year-old girl, who would say the most amazing things, like many young children. One time she was asked how she knew the answer to something. She replied, "I was born to know it." We are *all* "born to know it!" As adults, however, our intuition often ends up buried in our subconscious because of negative conditioning, over-analysis, and fear. Following your intuition provides unlimited resources for personal growth, empowering your soul. Extensive, redundant analyzing becomes unnecessary because intuition continuously leads you to your next right step.

If you want to enhance your intuitive skills, make time to relax and find the calm place within your being. Sit perfectly still for at least five minutes, twice a day, observing and focusing *only* on your breathing. This simple exercise causes you to turn off the continuous chatter and self-talk playing in your head and allows new ideas to surface from your subconscious into your conscious thought. Meditating eventually spurs you to be more aware of your internal wisdom, your center, your gut. Other activities such as writing, exercising, or singing offer similar benefits by allowing creative and intuitive responses to surface. Activities with repetition can provide an opportunity for your intuition and creativity to surface. By following your inner signals, you will begin to hear, feel, and know your intuitive voice. Through practice you will learn to select the right answers for yourself. Most people have feelings or hunches about events in their lives, although they do not always trust this knowledge. If you have shut down your wise internal cues, rediscover your instinctive powers, by incorporating some type of activity suggested. Then begin to practice *following* the inner guidance you receive — soon your ancient knowing will return.

In case you are skeptical of using a nebulous resource like intuition, experiment first with this concept on small happenings in your life, such as intuitively selecting which elevator door will open or who will be on the line when your telephone rings. As you test and practice the use of your hidden power on insignificant happenings, slowly incorporate this knowledge into more important everyday life situations, building your confidence. Making a decision based on intuition may require a leap of faith with no *proof* to support your selection. Sometimes the intuitive choice seems illogical. Following your gut instinct *appears* to require an element of risk, yet the opposite is actually true because your intuition is always right for you. A previous student of mine, Carol, a mother in her early forties, was on a weekend retreat away from her children. On Sunday morning, the day she had planned for rest and relaxation, she awoke very early for no apparent reason, dressed, and began her trip home. Her friends on the trip wondered why she was leaving early and not staying for more fun. At the time, Carol did not know the reason either; however, she knew that she was *supposed* to head home. When she arrived home she learned that one of her children had been in a car accident and needed her. Clearly, this was Carol's sixth sense providing her with information, even though there were no facts to support her action. She used knowledge to her advantage by willingly taking a leap of faith and trusting her instinct.

The trick is to truly know your internal voice and not confuse it with wishful desires or logic. Intuition offers security when the skill is honed, although this cannot be proven at the time. We may know when intuition is right in hindsight. Often this proof comes from those times we *knew* what decision to make but instead ignored our intuition and were then stuck with an unsatisfactory outcome. A friend of mine did just that when she got married for the first time. Her fiancé had lots of great qualities — fun personality, intelligence, great career, etc. — but *something* told her not to proceed with the marriage. She did anyway since there really was no reason to not move forward, after all she was in love. Three years later she got divorced. This is often the case with intuition, a nagging doubt that something isn't right; yet it can feel risky to follow when the choice logically seems right. My friend was probably afraid to let go of what she had, fearful that something better might not come. But we must ask the question, *Is something better than nothing?* I think not. Stay true to your feelings, sometimes it's all you have.

Throughout history many great people have followed their hunches when seeking solutions, making discoveries, or deciding actions. Orville and Wilbur Wright listened to their intuition and followed their inspiration by pursuing their idea for an airplane. People thought they were crazy and said, "It can't be done; people don't fly." The Wright brothers persevered, believing in their dream as they relentlessly continued to perfect their work until eventually they created an airplane that would fly. I encourage you to tune into your own hunches. The messages you receive while exploring your career options will help you eventually select a career. Feelings of knowing occur in all areas of life.

TAKE RISKS

How many times have you held yourself back because you feared the unknown? Superior achievements have happened in this world because people dared to risk. You can do the same. Some of your dreams may require you to override your fears about competition, ability, money, and family expectations. Prepare to make heroic choices. Everyone has fear, the risk taker feels this fear and then acts anyway. Heroes do what they know they must, in spite of their worry and anxiety — this can be you.

Fears come in all sizes and shapes. A hero is not just a military leader in the heat of battle or a fire fighter rescuing a baby from a burning building. A hero is someone faced with a choice, often for good or bad, honesty or silence, growth or stagnation, who then chooses that which is right and usually more difficult. It's easy to take the low ground. These *choices* appear every day of our life; it's just that we often don't pay attention to the opportunities for risk taking. They may be emotional, intellectual, or physical. A risk is anything that you think of doing, but talk yourself out of because you worry that you might feel foolish or uncomfortable. Risks are personal. Perhaps expressing your opinion at work or school might be a risk. Telling another person how you really feel about them might also be a risk. Trying a new sport, singing to a group, or going somewhere exotic may also be risks. Only you know what would be a risk for you.

Not risking can cut you out of the fun in life. At my birthday party this year many of my family and friends were toasting me, telling stories about our lives together. It was marvelous fun. Later a few of us danced, whooping it up, just having a gas. A couple of my friends looked on whispering to themselves. I waved for them to come and join in. My girlfriend said, "I can't, I feel so intimidated to dance around such good dancers." In my mind this was ridiculous! My friend has just cut off her own freedom to experience something she deeply enjoys because of the fear that she would look foolish. This friend possibly didn't give a toast for the same reasons. The end result is that we all lost. I didn't receive her love and involvement; she didn't receive the joy of doing.

Sometimes we are so unaware that we don't even know the areas where we have cut ourselves off from growing and experiencing life to its fullest. We become very comfortable within our *bubble*. You may want to shake up your perceptions by asking yourself the really honest questions: *What are my true feelings? Do I express my feelings openly and honestly? Do I enjoy what I do? Do I hold myself back? Are there things that I would like to do, but am not doing? What are my deepest fears?* Asking these questions will help you see beyond your comfort zone.

Favorable change occurs when you learn more about yourself, overcome your fears, and take action. Personal growth requires the ability to let go and trust that you will benefit from your new behaviors. Experiencing something new in life or questioning your beliefs and attitudes may cause you to feel vulnerable and out of control. You may feel nervous to act. But to just think and worry about what you want only creates more fear and self-doubt. To build confidence, focus on your challenge and think of other admirable risk takers. When I was in college, a teacher of mine showed a film about a 65-year-old woman who decided to master her fear of heights by learning to skydive. After viewing the film on overcoming fear, I committed to eventually skydive as a catalyst to work more aggressively through other challenging areas in my life.

Recently I felt myself stagnating, so I decided to finally follow through on my commitment to skydive. I felt petrified at the thought of jumping out of a plane and free-falling thousands of feet. Hours before jumping, I suffered tremendous anxiety. I was convinced that free-falling would be unbearable and that only after the chute opened would I enjoy the ride. I created a very frightening, *imagined* scenario for myself. Once out of the plane and in the air, however, my fears vanished and I felt exhilarated and thrilled. The experience was wonderful! The adrenaline rush and awesome view of the earth from my vantage point were breathtaking. I felt so peaceful as I floated to the earth. My anticipated fears and anxiety before the jump were much worse than the activity itself: my experience was nothing like my imagination.

Our minds are very powerful. We have a tremendous ability to imagine possible outcomes that inevitably are far more negative than the reality. Since skydiving was an unknown activity for me, I created ridiculous possibilities of failure, far worse than the actual experience of jumping. As you embark upon the task of turning your dreams into reality, know that you may be producing unnecessary fears for yourself. As you learn to reduce your anxiety and fears by *doing* that what you fear, new experiences will become easier and more enjoyable.

> *I must not fear. Fear is the mind killer.*
> *Fear is the little-death that brings*
> *total obliteration. I will face my fear. I*
> *will permit it to pass over me and*
> *through me. And when it has gone*
> *past I will turn my inner eye to see its*
> *path. Where fear has gone there will*
> *be nothing. Only I will remain.*

> Frank Herbert

When I feel anxious about a particular situation, I make every effort to change my fearful self-talk into calming, soothing affirmations of success. Challenge yourself to expand and grow into a more relaxed, confident, and happy individual, by overcoming your fears. Let yourself go so you can toast and dance, experiencing the rhythm of life!

SEEK A NURTURING SUPPORT SYSTEM

Making transitions in life requires support from others. Create a loving and encouraging circle of friends and family in your life who will encourage you to achieve your highest potential. Appreciate their support and provide the same for them as well. Life can be tough, filled with obstacles, so you want those closest to you to provide those "good going!" responses with pats on the back. Life's too short to listen to negativity and questioning of your judgment and choices. If you are around people who question your ideas and plans, especially if your path is different from theirs, select new environments and social settings. Sometimes people say things such as, "That can't be done; it's too difficult." or "What do you want to do that for?" or "That's not a real job!" Disregard any negative statements you hear. Believe in yourself and be around productive, supportive, and upbeat people.

Quite often criticism comes from jealousy. For instance, if you start planning a career change, the miserable people you work with, who have been in the same job for years, may become your loudest critics. Likewise, parents sometimes belittle their children's (adult children, too!) ideas because they themselves lack confidence, regret their own choices, or find their children's interests so different from their own. This type of response can be detrimental to your development, so stay away from negative people.

If faced with criticism of your dreams or lack of faith from loved ones, diplomatically express how you feel, laugh at their ludicrous statements, or leave the room! Depending on your situation, you may need time to work through any negative feelings towards the situation. Eventually, you will chuckle at the thought of someone else's opinion controlling your emotions and life. You will begin to take pessimistic comments you hear in stride and forget them. If you become upset, know that you have allowed another person's opinion of you to become more important than your opinion of yourself. Individuals who treat others with cynicism and judgment have often been treated in this same disrespectful fashion. At some time in their lives their ideas were squelched. Disassociate from negative people and learn to tune out gloomy messages from others. Remember: negativity breeds negativity.

Your exploratory journey will be much easier if you have confident, encouraging people around you who are open, eager, receptive, non-judgmental, and patient. As you explore, build your own inner strength and seek out caring people who validate your endeavors. To survive, human beings need love from each other, so send encouraging love messages to people near and far by telephoning, writing, e-mailing, or getting together. Sometimes just thinking a joyful thought can help create a loving atmosphere.

Knowing others who nourish, strengthen, and love you is vital to your success. Vicki, my brother's wife, went back to school and enrolled in two classes: *Art Appreciation* and *Study Skills*. At 10:00 p.m., the night before her finals, Vicki commented that she hadn't done her reading or prepared for her final exams. My brother Steve could easily have ignored her, told her not to worry, and gone to sleep. Instead he made her get up and pull an all-nighter. Steve showed Vicki what to study, quizzed her on her material, and brought her snacks and coffee. Steve's actions demonstrated support. Nurture relationships with people who put positive energy into your life, and give the same to them as well. Ask for help if necessary.

DISCUSS YOUR JOURNEY

Before you begin your planning, explain to the special people in your life how you feel and why you are exploring yourself and your life. Ask them to be patient and to provide you with the freedom and time you need to discover at your own pace. Ask them to be non-judgmental and supportive of you in your quest for a more fulfilling life. Communicate your feelings and love to your friends and family and thank them for believing in you.

Talk about how your investigation may affect you and in turn your loved ones because of the commitment you are making to your life. Explain the process and let them know that this takes a *minimum* of six months to search, select, and prepare for a career. Depending on your age, experience, and interests you may need *years* for search and preparation.

Discuss how your various options may affect your relationships and lifestyle. The process of uncovering your direction and purpose adds new dimensions and ignites positive feelings in relationships. Discuss with your loved ones your preferences, life goals, and how you will help each other during this transitional time.

If you are a young adult with parents concerned about your future, let them know that you're exploring and would delight in receiving their support and encouragement. If you feel pressure from them to make a decision, request they ease up on their need for you to have a plan immediately. Ask them to be patient. Reiterate how the process works and that you need time to explore. If you're just starting college or will be soon, the freshman and sophomore years are for savoring and sampling. In fact most freshman change their majors many times. There's plenty of general education to complete before you select a career or major. You are just beginning to learn about careers and options. Over 50% of incoming students are undecided, so accept your feelings of uncertainty — they're natural. Purge any self-doubt and know that you can be successful in many careers. What you choose now need not be forever. Reduce any anxiety by realizing that you help create your destiny. Explore at your own pace — without procrastinating, of course!

If you are making a career change or re-entering the job market, let your spouse, friends, or family know that you want to receive acceptance and encouragement. You'll have less time for daily tasks and socializing, so any assistance they can provide to lessen the burden of these responsibilities will help you greatly. You may struggle with life values and the trade-offs between time, security, and money — searching for harmony. Set your worries free; while you explore, imagine that you are 20 years old again. Adopting this perspective allows your mind to freely receive a wide variety of ideas without judgment and tension. Give yourself this gift. Say to yourself the loving things you would say to someone in your shoes. Many people will now have from three to five careers within their lifetime, so realize that you're not *too old* to make a change. Many adults don't even bother to explore what they might want; they *still don't know what they want to do with their lives!* You are exploring, so give yourself a hand.

Major life transitions bring about a myriad of emotions and issues. Our stress level increases. Transitional times in life such as selecting and training for a career, graduating from high school, moving out on your own, breaking up a relationship, meeting someone new, getting married, having a baby, getting divorced, surviving a catastrophe, and loosing a loved one cause turmoil and emotions from sorrow to elation, sometimes even chaos. The ebb and flow of life takes us on these journeys. We feel excited and out of balance. We want to laugh and cry. Both contentment and frustration overwhelm us. Eventually we merge the new with the old, becoming balanced again; however, this time as more actualized human beings.

We are often uncomfortable with these times of change, yet this is the process of life. Without change we cease to grow and without growth we stop living. *Live* spelled backwards is *evil.* Perhaps when we aren't living we are evil.

Look around and you will begin to see other people younger and older living their dreams. A recent Ann Landers column featured letters from older medical school students ranging from 40 to 65 years old. One 65-year-old man wrote that it took him three years to finally be accepted at a medical school. Tenacity, my friend! Other people are living their dreams, and so can you. Remember in most cases, it's never too late to be what you could've been.

The next chapter involves exploring yourself and selecting possible options. Keep your mind open. Relax, while we explore the best subject in the world: *You!*

If I hope, then I will try, and if I try then, I will achieve; if I achieve, then I will flourish becoming all that I am meant to be.

For in my birth I knew my path and in my childhood I played my song.
But I have forgotten why I am here.

So I move, step-by-step, closer to my destiny open and free.
Fresh and alive.
Ready to take on the new dawning, ready to swim in the sea of love, able to cherish that which appears.

I am open like a child, adventuresome like a teen, wise like an adult.

Revelations come as I explore, truth appears as I commit. My heart blossoms as I trust more fully. The Divine Love offers solace when I am unsure and appreciation when I am strong.

I do not know where my road shall lead, this matters not; as a traveler I freely accept my journey knowing that...

If I hope, then I will try, and if I try then I will achieve; if I achieve, then I will flourish and become all that I am meant to be.

Chapter Two

YOU - Sparkling, Spectacular You!

A human being is a single being.
Unique and unrepeatable.

John Paul II

Your essence encompasses a myriad of wonderful characteristics, beliefs, and ideas intermingled to form you. By knowing yourself — your values, interests, personality, and skills, you then have the ingredients necessary to uncover your path. Discovering who you are and what you want your life to represent provides a direction for your working life. People wanting to help improve the social ills of society go in a different direction than people seeking power. Exploring yourself gives you valuable insight into knowing what will ignite your spirit.

Open yourself up to a variety of possibilities. Risk! Explore! In this chapter you will become reacquainted with yourself, activating your mind into carving your chosen path. Imagine yourself as the director of your own life movie, visualizing each scene, selecting the theme, action, and location for your life. As mentioned in the first chapter, *Explore Self* is the first step of our *Creative Career Planner* — knowing *you*, the main character, is a crucial element for a good show. At this moment your goal is to simply *explore yourself*. Do not make a decision — this will come later. You will find out what you like and what's important to you. Your main task during this exploratory phase is to determine what you like and want, asking yourself the same questions over and over: *"Do I like this? Does this seem appealing to me? Is this interesting?"* Later we will consider the practicalities of options and goals. For now, anything is possible — there is no limit; you can be anything you want. Don't consider competition, training, possibility for success, etc. Your only criteria for judging during this chapter is *like: Do I like such and such?* You may already know many of your preferences. Your task is to become keenly aware of you and your needs. Focus solely on our first main question: *Who am I?* For the moment, disregard any other concerns and feelings unrelated to this question, as these are addressed in upcoming chapters.

Consider first what wishes you have hidden, folded in your innocent memory from sweet days when you exposed yourself, fresh and true. Many hopes have been blown away or buried. Now, you must courageously uncover your tender desires. We all have a part to play while on earth; thus, you must discover and fulfill your destiny. Your journey awaits. Businesses wait for you to start. Shows wait for you to perform. College degrees wait for you to earn. A teacher for the deaf, senator, book publisher, sports commentator, record producer, cartoonist — all wait for you to be. The choice is yours. Unleash your potential. Roll away from apathy. Dream a little. Dream a lot.

Temporarily focus only on who you are and what you like. Don't worry about finding a long detailed answer for the question *Who am I?* For now, just find small parts of your answer; eventually each piece will lead to your larger answer. As you explore, keep a list of your *wants* and *don't wants*. Don't worry about coming up with a job title at this point. On the following page, under *Pieces of My Dream* jot down your preferences at this moment. You might list such items as, *I want to help people* or *I don't want to have a set schedule*. No concern is too small. What type of environment do you prefer? How much money would you like to make? What drives you crazy? How much drive and motivation do you have to work towards a goal? Consider what brings you passion, lights your fire! This exercise, and others, will assist you in uncovering your motives, desires, and preferences. Return to your *Pieces of My Dream*, adding and changing when necessary and you, the precious, sparkling jewel, will be revealed.

And a man said, Speak to us of Self-Knowledge.
And he answered, saying:
Your hearts know in silence the secrets of the
days and the nights.
But your ears thirst for the sound of your heart's
knowledge.
You would know in words that which you have
always known in thought.
You would touch with your fingers the naked
body of your dreams.
And it is well you should.
The hidden well-spring of your soul must needs
rise and run murmuring to the sea;
And the treasure of your infinite depthswould be
revealed to your eyes.
But let there be no scales to weigh your unknown
treasure;
And seek not the depths of your knowledge with
staff or sounding line.
For self is a sea boundless and measureless.

The Prophet
Kahlil Gibran

PIECES OF MY DREAM

What I want   What I don't want

Finding your calling requires time, patience, and effort. During a period of change we often feel out of control because an unknown future lies ahead. We believe that knowing our future will bring us comfort which is partially true. Yet, selecting prematurely brings even more angst if the career is not the best fit. We do not know exactly what steps to take. This uncertainty causes us to feel uncomfortable, so we seek ways to ease our discomfort, sometimes making hasty decisions. Therein lies the paradox: to live a full life is to live with uncertainty; to eliminate uncertainty eliminates the spirit of life. The only thing certain about life is change. Thus, if you are not progressing forward in life, you are stagnating; because life is about transitions, adjusting, and growing. Give your all to your passions. George Bernard Shaw expresses the point this way, "I want to be thoroughly used up when I die. Life is no brief candle to me; it is a sort of splendid torch which I get a hold of for the moment and I want to make it burn as brightly as possible before handing it on to future generations." Once you accept the fact that life continuously evolves, then as you hold your torch, you will relish the opportunities that come your way. Your focus shifts. Instead of trying to control everything in life, you develop an accepting attitude, open and willing for change. Make transformation your norm, find comfort in the flux of life. You will create a flexible career plan for yourself, doing what feels right at each moment and directed towards a goal. Feel capable of achieving your most magnificent dreams!

CREATING YOUR MAGIC
Getting Rid of Past Demons

As you explore yourself, keep in mind your true desires. The words of Kahlil Gibran in his book *The Prophet* summarize the purpose of work: "Work is love made visible." What really makes you happy? How might your love manifest itself as work? You may feel frightened to reveal your spirit and your persona. Fantasize just a little. What do you find? What do you love to do? Have courage and dream. Dream big. Your dreams will be accepted by the Universe. Envisioning your future keeps you alive, excited, and vibrant. Follow the path of your soul, your yearnings, and happiness will bathe your body. Your work becomes your contribution to the world. As an extra reward, success will surround you. With all the clamor in our society, you may not hear your own wishes, so begin to listen carefully to your intuition and your heart.

By knowing your feelings, you will cultivate the courage needed to uncover your hidden wishes. Some people feel anxious and perhaps insecure with their new wisdom and power when they begin to change their lives. Committing to a career idea may feel uncomfortable because it is unfamiliar; a new choice represents what you would like to become — often something unknown. Sometimes we distrust our ideas until we become more secure and familiar with an unexplored way of being. During my own career search, the idea of being a writer appeared in my mind. This idea felt right. In the depth of my being, my spirit knew that I would eventually be a successful, published author. Yet, with all this sureness, I quickly began to doubt my ability to manifest greatness. My subconscious mind took over and criticized and analyzed my idea, deciding it was ridiculous, even though my heart knew what was right.

You too may have this internal struggle with your intuitive and subconscious. Respect each side of your being, but follow what you know is truly right. When thoughts of self-doubt permeate your mind, realize that they are only thoughts, not reality. You may feel incapable or anxious because you have not yet learned the skills necessary for a field of endeavor that interests you. It is normal to have feelings of self-criticism. Most people who undertake personal growth encounter some disbelief in their ability to transform their lives. Frustration at various stages of growth may occur while you change. Sometimes old, learned programming creeps into your mind, spouting untrue affirmations. Counteract negative self-talk with positive beliefs.

In addition to your beliefs, there are many other factors that influence your current perceptions including society, environment, peer pressure, family background, learning style, self-esteem, and personality. These factors, in turn, influence your career choice. Your history has shaped your current interests and abilities. For example, some people were taught to have a strong work ethic while others have slid by putting forth very little effort. Some people have been praised and others criticized. Certain groups of people, such as women and minorities, have been brainwashed into believing they are second best. Parents sometimes discourage children from participating in particular activities that may cause the children (including adult children) to doubt their own capabilities. Other individuals received very little parental nurturing in the areas of educational and career goals. And some people had wildly supportive parents who fostered their children's talents. Whether you lived in an environment with almost no support or in a very nurturing setting, explore and observe your past and how this influences the choices you make.

Almost everyone has some type of obstacle to overcome, even the people who appear the most fortunate. You have a unique combination of strengths and weaknesses that make you a deserving candidate for the fields that interest you. If you feel negative influences from the past are too great for you to overcome alone, then seek the assistance of a counselor, psychologist, hypnotherapist, support group, college resource person, and/or friend. To overcome negative conditioning, make active, conscious changes by facing the realities of your life; then make a commitment to reprogram your beliefs. Self-help books and seminars are also useful tools for assisting you with making positive changes.

Influences from your past, such as a bad childhood, a negative environment, growing up in an inner city, inadequate parenting, or a learning disability, may slow your current progress. If you have frustrating past circumstances, then view these as opportunities for changing. As trite as it may sound, the past is over, and you must focus on changing the present, so your future will be better. If appropriate, think about whether a counseling or support group might allow you to work through any past demons or beliefs that inhibit your current growth. If you're in school, seek support with study groups and a tutor. Joining a social club might just be the extra boost you need. Help is always available! Make smart choices now, moment by moment. You may have more obstacles to conquer than other people; however, the skills you learn in overcoming your roadblocks will make you a stronger and more capable individual. The words in *Psycho-Cybernetics* touch on this point:

> *We are built to conquer environment,*
> *solve problems, achieve goals and we*
> *find no real satisfaction or happiness*
> *in life without obstacles to conquer*
> *and goals to achieve.*

> *Maxwell Maltz*

Evaluate your personal history. A client, Sandra, had the subtle challenge of learning to trust her natural expressive and intuitive nature. The programming she had received in her family was to be logical, scientific, and competitive. But, because she is not the logical type, her instinctive actions and feelings were often not validated.

If she expressed an intuitive belief or feeling, it was often scoffed at because there was "no proof." Consequently, Sandra did not pursue her true creative interests because she was programmed to believe the subtle family message that "logical and scientific endeavors are better than nonscientific interests." Even though Sandra's experience was mild in comparison to some others, she was definitely influenced negatively and had difficulty knowing and trusting herself. This uncertainty caused her to feel frustrated with her career choices. As a result, Sandra invested time and energy in discovering her true nature, learning more about herself. She now values and follows her natural spirit. Consider what past demons may haunt your choices today.

Passionately surrender to your natural spirit. The more you honestly express your true yearnings and act upon your desires, the lighter and more free you will feel. The magic of life occurs by really living your essence within, not by playing the game of life by somebody else's rules. You must determine your own truth. The better you understand and know yourself and begin to actually make choices based on the true you, the more easily your life unfolds. You begin to flow with the natural rhythm of life, with the energy of higher good. You create magic in your life by submitting to your true essence.

VALUES -
Oh, Why Do I Do What I Do?

In this section you'll discover what forces influence your actions. Values drive behavior. To know what motivates you to take action helps you with your choice. If you feel strongly about a particular topic or belief, then you will naturally devote time and energy to support your passion. Feeling inspired about work you cherish and find worthy of your time helps keep you motivated and brings balance and happiness into your life.

What is meaningful to you? Vincent Van Gogh, for example, was driven by something entirely different from what motivates Bill Gates. Does creativity and self-expression vitalize you, like Van Gogh? Or perhaps power and money excites you more, like Gates. If you are driven by creativity and money, then being a movie producer like Steven Spielberg or a fashion designer like Anne Klein might seem thrilling to you. The possibilities are endless.

People usually feel happier when their career allows them the ability to express their top values. Sales representatives continue to close sales because of their aspiration for money and the independence that comes with money. Teachers, on the other hand, feel enthusiasm for teaching because of a passion to help people, feeling thrilled when eyes light up with understanding. Select a profession and life style compatible with your values. Whether you are a teenager or a mature adult, the question is still the same: *With the remaining part of my life, what do I want to be remembered for?* Don't concern yourself with creating a specific answer this moment; instead try on a few ideas for size, letting your soul lead you to the answer. Your dreams may be simple and humble, such as having a family and serving the community by being a nurse, police officer, or fire fighter. Or you may wish to contribute something grander, perhaps by being an entrepreneur, creating jobs for society or a research engineer, discovering a nonpolluting form of transportation. You may have several desires, related or unrelated. Perhaps you thrive on variety, security, and being in charge, in which case you might enjoy health care management or educational administration. Remember, changing careers continues to be fairly common and will be more so in the 21st century, so you may eventually experience several career dreams within your lifetime. Search deep inside your soul for your longings.

Sometimes a struggle occurs with competing desires. For instance, a client of mine, Melinda, an artistic spirit in her mid-twenties, was looking for a career where she could experience freedom of expression, yet she felt some dissonance because she also valued security. She knew that many creative careers, such as artist, dancer, or actor, are competitive and often not very secure. Later, however, she learned that some fields, such as interior design, graphic arts, or product development with a large company, do offer some stability. She decided to explore the more secure options, since they fit better with her values. She was willing to give up some of her creative freedom as a trade-off for more steady work.

Explore the values listed on the next page. Rank each value from most important to least important, writing them in the space below the list. This will help you determine your motivators. Sometimes thinking of the values in the extreme may help you clarify what is most important to you. For example, when deciding between the values *helping others* and *money* say to yourself, "Would I rather die extremely poor, but have helped people? Or would I rather die filthy rich, but have helped almost no one?" Obviously your life will not unfold in such extremes, nevertheless, considering the values in this vein helps you clarify what drives you. If you could only have one value in your work life, what might that be? You might want to write each value on an index card and move the cards around, exploring your reactions to the different combinations you arrange.

Another helpful exercise is to ask someone you trust to complete the values exercise and then discuss the results with each other. Verbalizing your thoughts and feelings helps you to clarify and solidify your conclusions. Learning about the behaviors of others helps you to better understand yourself. Ask people you know these questions: *Which five values motivate you? Does your current work or life style meet your values? If yes, how so? If no, why not?*

After you've decided your order, then the value on the top of your list should be your first choice. In other words, if you are only allowed one value, then your first value is most important to you; the second value on your list is your second choice, and so on.

Next to *each* of your top five values, write five reasons why the value is important to you. Your reasons may be very simple or elaborate. Any reason qualifies. If it's important to you, that's a good enough reason. For example, if *helping others* is your top value, list five reasons why you like to help people, such as: 1. to make the world a better place, 2. to feel good about myself, 3. to meet fascinating people, 4. to feel a sense of purpose, and 5. to make my family proud of me. Then move to your second most important value and list five reasons why it's important to you. Continue until you've listed five reasons for each of the top five values.

Perseverance is more prevailing than violence; and many things which cannot be overcome when they are together yield themselves up when taken little by little.

Plutarch

VALUES

- *money*
- *security*
- *family*
- *free time*
- *adventure*
- *variety*

- *prestige*
- *creativity*
- *fame*
- *power*
- *flexibility*
- *independence*

- *being in charge*
- *helping others*
- *intellectual stimulation*
- *work environment*
- *recognition*
- *co-worker relations*

My Top Five Values & Reasons Why:

Contemplate your list carefully and decide if you are satisfied with the order. If not, make adjustments. Do you see a theme flowing through your choices? Do any of your values relate to a particular field of interest? For example, the values *intellectual stimulation, helping others*, and *security* fit well with many health related careers, such as physical therapist, speech pathologist, or physician's assistant. The values *creativity, variety*, and *helping others* can be met by being a public relations specialist, graphic designer, or hypnotherapist. If you are studying in school, do your values fit with your current major? What occupations match your values? If you are already in a particular career, do your values fit with your current work? If you are unhappy with your work or school, there's a good chance that your values do not match with your current situation. Later you will gather options that fit with your values.

In addition to understanding motivations, realize that a variety of options will fulfill your purpose. Sometimes values are satisfied in a direct way. For instance, an individual who wants to help people can do so by working directly with people as an occupational therapist, counselor, or chiropractor. In contrast, helping people may also be achieved indirectly by working as a scientific researcher on a project that ultimately brings an important medical cure or as an owner of a business who provides people with employment opportunities.

Values may also be fulfilled by your hobbies, making work secondary. You might prefer to work in a low stress job mainly to pay the bills allowing your energy to be used more in your personal projects. A friend of mine in her thirties, Chris, manages a hotel as her "work work" yet she paints abstract art as her "life work." At this point in her life, establishing a stable career to raise a family is somewhat more important to her than living solely for her creativity. Eventually she may be able to support herself as a fine artist. In contrast, another friend, Tony, used to teach chemistry as his "work work" and politics was his "life work." He taught chemistry by day and attended political rallies, fund raisers, and city council meetings by night. He ran for the office of state assembly in his city and was defeated by a close margin; however, he still plans to eventually make politics his full time job. Soon enough, I'm sure, chemistry will be his past career and his passion will become his present career. Consider the various ways your values can be met. What type of contribution do you want to make to the world? Perhaps you want to leave an important mark

in history by contributing to science, health care, or education. Or maybe you just want to enjoy the good things in life, working more for money and free time. The choice is yours. And your choice of purpose greatly affects your lifestyle, so choose wisely and honestly. Ultimately make your selection based on your dreams and passions.

> *Go confidently in the direction of your dreams!*
> *Dare to live the life you have imagined.*
> *As you simplify your life, the laws of the universe will be simpler; solitude will not be solitude, poverty will not be poverty, nor weakness weakness.*
>
> Henry David Thoreau

Allow yourself the freedom to reveal what you truly desire.

Now, copy your top five values under the heading *MY TOP FIVE VALUES* on your *MAGICAL QUEST SUMMARY* located at the end of this chapter. This page is designed to help you organize your preferences while you explore. Once your *SUMMARY* is complete, you'll see how each aspect of you fits together easily like a puzzle.

YOUR ESSENCE - What I Like

Creating your purpose and knowing your values brings you one step closer to your ultimate goal. Let's now focus on your interests. What lights up your soul, causing you to radiate sparkling eyes and a spirited smile? What activities make you want to get up out of bed, stimulating passion in your heart? Many of the things you like to do can be translated into some type of career, perhaps even a new career that you'll invent to meet the needs of the market. Sure, some days we would rather not work at all, but since most of us must work, consider what you would enjoy doing so much you would do it for free.

The quick interest assessment, *INNER QUEST*, on the next page will assist you in determining what you like. Your results will reveal career options that relate to your interests.

INNER QUEST

DIRECTIONS FOR *INNER QUEST*: Read each item in each square. Circle any activity you *like* to do, even if you are not good at it or have never experienced the activity, but you think you would like it. Do not circle what you *kind of like*.

Next, total the number of circles you have for each column. Write the number on the small line at the bottom of each column.

Then, total the first two columns to get a grand total and place this total on the line below the small lines. Total the next two columns and place this total on the line below the small lines of these two columns. Continue this process until you have **EIGHT GRAND TOTALS**.

After completing *INNER QUEST*, evaluate your results. You should have two to four columns with many items circled. Do you notice any similarities between the items listed in each column? The columns relate to particular themes. Each two columns represents one of eight general types with characteristics and activities of people in these areas.

Let the facade drop, the pretension retreat,
and a sliver of openness appear.
Let the fear vanish and the worry float by.
My essence slowly surfaces.

Shadows move into sun.
Murky waters become clear.
My silhouette takes shape as I tunnel into the
depths of my soul.

New sights mesmerize, shining a glory of
understanding who I truly am.
Do I like this or do I like that? Hmm.
Naturally, easily answers flow.

I express my beauty within.
False gods no longer dirty my spirit.
The truth rings clear, harmonious, singing a
sweet song of freedom.
Godly love surrounds protecting, cherishing
and guiding.

INNER Quest

©1994 Tarin Frances

TOTALS — — — — — — — — — —

study astronomy	measure distances	study animal behavior	use a microscope	play computer games	analyze	do logic puzzles	research	read scientific material	study the environment	ask why?	watch DISCOVERY channel
be logical	solve math problems	take chemistry courses	study the ocean	study nature	program a computer	use a telescope	play chess	be intellectual	use a calculator	read National Geographic	study electronics
study a language	combine logic & intuition	solve word problems	take risks	think abstractly	be open-minded	originate new ideas	be independent	read the classics	visualize a movie scene	design	be innovative
explore the unknown	study the world	work outside the box	study great thinkers	invent	create systems	study trends	learn about people	study history	appreciate music	brainstorm	trouble shoot
be clever	read about art & music	design landscapes	direct a play	have creative expression	perform	coordinate clothes	explore great art	dress with style	select colors	visit art galleries	create music
study fashion	create ad slogans	daydream	make people laugh	decorate	be introspective	select fabrics	watch a play	do arts and crafts	design something	empathize	paint a picture
study sociology	write stories or poetry	develop others	teach others	search for truth	sing	create with words	understand other cultures	discuss life	study religions	meditate	use intuition
study the self	create	appreciate the unique	explore metaphysics	study families	appreciate beauty	study psychology	explore the soul	relate with passion	be flamboyant	write songs	communicate effectively
fight for a cause	express your point of view	deliver a speech	delegate	convince people	have an adventure	be in charge	be a club officer	see the big picture	be assertive	make decisions	sell things
take a management course	attend meetings	direct a fund raiser	have high energy	be persuasive	make things happen	start a business	debate	be in politics	lead a group	be fair minded	talk smoothly
care for the sick	express your feelings	care for elderly people	have a party	read about people	be understanding	study the human body	talk with strangers	study human behavior	care for others	play with children	talk on the phone
counsel others	learn about health	do charity work	be kind	work in groups	teach others	help a friend	read self-help books	listen	be sympathetic	lift weights	be friendly
be sensible	assemble things	care for animals	work with wood	build something	be mechanical	drive a boat	go camping	be practical	go scuba diving	use machines	go skydiving
drive vehicles	fix gadgets	repair an engine	use electronics	use physical strength	play sports	garden	ride a motorcycle	fly a plane	prepare food	use office machines	work outdoors
order supplies	follow a schedule	use a computer	set up a system	be efficient	balance a budget	do word processing	check details	be organized	be systematic	answer phones	prioritize information
complete forms	develop flow charts	check inventory	be conscientious	make arrangements	compile information	make follow-up calls	follow directions	do systematic bookkeeping	answer phones	file material	proofread

The first two columns are the *WIZARDS* or intellectual types. The next two columns are the *EXPLORERS* or the investigation types. The fifth and sixth columns stand for the *ARTISANS* or creative types. The seventh and eighth columns designate the *MYSTICS* or the spiritual types. The ninth and tenth columns identify the *RULERS* or decision-making types. The next two columns relate to the *HEALERS* or helping types. The next two columns identify the *WARRIORS* or physical, hands-on types. The last two columns indicate the *ADVISORS* or organizing types. At the top of each two columns is a blank line. Write the name of the category above each of their respective columns, i.e., write *WIZARDS* on the line above the first two columns; write *EXPLORERS* on the line above the third and fourth columns, and so on.

Select your top two to four favorite themes. The columns with the largest grand totals should represent your favorite types. A high number of circles for a particular category means that you will probably prefer careers that relate to that particular theme. You will probably have one to four columns with many items circled and one to four columns with very few items circled.

If you circled only a few items on the *INNER QUEST* assessment, you may want to reevaluate your choices. Perhaps you need to be more open-minded and less critical when deciding what is enjoyable to you. Some individuals with a small amount of interests truly haven't experienced enough activities in life. You may be a person who needs to try more things, take classes, travel, become involved in sports, try new hobbies, etc. (Remember our *risk* topic.) In other cases individuals who like only a few activities are just really focused and know what major themes sound appealing. Career planning then is more a reaffirming and fine-tuning of interests. If you have a small amount of interests, determine why this is the case.

Conversely, if you circled items from many categories and seem to have liked almost everything on the *INNER QUEST,* then you may want to reassess yourself. Go back to *INNER QUEST* and circle only the activities you love or could give an *A* or *A+* rating to. This will help you find stronger preferences, eventually leading to your career decision. Some people, however, truly have a tremendous number of interests. If you are one of these people, you may prefer to have a couple of careers at one time, a few careers throughout your life, and/or be in careers that involve a variety of themes, such as entrepreneur, company president, internet business owner, or movie director. Professions that people expand into businesses also generally involve characteristics from most of the themes. Paths such as a nurse owning a clinic, an actor producing movies, a chef owning a restaurant, a teacher developing a school, a truck driver creating a transportation service, or an athlete running a training camp all involve a myriad of activities and skills. If you're more eclectic, look for careers with room for expansion, growth, and creativity.

On the following pages read the portraits and careers that fit with each type. Focus on your top two to four favorite preferences from your *INNER QUEST* results and determine if the types describe you. Ideally, most of the portraits for your highest-circled category will describe you. Your second, third, and possibly fourth highest categories should also, for the most part represent you; of course there may be pieces of these descriptions that are not part of you. If not, read all the types and select the three to four that fit you best.

If you find major discrepancies between the descriptions and yourself, review your *INNER QUEST* results, perhaps making changes. Sometimes previous experience in a particular area influences results. Make sure you circled what you *like* to do, even if you're not skilled in that particular activity. In other words, don't circle something just because you know *how* to do the activity. Sometimes your interest in recreational activities influences your results. You might like certain activities for fun, but not for work. Contemplate your results.

If you find that none of the categories match your essence, then write your own portrait of your work characteristics and values. Perhaps use some of the information on the descriptions, selecting only the aspects that feel right for you.

Reflect on how your preferences fit with particular career options. Notice the differences between your favorite and least favorite descriptions. Perhaps share your results with someone you respect and who knows you well. Ask for this person's feedback.

Examine the various careers listed under your favorite descriptions and seriously consider each career as a possibility. Some careers are listed under more than one category as they fit well with a few of the types. Circle careers you might like *and* those you know nothing about. Be open-minded! Avoid ruling out options you know little about, as these may be your unpolished jewels. Curtail any negative self-talk so it won't prohibit you from selecting an option.

At this point, don't be concerned about your ability to be successful, the amount of time required to train, or the competition in a field.

Right now your *main* criteria for circling a choice is your *level of interest*. If you worry about your competency, imagine that you're excellent in everything you want to pursue. For example, if you hate school, imagine you love it. If you're 50 years old and worried about your age, imagine you're 20. Your only criteria are *like* and *dislike*. If you judge now, you inhibit your soul from blossoming forth; so resist critiquing in any other fashion, other than interest level! Pretend that you are shopping for a career as you would for clothing, a stereo, car, house, or mate — you're trying on, listening, test-driving, visiting, and dating. Ask yourself only one question, "Does this option seem appealing?"

Once you've explored these eight types, turn to your *CAREER OPTIONS LIST* and *MAGICAL QUEST SUMMARY* at the end of this chapter. Transfer your circled careers to your "shopping list" under your *CAREER OPTIONS LIST*. If your list of possibilities seems short, you may want to review the types in a more open-minded and curious fashion, selecting more options. Conversely, if your list seems unmanageable, you may want to review your list and be a bit more discriminating, selecting careers that you *really* like. Any amount is fine, however.

Under your *MAGICAL QUEST SUMMARY* find the heading *MY INNER QUEST RESULTS*. Write your favorite preferences with a small description of each type. You want to feel that your descriptions are the true you.

Your *SUMMARY* and *OPTIONS LIST* serve as an organizing tool designed to guide you in becoming clearer about you and your preferences. In summary:

√ *Read your top two to four descriptions.*

√ *Confirm that these types describe you.*

√ *Write your own type if the descriptions do not fit.*

√ *Circle at least five careers that you may want to pursue.*

√ *Transfer your results to the SUMMARY and OPTIONS LIST.*

The warmth of the sun reminds me of the desires within my soul.

The gentle breeze of air allows my worries to fly away.

Cool, calming waters take me to my deepest being.

As the day gently rises and sets earth grounds my essence leading with a gentle hand.

Nature offers vital powers for our daily living.

Thunder, wind, and rain stir the wild and primitive within our dormant selves.

Awakened we rejoice, relinquishing ignorance, praising passion, and thanking the turbulent and unruley.

Screaming to be free, we sing praise, Alleluia, thank God, Alleluia!

WIZARDS
(intellectual)

These people like to research and solve complex problems using their mind. Wizards are curious, logical, analytical, and independent thinkers. Often they dislike the corporate structure and prefer to explore solutions to various projects on their own. These individuals often have unconventional attitudes and they enjoy thinking through problems, especially ambiguous tasks.

Motivators:

intellectual stimulation and the unknown

Preferred industries:

- medical
- research
- scientific
- investment firms
- higher education
- engineering
- computer
- electronics
- law

Strengths:

- curious
- interesting
- original
- knowledgeable
- rational
- self-controlled
- objective
- introspective
- independent
- scientific
- abstract thinker
- scholarly
- theoretical
- calm
- controlled
- persistent
- practical
- perceptive

Weaknesses:

- may ignore feelings
- may take too long before taking action
- may often be asocial
- may be critical

WIZARDS
(intellectual)

actuary
aerodynamist
anthropologist
archaeologist
architect
archivist
astronomer
auditor
bioengineer
biologist
brew master
CAD designer
chemist
chiropractor
college professor
computer programmer
dentist
economist
embalmer
engineer
environmental scientist
ethnologist
financial analyst
geographer
geologist
health officer
industrial engineer
inhalation therapist
laboratory technician
legal assistant
map maker
mathematician
medical illustrator
microbiologist
museum curator
occupational safety specialist
optometrist
orthodontist
osteopathic physician
paleontologist
patent lawyer
pharmacist
phlebotomist
physical therapist
physician
physician assistant
psychiatrist
quality assurance manager
radiologic technician
research librarian
seismologist
statistician
systems analyst
technical writer
veterinarian
zoologist

EXPLORERS
(investigation)

Explorers offer an interesting blend of logical and emotional based skills. They feel as comfortable writing poetry as they do solving a calculus problem. Developing a large scale project with never ending possibilities intrigues this type. Explorers are usually creative, intellectual, open-minded, and extremely independent.

Motivators:

curiosity and adventure

Preferred industries:

- computer design
- film & television
- environmental
- political arenas
- communications

Strengths:

- imaginative
- dynamic
- avant-garde
- smart
- unique
- analytical
- driven
- intuitive
- global thinkers
- assured
- resourceful
- diplomatic
- adventurous
- open-minded
- sophisticated
- clever
- personable
- curious
- understanding
- logical
- analytical

Weaknesses:

- may become bored quickly
- may feel superior to others
- may have unrealistic expectations for others

EXPLORERS
(investigation)

advertising executive
ambassador
amusement park designer
automotive designer
book publisher
cinematographer
columnist
comedian
comedy writer
communications consultant
composer
computer network specialist
computer trainer
documentary developer
entrepreneur
environmental activist
film director
film editor
film producer
foreign correspondent
foreign service officer
genetics developer
graphic designer
hotel manager
intellectual property attorney
inventor
journalist
judge
literary agent
lobbyist
museum director
music producer
naturopathic physician
negotiator
orchestra conductor
pediatrician
perfumer
philosopher
photojournalist
political scientist
president/CEO
producer internet software
product developer
psychiatrist
psychologist
public relations executive
recording engineer
screen play writer
software engineer, advertising
systems
stock broker
syndicated cartoonist
television executive
toy manufacturer
trial jury consultant
venture capitalist
video game designer
Web page designer
Webmaster
wine maker
writer, fiction & non-fiction
yacht designer

ARTISANS
(creative)

glass blower
graphic designer
greeting-card editor
illustrator
interior designer
jeweler
magician
make-up artist
model-maker
movie critic
movie director
mural designer
museum curator
musician
music mixer
package designer
pastry chef
photographer
portrait artist
picture framer
restaurant critic
sculptor
set designer
special-effects artist
stained-glass artist
tattoo artist
taxidermist
visual merchandiser
voice-over actor

actor/actress
advertising copy writer
antique dealer
art critic
art teacher
artist
belly dancer
cartoonist
ceramist
chef
choreographer
circus performer
clown
comedian
commercial artist
cosmetologist
dancer
dance instructor
designer - clothes
costume
fabric
floral
furniture
jewelry
toy
display artist
entertainer
fashion coordinator
fashion model

ARTISANS
(creative)

These people like to create ideas and things using words, sound, or color. Artisans are sensitive, individualistic, imaginative, and intuitive. They do not work well with structure, preferring free nonconforming environments. They value beauty and esthetics. They like art, music, drama, and writing.

Artisans like to dress freely and expressively. They deal with problems through self-expression in art or other imaginative endeavors.

Motivators:

creativity and esthetics

Preferred industries:

- film and television
- entertainment
- advertising
- fashion
- design

Strengths:

- innovative
- unique
- ability to create beauty
- emotional
- experimental
- clever
- expressive
- stylish
- independent
- perceptive
- introspective
- process oriented
- versatile
- original thinkers
- flexible
- feeling oriented

Weaknesses:

- may have difficulty with follow-through
- not assertive about their own capabilities
- may be submissive
- may avoid direct relationships with others

MYSTICS
(spirituality)

Mystics enjoy the search for truth and the meaning of life. They instinctively connect to all types of people, fully appreciating the divineness of the human spirit. They look for emotional connection and open honest communication. They delight in the subtleties of life and the esoteric. To Mystics, life situations present many meanings with lessons revealing themselves in the unobvious; what meets the eye is not always the truth.

Motivators:

truth and harmony

Preferred industries:

- publishing
- film & television
- metaphysical
- psychology
- non-traditional education

Strengths:

- sensitive
- empathetic
- open-minded
- idealistic
- loving
- enlightened
- exciting
- peaceful
- joyful
- emotionally mature
- excellent communicators
- insightful
- imaginative
- dramatic
- perceptive
- diplomatic
- playful
- creative
- wise

Weaknesses:

- may live in a dream world
- may over-dramatize life
- may assume others relate to the esoteric

MYSTICS
(spirituality)

activist
actor/actress
adoption specialist
advice columnist
art therapist
astrologer
camp director
career counselor
child psychologist
civil rights activist
columnist
counselor
day-care director
diplomat
divorce mediator
drama coach
editor
feng shu specialist
gang counselor
genetics consultant
genetics counselor
greeting-card writer
herbalist
holistic healer
inter-cultural communications specialist
intuitive healer
marriage, family, & child counselor
matchmaker
mediator
metaphysical speaker
missionary
music therapist
novelist
numerologist
palm reader
performing artist
philosopher
poet
professor, arts & social science
psychic
psychologist
public relations specialist
radio talk-show host
religious leader
residence counselor
romance novelist
screen writer
sex therapist
singer
song writer
speech writer
talk-show host
tarot card reader
teacher
wedding consultant
writer
yoga instructor

RULERS
(leadership)

academic dean	loan officer
activist	lobbyist
activities director	management trainee
arbitrator	managers (all types)
administrator	motion picture producer
broker	motivational speaker
business owner	negotiator
buyer	newscaster
campaign manager	politician
camp director	production manager
caterer	promoter
CEO	property manager
city manager	program director
commodities trader	public relations specialist
community relations director	radio or T.V. announcer
consumer advocate	real estate salesperson
diplomat	record producer
district coordinator	regional sales manager
entrepreneur	restaurant manager or owner
fashion merchandiser	sales representative
financial aid director	school principal
foreign trade specialist	speaker
foreign services officer	stock broker
fund raiser	students-at-risk coordinator
funeral director	travel agent
hotel manager	umpire
importer/exporter	urban planner
judge	wedding coordinator
lawyer	wholesaler

RULERS
(leadership)

These people like to be in charge of others and make decisions. Rulers are energetic, persuasive, and outgoing. They like to see the big picture and enjoy making things happen. They have good verbal skills and are strong leaders, motivating others to complete the details of a project.

Rulers often dislike science and systematic things, avoiding long periods of intellectual effort.

Motivators:

money and power

Preferred industries:

- hotel and restaurant
- property management
- corporations
- real estate
- sales
- legal
- communications
- travel

Strengths:

- enthusiastic
- positive
- goal-oriented
- powerful
- confident
- dynamic
- risk takers
- flexible
- good communicators
- adventuresome
- lively
- ambitious
- self-confident
- sociable
- out-going
- direct
- zealous

Weaknesses:

- may be too materialistic
- may be inconsistent
- may neglect necessary research
- may be impatient

HEALERS
(helping)

These people like to help develop and solve problems of others. Healers are friendly, understanding, compassionate, and good communicators. They like to teach, serve, and care for others. In addition, they dislike working with machines or in highly structured environments.

Healer types avoid intellectual problem solving, preferring to discuss philosophical questions. They have good verbal and interpersonal skills.

Motivators:

helping and desire to make a difference

Preferred Industries:

- education
- health care
- childcare
- government
- social welfare
- personnel
- public relations
- customer relations
- recreation

Strengths:

- empathetic
- sympathetic
- helpful
- emotional
- caring
- understanding
- encouraging
- positive
- enthusiastic
- nurturing
- fair
- tactful
- generous
- cooperative
- cheerful

Weaknesses:

- may be too emotional
- may ignore factual information
- may have low mathematical abilities
- may become too attached to others

HEALERS
(helping)

- activities coordinator
- acupuncturist
- admissions counselor
- bartender
- camp counselor
- childcare worker
- college recruiter
- consumer advocate
- customer-service manager
- day-care owner
- dietician
- drug & alcohol counselor
- employment counselor
- esthetician
- flight attendant
- health educator
- high school counselor
- home economist
- interpreter
- labor relations specialist
- librarian
- manicurist
- massage therapist
- midwife
- missionary
- nanny
- nurse
- nurse's assistant
- nurse practitioner
- nutritionist
- occupational therapist
- park naturalist
- parole officer
- Peace Corps volunteer
- personal shopper
- personnel director
- personnel interviewer
- pet-sitter
- physical therapist
- physical therapist assistant
- police officer
- political scientist
- probation officer
- public relations specialist
- recreation leader
- recruiter
- rehabilitation therapist
- retail salesperson
- respiratory therapist
- school psychologist
- social worker
- sociologist
- special education teacher
- speech therapist
- teacher for the deaf
- teacher (all types)
- training specialist
- translator
- tour guide
- welfare director

WARRIORS
(physical)

People who like to work with their bodies and hands moving around, fixing, or making things. Realistic people are robust, practical, direct, and grounded. They often like to work alone.

Warriors usually do not want to work at a desk in a conservative office or business setting. They dislike office politics. They prefer to work outdoors or in an area with lots of space.

Motivators:

freedom and action

Preferred industries:

- construction
- parks and recreation
- industrial
- automotive
- agriculture
- printing
- sports
- trades

Strengths:

- up-front
- honest
- direct
- uncomplicated
- task oriented
- easy going
- mechanical
- athletic
- strong
- natural
- persistent
- calm
- good motor coordination
- good at building things
- sincere
- emotionally stable
- hearty
- rugged

Weaknesses:

- may start a project without enough planning
- may dislike abstract problem solving
- may have weak verbal and interpersonal skills
- may ignore feelings

WARRIORS
(physical)

agriculture technician
animal caretaker
auto body repairer
beekeeper
boat captain
camera gripper
camera operator
carpenter
coach
computer repair technician
contractor
cook
diver
dog groomer
driver
electrician
electronic technician
emergency medical technician
engineering technologist
farmer
firefighter
food broker
forestry technician
gardener
horse trainer
horticulturist
jockey
landscape architect
land surveyor
lifeguard
machinist
mechanic
painter
paramedic
park ranger
personal trainer
pet sitter
physical education teacher
pilot
plant breeder
plumber
police officer
professional athlete
racetrack manager
rancher
repairer
seamstress
search & rescue specialist
sheet-metal worker
sky diver
sound engineer
sports trainer
stunt person
tailor
tool & die maker
truck driver
veterinarian's assistant
welder
wildlife biologist
zoo keeper

ADVISORS
(organization)

accountant
accounting clerk
administrative assistant
admissions & records technician
appraiser or assessor
bailiff
bank teller
bank manager
benefits specialist
bibliographer
bookkeeper
budget analyst
building inspector
business teacher
card dealer
cashier
claims adjuster
collections agent
court reporter
credit manager
customer-service representative
data processor
dental assistant
desktop publisher
drivers education teacher
editorial assistant
employee-benefits specialist
estate planner
executive house keeper
health & safety inspector
health service administrator
immigration officer
insurance adjuster
insurance agent
insurance biller
IRS employee
laboratory technician
legal secretary
mail carrier
medical assistant
medical records technician
meeting planner
office manager
optician
payroll manager
payroll clerk
printer
proofreader
purchasing agent
rate analyst
receptionist
reservation agent
secretary
security guard
tax accountant
telephone operator
title examiner
translator
treasurer
typist
waiter/waitress
word processor

ADVISORS
(organization)

These people like to organize and follow through on details. Advisors are dependable, conscientious, and precise. They do not mind taking directions from others and working behind the scenes.

Advisors like to work in well-ordered environments doing systematic verbal and numerical activities. They often dislike free, unorthodox, exploratory behavior in new areas.

Motivators:

security and organization

Preferred industries:

- insurance
- health care
- travel
- government
- administration
- food & beverage
- accounting
- corporations
- banking

Strengths:

- organized
- thorough
- complete
- accurate
- punctual
- considerate
- quiet
- neat
- pleasant
- polite
- dutiful
- detail oriented
- stable
- controlled
- thrifty
- task-oriented
- consistent

Weaknesses:

- may be too rigid
- may be unwilling to change or adapt when necessary
- may be too rule oriented
- not philosophical

SKILLS -
Now That Sounds Fun!

Let's continue exploring what you enjoy doing, focusing on skill interests. Again you will determine what you like or what you think you like.

Before assessing your skill interests, remember that a skill is different from an aptitude. A skill or an ability is a learned and practiced aptitude. An aptitude, on the other hand, is a natural tendency towards a high ability in a particular area. Skills are the current perfected knowledge; aptitudes are the raw talent.

When assessing your skill interests use the criteria of *like* and *dislike*. Do not confuse how you learn with your potential to become excellent in a particular area. In other words, your current knowledge and the time and effort you need to learn something does not predict your future measure of excellence. Some people learn slowly and become outstanding in their field, while others learn quickly and do little with their potential. Some individuals have a small amount of *God-given* resources and develop these to their fullest potential. Still others have heaps of raw talent and never do a thing with their assets. All sorts of learning and potential variations lie between these extremes. Ultimately the time it takes you to learn is of secondary importance to your level of success, as long as you have enough tenacity to develop your potential.

A friend of mine who was a professional athlete told me that as a teenager he was the slowest runner in his school. That summer he practiced running every day until his feet were tough and callused. The next school year my friend was the fastest runner in the school and he eventually became one of the fastest runners in the world. He had the *desire* to develop his natural capacities.

To become excellent in a field requires dedicating time to developing the necessary skills. The old cliché that *success does not come overnight* is true! Cultivating success asks for patience and time. For example, a person who is an excellent chef has acquired this ability by working in a variety of settings, practicing for years, attending numerous classes and workshops, and reading magazines, trade journals, and books on the subject of cooking. This person has certainly had many trials and failures while exploring and adapting various cooking techniques. He or she may have learned slowly *or* quickly, but eventually became exceptional.

When assessing your skills, use your *desire* to perform particular tasks as the main criterion for checking items. Most likely, your favorite activities tend to involve your best abilities and highest aptitudes. Often individuals gravitate more towards activities they develop quickly; through this positive experience they easily practice these particular skills and learn swiftly. Nonetheless, sometimes people develop an ability in an area they do not like. For example, a student of mine, Jeffrey, excelled in math and science; however, he did not like careers related to these subjects. Instead, he was intrigued with, and drawn to, careers involving writing such as novelist, English professor, advertising copy writer, and journalist. He had the ability to express himself creatively, yet his grammar and sentence construction skills were underdeveloped. Even though Jeffery's writing skills were currently lacking, he had a high aptitude, as well as passion for writing. With practice and education, Jeffrey believed he would be able to greatly improve his skills; thus, he decided to pursue a career involving writing.

Sometimes individuals enjoy activities, but do not pursue them because they do not learn quickly. Learning slowly is not necessarily a reason to rule out an option. Select activities you like even if you are not accomplished in this area. What skills do you, or would you, like to use? Through your various life experiences with family, relationships, employment, volunteering, school, and hobbies, you have acquired valuable skills. With practice and time, you can attain additional strengths. You will also apply your current knowledge to future, possibly unrelated careers. These are called transferable skills. One of my clients, Rochelle, was tired of her position in sales and was considering employee training as a new option. She worried that she lacked the qualifications necessary for the profession. I assured her that she already had much teaching and communication mastery through her past sales positions. Some of her experience included effectively managing time, organizing orders, creating materials, giving sales presentations, and communicating with a variety of people — all the abilities needed for an employee training position!

Consider the various situations you can use a skill. Avoid letting negative experiences bias the possibility of using your expertise in a more positive situation. The **SKILLS CHECKLIST** on the next page will help you select your skill preferences. Read the directions and check the skills you like to use or would like to use.

SKILLS CHECKLIST

1. Read the skills below. Put a check next to each skill you enjoy using. If you are good at a skill, but do not like it, do not check the skill. You are determining your interest, not your ability in each skill.

2. For each column, total the number of checks. Write the totals of each column in the parentheses at the bottom of each column.

3. Read *all* the skills you checked. List your ten favorite skills on the lines listed at the bottom of the page.

analyzing	anticipating	adapting	accepting
appraising	critiquing	conceiving	clarifying
comparing	determining	conceptualizing	conveying feelings
detecting	discovering	decorating	creating ideas
diagnosing	enlisting	designing	developing
dissecting	evaluating	displaying	dramatizing
estimating	finding patterns	drafting	empathizing
examining	improvising	drawing	empowering
experimenting	innovating	estimating needs	enlightening
inspecting	investigating	imagining	enlisting
measuring	locating resources	making layouts	fantasizing
questioning	predicting	photographing	meditating
researching	seeing relationships	shaping	perceiving
reviewing	synthesizing	sketching	relating
screening	using insight	styling	teaching
( )	( )	( )	( )
arranging	advising	adjusting	accounting
assigning	caring	assembling	budgeting
conducting	counseling	balancing	calculating
confronting	curing	building	checking
coordinating	encouraging	climbing	classifying
delegating	explaining	constructing	collecting
finding short cuts	guiding	crafting objects	controlling
influencing	helping	delivering	counting
leading	informing	fixing	distributing
making decisions	listening	installing	editing
mediating	motivating	lifting	enforcing
negotiating	nursing	operating machines	ordering materials
persuading	offering support	preparing	organizing
planning	protecting	producing	recording
supervising	rehabilitating	repairing	retrieving
( )	( )	( )	( )

1. _____ 2. _____ 3. _____ 4. _____ 5. _____

6. _____ 7. _____ 8. _____ 9. _____ 10. _____

The results from your *SKILLS CHECKLIST* should be similar to your *INNER QUEST* results. The columns on your *SKILLS CHECKLIST* correspond directly to the same eight types described for the *INNER QUEST* columns. The first column on your *SKILLS CHECKLIST* list represents the *WIZARDS* or intellectual careers. The next seven columns (moving across the page) are in the same order as the *INNER QUEST* columns: *EXPLORERS, ARTISANS, MYSTICS, RULERS, HEALERS, WARRIORS,* and *ADVISORS.* Write the appropriate names above each column. The column with the largest number of checks should be your favorite work type, similar to the outcome of *INNER QUEST.* Your second highest number should represent your second favorite type, and so on. Compare your *SKILLS CHECKLIST* results with your *INNER QUEST* results. Determine if you have the same top two to four categories for each assessment. If your results are different, consider why you liked a particular theme in one instance, but not in another. For example, if you circled *care for others* under the *HEALERS* category on the *INNER QUEST* sheet, you should have checked caring, listening, and encouraging under the *HEALERS* category on the *SKILLS CHECKLIST* because these are the skills used to help others.

Next, on your *MAGICAL QUEST SUMMARY* write your top ten favorite skills under the appropriate heading: *SKILLS CHECKLIST.*

YOUR PERSONALITY -
Oh, I Wouldn't Say That!

Throughout history various writers, philosophers, and psychologists have defined four general personality types as a way to understand differences and similarities among people. Hippocrates referred to the four humors: sanguine, melancholy, choleric, and phlegmatic. Shakespeare cleverly described his characters using metaphors and other provocative descriptions using the four elements of personality: Fire, Water, Air, and Earth. Carl Jung introduced the concept of "type" or "function" to modern day psychology, stating that behavior is motivated by our "archetype." David Kiersey and Marilyn Bates in their book *Please Understand Me: Character and Temperament Types* discuss the four personality types of the Greek gods, with Dionysus teaching Joy, Apollo representing Spirit, Prometheus portraying Science, and Epimetheus providing Duty. Characters in movies, stories, fables and mythology exemplify the motives and desires of these types. Obviously, human beings possess a myriad of traits, characteristics, and beliefs, yielding unique individuals; still, identifying these four general groupings allows for better understanding of ourselves and others. Our primary personality motivates our behavior. Some individuals have a couple of personality types that influence behavior. Determining where you fit within these four types provides another way to know yourself better and to select careers that fit with your personality.

On the next page you will find *THE ELEMENTS,* a short inventory designed to assist you in determining your favorite general personality preferences. If you are an intellectual leader, for instance, your direction is different from a creative helper. Although an assessment cannot measure the subtle nuances of your essence, it can give general information, steering you to the right paths. Use this information to select careers that fit with your persona.

First, read *all* the adjectives listed below. Then, decide which words describe you best. From *all* the adjectives listed, circle the *top 25 words* that describe you best.

If you have anything really valuable to contribute to the world it will come through the expression of your own personality, that single spark of divinity that sets you off and makes you different from every other living creature.

Bruce Barton

THE ELEMENTS

FIRE

adaptive adventurous authentic bold canny clever cooperative daring determined direct dynamic electrifying enterprising expressive exciting friendly impatient impulsive industrious influential insightful inspiring lively pioneering powerful precocious quick resourceful sagacious sharp spontaneous unplanned vivacious venturesome witty zealous   **total words circled -** ____

WATER

affectionate artistic aware caring catalyst changeable compassionate compatible creative devoted dramatic dreamy eager emotional empathetic enthusiastic harmonious humanitarian idealistic imaginative intimate intuitive impressionable passionate peaceful perceptive psychic receptive responsive romantic sensitive sensual spiritual tactful understanding warmhearted

total words circled - ____

AIR

abstract accurate analytical argumentative articulate astute candid controversial cool-headed fair curious discerning impartial impersonal independent inquiring inquisitive inventive intellectual investigative knowledgeable logical nonchalant objective open-minded questioning persuasive philosophical rational research-oriented restrained rigorous skeptical subtle theoretical versatile

total words circled - ____

EARTH

amiable approachable calculated calm compliant congenial constructive conventional decisive dependable easy-going frank genuine gracious helpful kind meticulous orderly organized patient peaceful planned persevering pleasant practical productive realistic responsible savvy sensible sincere stable steadfast thorough traditional trustworthy

total words circled - ____

Count the number of words you have circled for each category and write these numbers in the appropriate spaces below:

FIRE - _____ **WATER** - _____

AIR - _____ **EARTH** - _____

Next, from the four categories on the following page, select the one group that seems most like you; then choose your second, third, and fourth favorite categories.

FIRST - _____ **SECOND** - _____

THIRD - _____ **FOURTH** - _____

Your first choice from these selections will most likely be the category that has the largest amount of words circled. Determine which group of words fits you best. This grouping provides you with another theme for you to investigate for increased self understanding. Use this information as a guide.

For some individuals one or two main themes do not describe their personality. These people instead have a combination personality, possessing traits from all four elements. If you answered honestly and found that you fit into more than two themes, you simply have more options to consider! Focus on the words that you circled, using these to evaluate your career options when we come to decision-making.

On the next few pages are general illustrations of the four elements along with recommended careers for each type. Read the descriptions and careers that fit your top two favorite elements. Again, circle careers you *might* be interested in pursuing and those that are unfamiliar to you.

Some careers are listed under more than one element as they fit well with these different types. Also, sometimes people become worried if the career they are considering is not listed under their element list. Not a problem. Remember interest inventories serve only as a catalyst to move you closer to your niche. They are not designed to *tell you* what you should become, instead they only offer *suggestions* for you to consider. Ultimately you sift through the information provided and then create your own career description.

Again, at this time you are just exploring, not committing to options, so be open-minded when selecting possibilities. Later you will make a decision.

FIRE

Eat, drink, and be merry! is an accurate motto for the Fire type. The Fire personality prefers doing rather than talking, acting rather than watching, and exploring rather than researching. Fire people are the risk-takers of the world, excellent at negotiating and troubleshooting. They excel in many different fields but prefer careers that are action-packed and changing, such as the paramedic, air-traffic controller, or athlete.

Fire personalities live by the seat of their pants, primed for the next crisis. They are the high profile politicians, stock brokers, and business people of the world, the heroes of action movies. This type is found in most career fields as long as there is sufficient visible activity. For example, most Fire types would suffocate doing long tedious research, unless of course it is outdoors or connected to an element of excitement. They prefer to be active with change in their environment. Freedom and variety motivate this type. Using their five senses with tangible work projects also motivates this attractive type. Fire personalities would rather show you than tell you.

As managers and teachers, Fires will often have endless hands-on activities, perhaps meeting in new locations or scheduling outdoor activities or field trips. A fun game or competition incorporated into getting a mundane project completed invigorates the Fires. If possible, they prefer to add an element of play to work. This type often will change his or her mind or make decisions at the last minute, adapting as they go. This may result in the Fires adjusting and manipulating rules and policies to fit the needs of a situation. Sometimes these traits are particularly annoying to the Earth type who prefers more stable, grounded plans.

Fire types may shy away from discussing feelings and problems, preferring to ignore heavy issues. Consequently, they move quickly into the lighter parts of conversation, usually making them friendly and easy to converse and banter with. Fire personalities are generally good-natured and possibly more carefree than the other elements. They are direct and complimentary towards others, not threatened by the accomplishments of others. They live in the present moment, naturally forgetting any past disturbances or problems. Worrying about the future or lamenting about the past usually would not be a focus for a Fire type. Instead they are primed for the next task on hand; they like to keep moving. Never allowing a dull moment, Fires want to have fun. They can become restless if life becomes too routine, sometimes creating some excitement — good or bad, if necessary. They often put projects off until the last minute. Fires work best with some amount of pressure, such as deadlines or possibly a crisis situation. Fires are motivated by action.

The suggested career list for Fires is diverse, yet, a common theme amongst most of the options is change, variety, adventure, or risk. Whether the career is in the science field, i.e. an orthopedic surgeon, or in the creative area, i.e. designer, a hands-on excitement emerges as a product of the career and the life that a Fire type brings to the profession. Although Fire types can do well in school, they often find the structure of traditional schools and colleges mundane and dull as the Fires prefer to learn as they do and experience.

SUGGESTED CAREERS FOR FIRE

actor/actress
airline flight attendant
airline ticket agent
antique dealer
architect
art teacher
athletic trainer
automobile salesperson
broadcasting announcer
cartoonist
caterer
consumer financial advisor
cosmetic salesperson
customer service representative
dance therapist
designer (any)
electrologist
emergency medical technician
entrepreneur
escrow officer
executive chef
exercise physiologist
exotic dancer

fashion coordinator
fashion designer
fashion display specialist
film producer
fire fighter, chef or inspector
floral designer
flying instructor
football coach
fund raiser
graphic designer
hair stylist
home economist
hotel manager
industrial arts teacher
interior designer
lawyer
legal assistant
lobbyist
masseur/masseuse
medical assistant
modeling instructor
museum exhibit designer
music therapist
neurosurgeon
news assistant or caster
news reporter
nurse anesthetist or midwife
nursing home therapist
nutritionist
occupational therapist
optician
oral surgeon
orthodontist
orthopedic surgeon
paramedic
performing artist
photographer
photojournalist
P.E. instructor
physical therapist
physician
probation officer
professional model
psychiatric nurse
public health educator
public relations specialist
real estate agent
recreation therapist
respiratory therapist

sales manager
social worker - all types
special event coordinator
speech pathologist
sports marketer or promoter
stockbroker
teacher, any
television director or producer
travel agent

WATER

To thine own self be true sums up the Water's outlook on life. Authenticity combined with love describes the Water's need; therefore, they are often the poets, writers, philosophers, and humanitarians of the world. They continuously explore their own nature, searching for a deeper meaning of life and purpose, ever involved in self-actualization. The Water type thrives in peaceful, harmonious, gentle atmospheres. Because of their desire for harmony and creativity, they often flourish in the creative arts and social service fields, finding business atmospheres hostile and harsh. However, Water types that do work in the corporate environment add a refreshing balance to the competitive nature of business. If working in business they find a better fit in personnel, sales, advertising, public relations, and management.

Water types make excellent friends and confidants, always ready to lend an open, empathetic ear. They fully understand the needs of others, often before others themselves know how they feel. The Water personality instinctually feels the pain and joy of mankind. They are excellent at bringing people together to work for the common good. Because of their excellent ability to communicate and understand people, Water types excel as teachers, counselors, negotiators, and mediators. This type feels compelled to meet the needs of individual; thus, they often shy away from cost-cutting decisions in business that may cause suffering to employees.

Oftentimes the Water type may become restless with work and relationships if human interaction becomes meaningless. They want to be appreciated and feel connected to their work and the people in their lives. If environments and relationships lack this personal nature, the Water type begins to feel down and perhaps even angry. To them, there is nothing worse than the dismissal of a caring and understanding attitude towards others. Groups and organizations benefit greatly if a Water type is on board as they bring diplomacy and a personal connection most of the time to any setting. Water types make others feel understood and related to as usually these types have a natural ability to listen authentically — others feel as if this *type is in their shoes*. Because of their expertise in this area, Water types may feel alone and not understood as other types generally are not as skilled in the fine delicate nature of creating and providing empathy in personal relationships. The catalyst for others, they may feel lonely unless another Water type is available to listen and nurture, naturally filling the void.

Although this type is sensitive and perceptive they are by no means weak. Unfortunately other elements may find their empathetic nature as something to take advantage of. Being good at communication, however, Water types eventually learn to express their feelings when being treated unfairly. This is an unpleasant task to this type, but they begin to realize that they are often the only ones seeing life through rose colored glasses. They are psychic and intuitive, and others may unknowingly hurt the feelings of this personality. They find dishonesty distasteful and believe that human beings really could all live in harmony with each other, only if everyone could agree to live according to a high code of ethics, instead of just living by rules. While the Fire type is motivated by action, the Water type searches for harmony and love.

SUGGESTED CAREERS FOR WATER

actor/actress
advertising manager
art director
artist
artist's agent
astrologist
book salesperson
broadcasting director
burial-needs salesperson
career counselor
casework supervisor
child psychologist
classical music composer
clergy member

college counselor
college professor, arts & humanities
college recruiter
counselor
day care director
dean of students
designer (any)
employee welfare manager
employment counselor
engineering psychologist
fashion coordinator
film producer
financial services sales agent
foreign student adviser
fund raiser
geriatric social worker
gift shop owner
graphic designer
high school counselor
hypnotherapist
image consultant
industrial psychologist
interior designer
internist
labor relations specialist
literary agent
lobbyist
marriage & family counselor
model & modeling instructor
museum exhibit designer
music therapist
naturopathic physician
newspaper editor
news reporter
nursing home therapist
occupational therapist
parole officer
pediatrician
personal manager
personnel administrator
physical therapist
physician
playwright
poet
political science professor
principal
psychologist
public relations specialist
real estate agent

recreation leader
residence counselor
school social worker
scriptwriter
secondary school teacher
securities manager
social director
sociologist
special education director
stockbroker
summer camp director
talk show host
teacher, art
teacher, K-6
teacher, theater arts
wedding consultant
writer

AIR

The Air personality thrives on knowledge, learning, and intellectual stimulation. These individuals are information-seekers and complex problem-solvers. Air types are the inventors, scientists, and visionaries of the world, desiring reasons and explanations for its functions. They are the pioneers of the 21st century information highway. Thus the Air types often dominate the computer design and programmer positions. *To know* is the theme of the Air type; thus, they abhor not knowing. Often they have extensive facts and trivia stored in their complex minds. Debating and analyzing come naturally to the Air type, and they can be fiercely competitive, sometimes taking the opposite side of an argument — just for fun!

Very curious by nature, this type does well in most careers, although they are not always attracted to areas involving intense people contact such as child care or customer service.

The Air personality is excellent at objective, accurate observation, which serves them well in any type of research. This type, however, sometimes allows their intellect to outweigh their emotions, causing conflict when personal feelings enter into a situation. In addition, they may spend too much time gathering information, causing an unnecessary delay in decision-making.

The Air type enjoys discussion and exploration of politics, scientific discoveries, and new inventions. To not know or to be without information is very uncomfortable for this type. While Water types are intuitive and analytical when dealing with people and human emotions, Air types do well in a similar fashion when processing heaps of data and facts, using intuition, analysis and abstract thought to solve problems. They would prefer to not apply this similar process to their own emotions, however. Discussing their personal feelings and insecurities are events the Air types would just as well avoid all together. Sometimes this makes the Air type seem coldhearted which is usually not their intention as they are usually fair and rational; they just aren't showing the emotion that's deep inside.

An Air type is usually a quick thinker with a dry wit and an interesting conversationalist, becoming bored without something thought-provoking to discuss or think about. They value control and dislike being overcome with emotion. They may be rather cool and reserved when conversations veer towards emotional feelings as this is often uncharted territory for Airs. As the Water type searches for self-understanding and emotional exploration, the Air type hungers for knowledge and intellectual investigation.

SUGGESTED CAREERS FOR AIR

academic researcher
actuary
advertising account executive
anthropologist
archeologist
architect
botanist
buyer
chemist
city planner
criminologist
cryptanalyst
cytologist
demographer
dramatic coach
earth scientist
ecologist
engineer
engineer technologist
entomologist
entrepreneur

environmental scientist
executive banker
film producer
foreign correspondent
fund raiser
geneticist
geographer
geologist
geophysicist
horticulturist
industrial designer
information scientist
information systems analyst
intelligence research specialist
investigator
investment banker
inventor
interior designer
international lawyer
judge
labor relations consultant
lawyer
literary agent
lobbyist
management analyst
marine biologist
market research analyst
mechanical engineer
metallurgical engineer
meteorologist
microbiologist
mineralogist
movie director
neurologist
news analyst
newspaper columnist
newspaper editorial writer
nuclear engineer
nuclear physicist
ocean engineer
oceanographer
paleontologist
pharmacologist
photojournalist
physical anthropologist
physicist
political scientist
politician
psychologist

publisher
radiologist
real estate agent
recording engineer
research psychologist
seismologist
sociologist
space physicist
statistician
systems analyst
tax fraud investigator
web page designer

EARTH

Work first, play later sums up the responsible nature of the Earth personality. The Earth type is the Rock of Gibraltar, the traditionalist, the structure for our communities. This type can be counted on to follow through with his or her word. Without the Earth type, chaos would reign. Though sometimes serious in nature, this type is usually thoughtful, understanding, and loyal. Earth personalities have the ability to focus consistently on a particular project to completion. Usually humble and modest, these types often surprise others with an unexpected specialty or area of expertise.

The Earth personality has a need to serve; therefore, they often work in the medical professions, as well as in business, government, and the trades. Since these types are realists, they usually are skilled at practical, concrete activities involving the five senses, such as accounting, finance, and management. Work that's measurable with a right and wrong way of completing is more preferable to the Earth type than tasks involving abstract thought and variation. The facts are most important to the Earth's way of thinking rather than personal bias and situational information. They like to work with structure and procedures, preferring change in small doses. If Earth types find themselves interested in the creative arts, they often opt for a more secure position or choose to experience their creativity through their hobbies (unless they have strong Fire or Water characteristics).

In personal relationships, the Earth type is stable and predictable. Usually good-natured and calm, this type appreciates the traditional aspects of family, honoring holidays and other ceremonies. They are often conservative and polite, very friendly if more extroverted, while reserved if more introverted. This type is extremely loyal and responsible. They usually follow through on the details of any project they find interesting.

The Earth types are the caretakers, nurturers, and hosts of work and family, making sure others are content and striving to keep stability in our world.

SUGGESTED CAREERS FOR EARTH

accountant
acupuncturist
aircraft inspector
airline dispatcher
airport manager
alcohol/drug counselor
appraiser
auditor
automobile service manager
bank operations officer
brokerage manager
building materials supplier
caterer
child care helper or manager
chiropractor
collections manager
college admissions administrator
commercial banker
computer programmer or operator
construction estimator or inspector
contract specialist
controller
credit analyst
customs-import specialist
dental assistant or hygienist
dental laboratory manager
dentist
department store manger
dermatologist
dietitian
electrical inspector
engineer
environmental specialist
escrow officer
estate planner
financial analyst
fire inspector
food & beverage manager

funeral director
gardener
golf club manager
health officer
highway inspector
historian
home economist
hospital administrator
hotel manager
import-export agent
international banker
lawyer
librarian
loan officer
manager
medical administrator
massage therapist
occupational therapist
officer manager
optician
paralegal
park superintendent
patent attorney
pawn broker
personal manager
personnel administrator
physical therapist
police officer or chief
postmaster
prison warden
purchasing agent
radiation therapist
respiratory therapist
secretary
securities/brokerage manager
social worker
speech pathologist
stenographer
systems analyst
teacher, K - 12
veterinarian
wedding consultant
wholesaler

Now, that you've reviewed your personality preferences and selected options from the career lists, turn to your *MAGICAL QUEST SUMMARY* and *CAREER OPTIONS LIST*. Under the heading *MY ELEMENTS* write a summary of your personality type or types: *FIRE,*

WATER, AIR, or *EARTH*. Then list at least five new career possibilities under your *OPTIONS LIST*.

INTERNET ASSESSMENTS – More About Me!?

At this point you hopefully have a greater understanding about yourself and several career options to consider. If, however, you want to take more assessments then you may find the following internet sites helpful:

Campbell Interest & Skills Survey -
http://assessments.ncs.com/assessments/tests/ciss.htm

Enneagram Personality Assessment -
http://www.enneagraminstitute.com/
http://www.ideodynamic.com/enneagram-monthly/
http://www.prosperity.com/enneagram/

General Assessments -
http://www.prospects.ac.uk/cms/
http://www.niefs.net/intera.htm

Keirsey Temperament Sorter -
http://www.keirsey.com

The Self Directed Search -
http://www.self-directed-search.com/
http://www.self-directed-search.com/aboutsds.html

Values Assessment -
http://www.prenhall.com/success

These various inventories merely provide more information for self discovery. Decision-making involves much more than taking assessments. Uncovering your purpose is your next step. Following this you will explore your options.

The remaining chapters assist in solidifying your goals, moving from a general idea to a more specific plan of what you want to do.

MY PURPOSE -
Let's Discover!

The exercises and ideas you've completed so far provide insight into selecting your purpose. Another way to approach the topic is to say, "Why will I work?" Discovering your purpose is different than selecting the actual career or careers you will pursue. It is broader, defining the style or feel of your work, providing a loose structure for the direction that your work life will take. Basically you want to write a mission statement for yourself — one or two sentences that explain why you work. The mission statement makes deciding which career or careers to pursue much, much easier.

To discover your answer, brainstorm, discuss, write, and meditate about your *Magical Quest Summary*. Look at your top values to determine the main theme behind your work. Your top skills from the *Skills Check List* and strengths from your top *Inner Quest* types both provide the types of activities you would like in your work. Use this information to define a purpose. You may want to write each item on an index card. Then place the cards into clusters based on similarity. You can also place the cards in order of importance. Notice how you feel. At the end of this chapter is a page titled *Notes For My Purpose* for you to write down ideas and phrases that come to mind. Don't judge what comes up for you. These notes help you eventually write your finished statement of purpose. Allow your mind to process your ideas while listening to your heart.

Next, look for themes and ideas that are woven through your preferences. Are you leaning towards something in the helping or creative areas of work? Are you more analytical and business-minded? Or is there an outdoor, adventurous streak showing up in your preferences? There is no right or wrong in this activity — what you select is merely based on *your* desires. Some purposes are simple, others complex. Some are spiritually meaningful, others extravagant, filled with power. Consider what motivates and inspires you. Examples of purpose or mission statements are:

- "To entertain and enlighten the world."
- "I pledge to provide support for children in the United States."
- "To make tons of money in business as a leader using analytical skills."

- "To use hands-on and problem-solving skills in a technical environment."
- "I want to work outdoors helping to end racism."
- "To be rich and famous working in a creative environment."
- "To help people in a positive manner that allows me time to raise a family."

Another way to explore your purpose is to ask yourself what you want people to say about you after you die. Don't think of this in a morbid fashion but rather as an exercise to fantasize about your future. What type of legacy will you leave the world? These answers probably tie in with your summary results which lead to your statement of purpose. Writing your statement helps you become very clear about how you want your future to unfold. Again your purpose needn't be anything grandiose. The criteria is that it fits you!

If an answer is not jumping out, give it time to incubate. Your mind, body, and soul must come together; then ever so slowly, your intuition reveals an answer. It will not be forced. It can be helpful to discuss your feelings and ideas about your summary and your purpose with someone who cares about you. Journal-writing and meditating also assists in releasing this answer. You may need to move on to explore careers (discussed in the next chapter) before you can establish your purpose for working. Then return to this section. Do what works for you. If you have tried a variety of methods for uncovering the answer and nothing fits just yet, then let it go for a while. Save your notes, however. Don't dwell on the need to know, grinding your brain. Just forget about your mission statement for now. Something will pop up, quite possibly when you least expect it.

Definitely select your purpose at some point. If it's not flowing to you now, then perhaps gather more information about your options and then explore. Don't fret. If you feel really frustrated, turn your mind off and give it a rest! During your career planning process, an answer will appear as long as you follow the suggestions I am offering.

GUARANTEED SUCCESS - You Mean, Have My Dream Come True?

Together, we have uncovered many options. You've learned new things about yourself or reconfirmed what you already knew. Possible career ideas have been flowing through your mind as you've considered the roads you might take. You've been asking questions like, *What do I like about such and such option? What will my life movie look like?* You've been exploring, dreaming, wondering, and searching. You know that anything is possible. When the time is right, you will make a selection for your future career or careers.

Sometimes our deepest desire lies just below the surface, but we avoid acknowledging these feelings. Worries and concerns may hold us back, obscuring our vision of what we know is right for our future. We know our purpose, but cannot see. We know our essence, but cannot feel. We know our next step, but cannot move. We do not believe. So, for just this moment, take that next right step in your mind and imagine you could have *any* career, *any* occupation, *any* lifestyle you fancied, that no barriers exist. Erase any negative factors and influences that would prevent you from living your dreams. For a moment, do not concern yourself with the competition, future of the job market, family pressures, or societal influences. Ignore any concerns you have about your age, appearance, marital status, family, financial responsibilities, intelligence or abilities. Imagine that your fairy godmother *could* appear, wave her magic wand, and poof — there would be your answer, your desire. If you lived in a perfect world without worries, concerns, or problems, what career would you select if you were *guaranteed success*?

Explore the fantasy career or careers to this answer. Imagine, visualize, feel, smell, and taste the spirit of your desires. If you don't know, take a guess and make a choice just for today. What is your wish today? If you have several fantasy careers, explore each one of these in detail. Specifically, what would your days be like if you pursued any one of these ideas? Who would you interact with? On the next page explain in detail what you would do moment by moment. Describe your work setting. Write a very specific scenario of your dream describing the who, what, and where of your vision. Make up characters and scenarios that would happen while you work. What motivates you to pursue this idea? The ex-

ercise of writing about your dream(s) may serve as a catalyst towards making them come true. If this task seems too overwhelming, return to this activity after you've completed the suggestions offered in the next chapter: CAREERS.

*The small whisper within my chest aches to be heard.
Its subtle knowing silently makes its presence.*

*Daily detors of society rumble; cars, trucks, and planes destract the sounds inside.
Advertised rules for living noisely clutter my mind; chitter chatter, shoulds and woulds obstruct the vision.*

*If I could see clearly, then I wouldn't be blind.
If I could hear easily, then I wouldn't be deaf.*

If someone would listen then I would say the truth.

That my seed of Creativity yearns to be free, that my whisper longs to be heard, that my knowing has been unleashed.

I am complete.

MY DREAM CAREER -
If I were guaranteed success...

LIVE THE DREAM -
And, How Do I Do That?

Are you ready to begin your dream today? It's a bit frightening to realize you can actually experience all you have ever fantasized. With enough determination, passion, and commitment, you can make your dreams a reality. Maybe you do not have an immediate answer to the question in discussion — no problem, continue reading. Or maybe you need more skills to pursue your dream; if so, begin now to improve your skills. Perhaps you do know exactly what you desire, then begin now. Everyone wishes to live their dreams, so why not do just that? Live your dream! Skip to Chapter Five - *GOALS* and *get started*!

On the other hand, you may be skeptical about this fantasy concept and do not believe it possible. After all, you might say, "Work wasn't made to be fun." "There's a lot of competition, you know." "Only the lucky few ever have a life full of excitement." Perhaps you have some very good, logical reasons why your wishes won't come true. You may even have physical limitations that keep you from your dream career. After all, if you're deaf, you probably won't be a police officer. If you're 30 and want to be an NBA basketball player, but you've played very little sports, it's probably a tough dream to achieve. For most people, however, their dreams can become reality if they want to work at it. I had a student who didn't start figure skating until she was 19 and then she skated professionally. When I met her at 50 she was still skating and teaching others to skate! An actress had her first substantial television role on the show *Northern Exposures* when she was in her 60s. I knew of a janitor for a school, who after years of working, decided to go to school herself. Eventually she became a teacher and finally achieved her dream. The possibilities are endless.

Fantasies don't guarantee success, but with enough determination, preparation, and belief, your dreams can come true. By taking small steps towards the completion of your goals, they will eventually become reality. Consider how much effort you want to put forth to achieve a dream. Quite possibly the reasons you give for not living your dream may just be excuses. Perhaps you're using some of the following rationalizations to justify why you can't live the reality you desire:

- There's too much competition.
- I am not talented (or smart or ...) enough.
- I don't have any experience.
- My partner doesn't want me to change.
- I am too old.
- I can't move.
- I can't afford it.
- I don't have enough money.
- There are no jobs in my town.
- I might fail.
- I have children.
- I am a minority.
- I am too young.
- I have a family business to run.
- I have a mortgage payment.
- My family doesn't approve.
- I am a man.
- I am a woman.
- It will take too long.

If you believe these statements, then you may feel more comfortable selecting a career that you like less than your dream, something you feel is safer and more realistic. But truly, what is realistic? Is landing on the moon practical? Is sending messages through wires realistic? What about repairing a human heart, seeing people on a TV screen, or selling two million CDs? It's intimidating to go for the impossible — the choice that may cause the people you know to say, "Oh, I don't know about that! You're crazy; that's too competitive!" And, pursuing the impossible usually requires lots of time and effort. Maybe you just don't want to work that hard.

We may feel discouraged because we feel inadequate or afraid of tough competition. Other times we concoct ridiculous reasons as to why our idea will not work. Psychologists have studied winners, however, and found that high intelligence, good looks, talent, or wealth *were not* the factors that brought prosperity. The common denominator among successful individuals was their *desire* to achieve their goal. Brian Tracy, a motivational speaker, states in one of his success tapes that these people are "unstoppable." Within their desire is the ability and willingness to complete goals steadily, step by step. Success takes time. Many people plod along diligently, eventually arriving at their destination, just like the turtle in *The Tortoise and The Hare*.

So the question still remains: *Why limit yourself?* Preferring to ignore their potential; many people do support limited viewpoints, not expecting their lives to be wonderful. Les Brown, a popular motivational speaker, mentioned on one of his videos "that most great ideas are taken to the grave." I'm sure you don't want that for your life! Individuals who believe differently experience lives of much happiness. Perhaps a limited existence is the result of limited thinking. Why not choose the path you desire? Choose the one that feels best for you, however unassuming or magnificent.

Actor Christopher Reeves epitomized living one's potential as he spoke at the 1996 Democratic National Convention in his wheelchair. His spinal cord injury has not halted his journey to pursue his passions. Not only was his life before his injury filled with many interests, he has continued to courageously and gracefully live with purpose. Reeves has directed a movie, written a book, and is active in politics. His message at the Democratic National Convention focused on potential. He encouraged Americans to adopt the NASA astronauts' motto: *Nothing Is Impossible.* He reminded us all that being an American is believing that dreams can come true — a principle the United States was founded and built on. Make *Nothing Is Impossible* your motto.

What if the majority of people believed in abundance, a belief that everyone can experience *their* personal best? Our world would be very, very different. With more people believing in and achieving excellence, greatness occurs. Fortunately, many people do live their vision, never doubting their power. Remember George Burns' advice: "Do what you love and you'll never work a day in your life." Why not adopt this idea. Create an open-minded, optimistic perspective knowing that *you* can live your dreams? *The Bible* supports this similar belief in Mark 2:24, "What things so ever you desire, when you pray, believe that you receive them, and you shall have them." Shakti Gawain in her book *Creative Visualization* states a similar theme in a more modern style:

> *Every moment of your life is infinitely creative and the universe is endlessly bountiful.*
> *Just put forth a clear enough request, and everything your heart desires must come to you.*

Won't you join all the positive people in the world and begin to live the life you imagine? Life would be grand and unlike our current existence if the majority of people embraced this glorious concept of self-empowerment — a beautiful scenario to imagine. How exciting it is to know that your life can be like your vision, if you *choose* to believe that anything is possible.

To begin your task, you must have infinite tenacity and willingness to grow. I remember Cathy, a young, 25-year-old single parent I counseled one summer. At the beginning of each counseling session she would tell me about her Alcoholics Anonymous meetings and how she was doing so well. Her eyes would light up as she talked about a picture she was painting or a play she was auditioning for — all volunteer work. Cathy told me she wanted to be a dental hygienist and that school was her first priority. I asked her why she selected this career instead of something creative? She informed me that it would be a good way for her to support her daughter and herself, but she never mentioned her love for being a dental hygienist. Since Cathy showed little excitement when speaking about the dental field, yet radiated enthusiasm when speaking of her creative projects, I suggested that she might select a career involving art or acting, such as working in advertising, graphic arts, or movies. "No," she said, "it wouldn't work." She decided that the competition was too much, even before she gave it a chance. We discussed the concept of living dreams; however, she seemed more interested in the requirements to be a dental hygienist. I planted seeds, although I had no idea if they would sprout.

A year later as I walked across the college campus where I worked, Cathy came running up to me enthusiastically with a huge smile on her face. She had a gleam in her eye and a cute, new stylish haircut. She told me she had taken an art class and her teacher had encouraged her to submit her portfolio to The Art Center in Pasadena, California. To Cathy's surprise she was accepted. She was ecstatic. Being a dental hygienist was out, and she was on her way to living her fantasy. You'll never know what is possible until you invest yourself and take some action toward this desire. Follow your own rhythm, just as Henry David Thoreau writes:

If a man does not keep pace with his companions, perhaps it is because he hears a different drummer.

Let him step to the music which he hears, however measured or far away.

As you begin to explore your career possibilities, cultivate the qualities of drive, desire, and persistence. Courageously carve your own path.

WRAP UP -
On To Careers, Yikes!

Your next step entails learning about the careers you might want to pursue. You want an expanded list of options so that in the end, when you do make a selection, you will feel confident with your choice. Now is not the time to select your career (unless you're 100% sure of what you want!). Now is the time to continue exploring. Review your *MAGICAL QUEST SUMMARY* and confirm that it describes you. Your *SUMMARY* is just that — an overview of you, highlighting your preferences including your *values, inner quest results, skills,* and *elements.* Look for the themes running through your assessment results. Evaluate your purpose, your mission statement. Examine and ponder your *SUMMARY.* Most likely, the careers you've selected for your *CAREER OPTIONS LIST* fit well with your *SUMMARY* results. If you look closely, your career answer may be visible. Meditate over your results. Don't rush for a decision. Remember that you are still in the inquiring phase, so stay open-minded and postpone making a decision until you've investigated your options. Examine your results carefully; determine if you want to make any changes on your *SUMMARY* or *CAREER OPTIONS LIST.*

In the next chapter you'll receive suggestions on how to investigate your options, consider the ramifications of each, and try on for size a variety of careers, as if you were shopping. Concentrate on understanding the specific characteristics of each career option. You will look into the careers you wrote on your *CAREER OPTIONS LIST.* For each career you're considering, get an accurate picture of what it entails. Learning the specifics of your options provides you with information necessary to make a thoughtful decision. Your choice won't be based on the glamour or the image of the career. Instead, it will be based on reality and your preferences.

If you do not have enough possibilities to explore, review your *inner quest, skills,* and *elements results* and their corresponding option lists for more possibilities. At the very least choose the 10 best options, even if the ideas do not thrill you. Perhaps you overlooked unfamiliar careers or made biased judgments in your selections. Reflect on the careers you know nothing about, as who knows what they may offer? An unknown option might just be your buried treasure!

Next, in Chapter Three — *CAREERS,* we will address how to explore your options which ultimately aides you in selecting an option (or options) that fits your purpose. Discussion of specific resources and ways to discover information about your alternatives begins. As you continue your exploratory journey, remember the words of Helen Keller: "Life is either a daring adventure or nothing."

The synchronicity of life reminds us that all unfolds perfectly, provding lessons, taking us outside ourselves.

We become more.
We become stronger.

Critical ideas from minds well meant vanish from our psyches.

We learn to trust the truth, the pure, the next right step that waits within our hearts.
Spirit guides with unconditional love.

MAGICAL QUEST SUMMARY

MY TOP FIVE VALUES

MY INNER QUEST RESULTS

MY TOP TEN SKILLS

MY ELEMENTS

CAREER OPTIONS LIST

NOTES FOR MY PURPOSE

Chapter Three

CAREERS - So Many Careers, So Little Time

Open up to a birds-eye view.
Soar above like an eagle seeking,
  searching for the perfect perching place.
Is this the space you'll call your own?

Seeking your life purpose is an unfolding process, so allow yourself the freedom to be undecided about your future. You began exploring with some ideas. Through the activities in this book, you're expanding your choices. For the time being, investigation is your main goal. Expanding and considering many options ensures that you will ultimately select the path that's best for you. If you don't search in this fashion, you might miss the ultimate. The unsure, "I'm exploring" space is where you'll be for a while. Accept this place. It's OK to be unsure about your future. Relax and just hang-out in uncertainty. Then you'll begin to seek the thrill of your adventure, surveying the byways you might take. The path is exciting, filled with wild possibilities. Let yourself go; bask in the dreamy potential of your life. You're creating the career you want, moving with the ideas that come to your mind. If you feel confused and unsure, congratulations, you're right where you're supposed to be! You're right on target! Now is *not* the time to have your life all tied up into one neat package, knowing your exact direction; now is the time be sloppy, crazy, and free. For that matter, it's best to be flexible and open throughout life.

You embarked upon your journey in the light, but quickly moved into darkness to the uncovered spaces of your soul. You began knowing some things about yourself and had a few career options. Now your self-knowledge has increased and your avenues widened. Asking yourself tough life questions brings a myriad of answers as well as fog and haze. Yes, being uncertain may be how you'll feel for a while until you have more information. Plunge into your mission with enthusiasm, continuing on the road to clarity. Pay attention to the desires of your heart as you acquire knowledge.

Gathering facts and information about your options is crucial in creating your life-movie. The specifics you find will lead you to your foundation: the who, what, where, when, and why. Will your life-movie be an intense drama or a thrilling high packed action-adventure? A set in a national park is much different from a recording studio. Conducting a business meeting gives a totally different feel than leading pre-school children in an arts and crafts activity. So as you read and discover careers, imagine yourself actually doing the job: How do you feel? What is it like? Listen to the soft whisper of your soul. Your *desire* is your main criterion for an option at this point — remember we'll evaluate the other factors such as competition, salary, and training later. Massaging your heart in this fashion leads you to your ultimate answer.

Investigate many options. Depending on your situation, you may want to consider short and long term career goals or a couple of careers that you can do concurrently. Also you may want a few careers throughout your life, maybe one for the first 10 years, the second for the next 10 years, and so on. Be open and free. Avoid negative judgments while you dig, ready to shoo them away if necessary.

I urge you to make sufficient time to explore your possibilities by reading and talking to people working in the fields you like.

Most of us spend the majority of our life working, so it makes sense to devote time to learning about our options *before* making a commitment. Yet many people commit to a career, train, and begin working only to find that they dislike the field. Amazingly, information about buying automobiles, furniture, and appliances is more sought after than information about careers. Finding data about careers can be obtained at a library, a college career center, on the Internet, or by talking to people doing the particular career. It's far better to spend time gathering information now, *before* making an investment, than later after you've trained for something new.

We live in a society where individuals spend more time planning a vacation or buying a car than planning their careers. As you explore your options, keep the question, *What's my purpose?* in the back of your mind. Study your values and options and your purpose may be revealed to you. Journal writing, meditation, and prayer can bring your wishes to the forefront. Remember that your purpose may be simple and pleasure-oriented or perhaps more complex and profound. Consider what type of contribution you want to make to the world. As you explore, ask for guidance from your Higher Power and you will be shown the next right step. The information you obtain helps your answer unfold, bringing you closer to a decision. Within your inner soul you already know your destiny; you're simply bringing it into your conscious mind. Slowly you uncover your purpose. Time spent now, to learn the realities of a career, saves you time later.

Follow the suggestions given in this chapter to learn more about the possibilities, and I promise you'll eventually feel happy about your work. Examination now eliminates the hit-and-miss job search later. Reserve time in your busy schedule, making this investigation your priority, even if it means socializing less, taking a day off work, or postponing an obligation. If you're in school, don't wait until you graduate to begin delving into your options. Do it now! If you're feeling nervous about a change, talk with people you trust about your feelings. If you're already working, don't use the excuse of "no time" to avoid exploring. Folks make time to see a movie or attend their child's event, so make time for you. If you dislike research, think of it instead as a journey into your future — a shopping trip, a date, or a search for buried treasure. You're designing your magical career path! There will be no pay-off now for researching, no tangible benefit. Your reward comes later when you find yourself passionately going to work with a smile on your face, feeling grateful for your life. Now is the time to determine how you really feel. Now is the time to try on. Now is the time to test the waters.

Most of my students and clients report that once they started hunting, they really enjoy learning about their options. They are amazed at how much information is actually available and how the knowledge they gain really assists them in making a decision.

Various resources exist that describe careers in detail. On the next few pages you will determine what to look for and where to go.

AREAS TO EXPLORE -
Oh, That Sounds Good.

Most of the books and career resources in libraries, bookstores, and career centers provide similar information. A myriad of resources exist. Each book does not list every career. If one resource does not have the option you want, move on to a different source. When seeking specific information about each career, examine the following:

- **JOB DUTIES** - What is the nature of the work? Find out exactly what you would do on the job. What types of duties does this work require? What percentage of time do the main duties require? How much variety is offered? Consider how you feel and what you think about the option. Visualize yourself doing these particular activities. How does it feel?

- **PERSONALITY AND SKILLS** - What specific skills would you need to excel in this field? What type of people do this work? For example, are they quiet, methodical, and detail-oriented; or outgoing, talkative, and enthusiastic? Do you seem to fit with this group?

- **SALARY AND REWARDS** - What are the beginning, average, and high-end salaries for this career? What intangible satisfaction would you obtain from this type of work? What are the opportunities for advancement? What career paths are possible?

- **TRAINING** - What type of training and education is required to enter this field? Is a particular certificate, license, or degree required? Are you interested in committing to this level of training?

- **WORK ENVIRONMENT** - Where would you perform this work? What type of businesses hire people in this field? Is self-employment an option? Can you freelance or work at home? Do you need to be a self-starter for this profession?

- **JOB OUTLOOK** - What is the projected long-term demand for this career? Is it expected to grow, remain the same, or subside? What is the competition? Are you willing to put forth the effort necessary to be successful in this field? How much risk is involved?

- **SOURCES OF ADDITIONAL INFORMATION** - Where can you obtain more information about this occupation? What are the professional organizations associated with the field? Write these associations for more information about the careers you really like.

Most reputable career resources cover these categories. When reading about a specific job, visualize yourself in that position and notice your gut feeling. Are you getting a *hit*? Does this option fit with your perception of your life-movie? Do you like the job duties of this option?

WHERE TO GO - I'm Ready To Learn.

Public libraries, universities, community colleges, community centers, women's centers, adult education offices, and book stores usually have some type of printed career publications in the form of books, pamphlets, and brochures. Visit any of these locations and utilize their services. Most materials include all the basic information you need to know about a career. Some locations may also have computerized guidance systems. These user-friendly systems give printouts of specific careers. The internet offers many career research sites as well. Be insatiably curious on your adventure. Call any of the suggested agencies and ask for what you need. If you're bewildered and not sure where to start, call the mayor's office or the local Chamber of Commerce. The people working in these offices are usually eager to help and will know where to direct you. Ask for what you want.

Community college career centers are the best kept secret. Most people remain unaware of the abundance of material available at these locations. Typically, the centers are open to the public with friendly, knowledgeable career technicians. Usually, you don't have to be a student to use the resources. Check them out! If you don't find what you need, move on to another source such as the internet, library or bookstore.

Finally, the most enlightenment and insight you can find comes from speaking to people about their careers and observing their work (to be discussed later in the chapter). There's no substitute for human contact. Many subtle nuances can be gleaned from a chat with someone who's doing the career you might pursue.

THE INTERNET

A wealth of information is available through various sites, such as *Compuserve, America Online,* Web pages, news groups, and chat rooms. Linking yourself to the Internet connects you with the whole world, allowing you to communicate with people who may be able to help you. Search for information using the career title or field. You might hook into a chat room related to your career interests. Ask for specific information about the career (as discussed previously) and perhaps ask the informational interview questions listed further in this chapter. Information and actual sites on the Web change daily. Following are some sites that were available at the time of this printing:

General Sites About Careers:

Bridges Career Exploration -
http://cx.bridges.com/

Career Exploration -
http://www.khake.com/page2.html
http://www.webcoin.net/html/careernames.html

Occupational Outlook Handbook -
http://www.bls.gov/oco

Professional Associations -
http://www.seekingsuccess.com/assoc.php3
http://www.marketingsource.com/associations/

Specific Information By Subject:

Accounting -
http://www.aicpa.org/index.htm
Anthropology -
http://www.practicinganthropology.org/
Aquatic Science -
http://www.aslo.org/aquatic.html
Art & Architecture -
http://www.library.american.edu/subject/art/org.html
Arts & Entertainment -
http://web.princeton.edu/sites/career/undergrad/
Industries/a&e.shtml
Business Management -
http://www.b2gfree.com/associations.htm
Chemistry -
http://libwww.syr.edu/research/internet/chemistry/
societies.html
Creative Freelancers -
http://www.freelancers.com
Criminal Justice -
http://www.unl.edu/crimjust/PROFESSIONAL.html
Computer Science -
http://www.khake.com/page17.html
Education -
http://www.k12jobs.com

Engineering -
http://www.khake.com/page53.html
English -
http://www.wm.edu/CAS/english/handbook.php
Finance -
http://www.saludos.com/cguide/bguide.html#finplanners
Geography -
http://www.aag.org/
History -
http://www.library.csi.cuny.edu/dept/historymajor.html
http://www.theaha.org/
International Studies -
http://www.apsia.org/apsia/career/career.php
Mathematics -
http://mathforum.org/mam/planning/societies.html
Medical -
http://www.askdrwalker.com/
Military -
http://www.todaysmilitary.com/
Music -
http://www.khake.com/page48.html
http://www.acreativestate.com/
Nursing -
http://www.nursesworld.com/prof.asp
Parks & Recreation -
http://www.coolworks.com/showme/default.htm
Outdoor & Environmental -
http://www.princeton.edu/~oa/careeroe.html
Philosophy & Religion -
http://www.udel.edu/apa/index.html#apaonline
Physical Education & Health -
http://www.udel.edu/CSC/health.html
Physics -
http://phyastweb.la.asu.edu/links/proforg.asp
Political Science -
http://sobek.colorado.edu/POLSCI/RES/assoc.html
Psychology -
http://www.psywww.com/
Science -
http://www.aaas.org/
Sociology -
http://www.asanet.org
Special Education -
http://www.kusd.edu/favorite/bookmarks/special_ed.html
Theatre -
http://www.scu.edu/careercenter/resources
majorsandcareers/theaterdance.shtml

Exploring these sites may lead you to other sources.

CAREERS - So Many Careers, So Little Time 73

PRINTED MATERIALS

Next are some of the most common career resources available in libraries, career centers, colleges and other agencies offering career services. They are also available for purchase:

• The Occupational Outlook Handbook

(http://www.bls.gov/oco)
This book offers detailed descriptions of the more popular occupations in the United States. It also includes general labor trends for the next ten years. It is published every two years by the United States Department of Labor. It is available on the internet and may be ordered from JIST publishing:

JIST Publishing
8902 Otis Avenue
Indianapolis, IN 46216-1033
Phone: (800) 648-5478
http://www.jist.com/

• Chronicle Guidance Publications

66 Aurora Street,
Monrovia, NY 13118-3576
Phone: (800) 899-0454
FAX: (315) 497-3359
e-mail: CustomerService@ChronicleGuidance.com
http://www.chronicleguidance.com/

This publication covers over 800 descriptions of careers in loose-leaf form. Some of their titles include Cruise Directors, Sports Instructors and Recreation Workers.

• The Encyclopedia of Careers & Vocational Guidance

J.G. Ferguson Publishing Company
200 W. Madison, Suite 300
Chicago, IL 60606
(800) 322-8755
http://www.fergpubco.com/
These four volumes describe careers in over 70 industries, giving descriptions of 2,300 occupations.

• Vocational Biographies, Inc.

P.O. Box 31
Sauk Center, MN 56378
Phone: (800) 255-0752
FAX: 1 (320) 352-5546
http://www.vocbio.com/

These loose-leaf biographies offer over 2,000 personal interviews with people in a variety of careers and specific facts about the career, e.g., Visual Merchandiser and Copy Writer.

VGM - Vocational Guidance Management

McGraw-Hill Companies
P.O. Box 545
Blacklick, OH 43004-0545
Phone: (800) 722-4726
http://www.booksmcgraw-hill.com

VGM offers three series of books:

1. VGM Professional Career Series. This series includes 14 volumes of career opportunities in different industries with up-to-date information about each industry. For example, *Careers In Accounting* and *Careers In High Tech* are two of the titles available.

2. Careers For ... & Other ... Types. This is another excellent series which describes careers in particular industries, offering such titles as *Careers For Travel Buffs & Other Restless Types, Careers For Nature Lovers & Other Outdoor Types, Careers For Film Buffs & Other Visual Types* ... and *Careers For Culture Lovers & Other Artsy Types.* Numerous other titles exist.

3. Opportunities In ... These books also outline a variety of industries with such titles as *Opportunities in Forestry* and *Opportunities in Television & Video.*

If you wish to order your own books or pamphlets, contact the companies directly. Or you may want to contact the distributing organizations. The following companies sell many of these books, as well as a variety of other career related resources:

Meridian Education Corporation
P.O. Box 911
Monmouth Jet, NJ 08852-0911
Phone: (800) 727-5507
FAX: (888) 340-5507
e-mail: custmserv@meridianeducation.com
http://www.MeridianEducation.com/

NIMCO
103 Hwy 81N
P.O. Box 9
Calhoun, KY 42327-0009
Phone: 1-800-962-6662
e-mail: support@nimcoinc.com
http://www.nimcoinc.com/

Peterson's
2000 Lenox Drive
P.O. Box 67005
Lawrenceville, NJ 08648
Phone: (877) 433-8277
FAX: (609) 243-9150
e-mail: support@petersons.com
http://www.petersons.com/

Purchasing books in your areas of interest may be more convenient than using the internet or going to a center or library; however, many public libraries also offer adequate career reference sections.

COMPUTER PROGRAMS

Several worthwhile computer career guidance systems are useful for research and self-assessment. Usually these are available for use through college career centers or government employment offices. A few of the more popular programs that may be available in your area are: *SIGI, EUREKA,* and *CAREER & COLLEGE QUEST.* Depending on the program, it may provide descriptions of careers and information on colleges, financial aid, scholarships, job search, resume writing, owning your own business, and the military. *EUREKA,* for example gives descriptions on several hundred occupations in California, with salary and demand projections just for the state. *CAREER & COLLEGE QUEST* includes the largest bank of financial aid information, covering scholarships, grants, and loans. In addition, the programs often offer interest inventory assessments that give a list of career options based on the answers you input. These programs are easy to use. Usually printouts of the information are also available.

COLLEGE PROFESSORS & COUNSELORS

Another idea for gathering knowledge about your options is to speak with the individuals teaching the disciplines you may be interested in pursuing. Telephone or visit college professors and vocational school instructors who teach disciplines related to your particular areas of interest. Educators should know the pulse of the industries they teach. Ask them to describe the jobs graduates of their programs pursue. They may be able to refer you to speak with a graduate or other organizations. You may even come across a new option. If you're not sure which schools offer the programs you like, ask a college career or counseling center or reference librarian for a referral. As you continue to seek information for your future, keep in mind the words of Jim Rohn, a well-known personal development teacher: "I find it fascinating that most people plan their vacations with better care than they do their lives. Perhaps that is because escape is easier than change." Embrace change with enthusiasm. Do not overlook the necessity of thoroughly understanding your options. We're talking about your life! It deserves your undivided attention and care, so do not shortchange yourself during this most crucial phase of your planning!

PROFESSIONAL ORGANIZATIONS

Almost every career area is affiliated with a professional association. These groups gather people together who want to keep abreast of the growth and changes within their particular field. The association usually offers a newsletter or trade journal that covers trends and issues in the industry. Write the professional organizations to request information about the careers you are considering. You might want to include a self-addressed stamped envelope. Most career resources list the addresses and telephone numbers of these organizations and associations. Most public libraries have directories that offer this information.

Additionally, you might consider attending meetings or seminars offered for the people in your fields of interest. Observing a room full of people from a particular industry is a fantastic way to learn the style and type of people in that field. And to determine if you fit with the group. A room full of trial attorneys is much different from a room full of elementary school counselors. Speaking with people at these gatherings gives you the opportunity to learn more about the profession and the topics the members consider important. Your interest in the career may increase or wane depending on your observations. You usually don't need to be a member of the group to attend an event.

INFORMATIONAL INTERVIEWS

An *informational interview* is a meeting that you arrange with someone who works in a position you might like. During the meeting you ask the person questions about his or her work, i.e., "What are the positive and negative aspects of your work?" You learn a great deal about the job and work environment. Talking to people in their work settings gives you the opportunity to discover the nuances of a profession not expressed in written material.

Usually, people are receptive to the idea of an informational interview. For a short time you become a journalist and your interviewee becomes a celebrity of sorts. People love to talk about themselves, so you should have favorable results when searching for someone to interview.

Some of my students have felt reluctant to call a stranger, or even someone they know, to ask about his or her career. Understandably, you might feel awkward at first; however, almost everyone I know who has conducted an informational interview experienced positive results! Most students report that the interviews *greatly* help them with making decisions about their futures. Many individuals gained a new contact, and some were even offered training or a job.

If you already have friends or acquaintances in the fields you're considering, of course, contact these people. They may know a friend-of-a-friend they can hook you up with. On the other hand, if you don't know anyone working in the occupations you like, make a cold call — just explain your purpose for calling. Use the telephone book, information operator, Chamber of Commerce directory, or library reference materials to locate businesses, organizations, or individuals. Be optimistic and open-minded. You may need to make a few phone calls before actually finding the right contact. If you don't immediately receive the results you desire, try another person. Ask the people you interview if they can connect you to other people in your areas of interest. Reach

people using the following ideas:

- friends-of-friends, and neighbors relatives, even distant relatives
- past and present teachers & professors
- the Internet
- professional and charity organizations
- yellow pages
- Chamber of Commerce mixers
- political events and fund raisers
- newspapers
- library reference materials
- past/present colleagues, supervisors, & clients
- service people (i.e., your doctors)

When telephoning a contact, explain that you are in the process of exploring your options and are considering a career in his or her field. Most people are genuinely interested in helping, as they remember the people that assisted them when they began their careers. Explain to the person that you find their position intriguing and would like more information about the occupation. State that you are *not* looking for a job, but would only like to ask a few questions about the nature of their work. Visiting the work site is important. Of course, this takes more time, but seeing the environment gives you the opportunity to observe the subtleties of a profession that you cannot notice in a telephone conversation. You will know if the surroundings give you that coming home feeling. (Or at least a close-to-home feeling!)

Be flexible and courteous when you call to arrange an interview. Ask for an appointment that would suit your interviewee best. If you don't find someone amenable to your request, select someone else. Be persistent until you speak with someone willing to give you some of their time.

You may have better success going directly to the place of employment instead of using the telephone to schedule your appointment. For example, folks like teachers, contractors, film crew members, and restaurant managers are often difficult to reach by telephone since they are usually in the field working. It might be better to stop by their work site during a lull.

Be creative when seeking an interview with people in more competitive or high-profile careers such as actors, artists, astronauts, CEOs, movie producers, professional athletes, senators, or writers. People in these positions may be more accessible than you realize. Making a simple phone call to directory assistance might just lead you to the person you seek. Sometimes all you have to do is go to their place of employment and ask! If making a few phone calls doesn't work, go to the work place, a meeting, or a convention where such people might attend. Athletes may be at their training camps — just hang out and introduce yourself. Senators and CEOs will usually respond to a letter, if they can't be reached by telephone. Schools, seminars, and training workshops are also good places to try. Writers and actors and other creative types often teach workshops and lecture through university extension programs or association gatherings — you might attend one of their classes and introduce yourself after the event. Also, you can meet writers and artists at book-signings or gallery events. Again, be assertive and request an interview after you introduce yourself. Rona, a client in her late thirties, was interested in being a cartoonist, so she wrote letters to her favorite cartoonists like Charles Schultz (*Peanuts*) and Cathy Guisewite (*Cathy*) to set up her interviews. Take risks and be daring! If you feel frustrated about contacting someone for an informational interview, remember that seeking employment in these competitive fields will be even more challenging, so be assertive and persistent. Getting an informational interview is the easy part!

If you live in a small city or rural area and the people who work in the careers you like don't live or work in your community, you might need to obtain most of your information over the telephone, through the mail, or via e-mail. For your interviews, however, consider taking a short trip to the closest metropolitan area, scheduling appointments prior to leaving with people in your areas of interest.

Once you set your appointment, be courteous, arrive on time, and show genuine interest. Some of the questions to ask are:

1. What are your job duties?
2. What are the positive and negative aspects of your work? Why do you feel this way?
3. How did you decide to get into this field and what steps did you take to enter this field?
4. How did you feel when you decided to enter your field — scared, worried, excited? Why?
5. What surprises did you learn about your field that you did not know about before entering?
6. If you could change the past, would you make the same career choice? Why?
7. What personal qualities do you feel would be most important to have in your work and why?
8. What career paths are available within this field?
9. How competitive is it to enter your field?
10. What advice would you give to someone entering your field?

If your interviewee has a tight schedule, then ask only the first five questions, as these are the most important. After your interview, send a thank you letter, either a typed business letter on professional paper or a handwritten note on nice stationery.

Conduct a few interviews. One interview doesn't necessarily give you an accurate picture of an option. More interviews will help you become increasingly clear about your future. Consider conducting an interview once a week until you've obtained enough information. They're entertaining and invaluable. The interview often enables you to make a decision. Jeff, a friend of mine, decided through his informational interviews that the business environment would be too stifling and serious for him. Initially, he felt that he might enjoy being a manager because he had worked in this field and done well; his passion, however, was working with children, possibly teaching. Jeff believed pursuing management the wiser choice because management generally pays more than teaching. After his first interview with a business manager, he decided to investigate teaching. He interviewed a couple of teachers and spent time observing in the classroom. Jeff commented on these experiences, "It was like going home. I just knew teaching was for me." He made up his mind and ultimately pursued teaching. His interviews paid off.

Some people feel *really* uncertain about the world of work and where they fit. If this sounds like you, then consider getting some type of job for about six months that gives you the occasion to meet lots of people. You might consider such jobs as a bartender, waiter, front desk hotel clerk, concierge, cab driver, salesperson, health club worker, or bottled water deliverer. Through your interactions with customers you will meet a variety of people, allowing you to conduct mini-interviews daily! You'll have people coming your way, providing almost limitless opportunities to ask questions.

As you move into the flow of exploring, be prepared to bump into people unexpectedly. The magic of syncronicity may happen to you. One of my students, Melanie, found herself meeting lots of people in the career areas she was considering, so she put the interview questions on an index card and began carrying the card in her wallet. When she met someone interesting, she was prepared to ask questions.

Another student, David, had a completely unexpected meeting with someone in a career he was considering: an FBI agent. At the time David, was a bank teller. One day the bank was robbed while he was working. He was shaken by the experience but was, nevertheless, able to assist the FBI agent assigned to the case. My student patiently answered all the agent's questions. After the report was complete, the agent made the mistake of saying, "And do you have anything you would like to ask me?" David whipped out his index card and said, "As a matter of fact I do." He fired away with his questions as the agent squirmed and politely answered. You just never know when you'll meet someone who can help!

JOB SHADOWS

A job shadow is similar to an informational interview, but in instead of interviewing the person you follow someone in a career you like for a day or half-day observing their experiences. This encounter lets you really see the ins and outs of the career. If you develop a good rapport with your interviewee, ask if you may return to observe that person in action. It's often an easier transition to shadow a person you interview since you've already established a relationship. Making a cold call just for a job shadow is a bit awkward. People are generally more receptive to participating in an interview first and then a job shadow. Like the informational interview, people usually agree to these requests because of their desire to support others. In fact, you are paying the interviewee a compliment by showing interest in this person's work.

During your job shadow keenly observe your surroundings and the happenings of the day. Notice the type of people you encounter and the problems they solve. Ask yourself, "How do I feel about this option? Does this particular place seem like the right life-movie set for me? Are these the characters I would like in my life-script?" This first-hand contact provides data for the

rational, emotional, and intuitive parts of your mind to collectively make a decision when the time is right. Observing directly clears up misconceptions and unrealistic views of careers. Some of the glamour disappears and you see the reality of the work. Do you like the job duties? Do they fit with the type of plot you want for your life screenplay?

Remember to show your appreciation by sending a thank you note, taking the person to lunch, or giving a small gift, such as flowers, a plant or book.

In addition to receiving information about a possible career, you're developing contacts. Cultivate relationships with people working in the careers you like. Keep in touch by periodically sending a short note, sending an e-mail, or making a quick telephone call. Ask a question or two about the industry or share something interesting. Later, when you're ready, you may want to call them for employment opportunities and contacts.

CLASSES, SEMINARS, AND LECTURES

Once you've done your preliminary research by reading and conducting informational interviews and job shadows, you may want to take a class or attend a seminar or lecture related to the fields you are considering. For example, a client of mine, Alicia, had an interest in multi-media, so she attended a seminar at a university extension program which provided an overview of this new field. She met the instructors of the program and people working in the field, all at a relatively low cost, time, and risk investment. Eventually, Alicia went into multi-media as a writer and graphic designer feeling confident with her decision, since she had spent time exploring.

Community services, community colleges, university extensions, professional organizations, and community groups offer a variety of courses that may be in just the area you want. Community service courses are offered through their own department or through the Parks & Recreation Department, depending on the organization in your city. These courses meet one to eight times, depending on the class structure, and generally cost from $20 to $80. University extension courses are available through major universities. Costs range from $25 - $500 a course, depending on the organization and length of meeting. Some classes meet once for three hours while others meet once a week for 15 weeks. Typically, these offerings are open to any community member. Take advantage of these opportunities!

Check newspapers, newsletters, or professional journals for times and locations of other workshops and seminars. The business section of your newspaper often lists upcoming events weekly. Telephone organizations directly or contact people in the field for information about classes offered through the association. Libraries are also a great way to learn about lectures and seminars. Call your local library and speak to a librarian for assistance.

INTERN AND VOLUNTEER

Another beneficial way to examine career fields is to participate in an internship program usually available through various schools and colleges. An internship consists of short-term, usually non-paid, hands-on training in a particular field. The department representing your major and the university career center usually post internship programs. However, you can initiate an internship on your own by contacting an organization of interest directly and offering your services. An intern may work in several different departments within the chosen field. When arranging your internship, outline what you would like to learn so that your experience will be meaningful. Interning is invaluable. You will gain not only marketable skills necessary for the field, but also contacts in the industry that may lead to paid employment.

Like interning, volunteering your time can also satisfy your curiosity about a particular career. You will learn about an industry and make contacts. Volunteering offers a win-win situation since the employer receives free labor and you gain valuable hands-on experience. Select places that employ people in the careers you like. Your commitment can be as little as five hours per week — just enough for you to learn about the business. Gabriella, a former student, was really unsure about her career path, so she spent a week or two volunteering at the places where her friends worked. It was an easy, non-threatening way for her to explore different industries and to gain exposure to the careers she was considering. Because of her status as a free employee, her level of obligation and pressure to produce lessened. Employees are more apt to share with you their experiences and not calculate your productivity when you're working for free. As a visitor, you acquire the freedom to ask questions and spy!

Volunteering or interning in your career area provides many benefits. First, you try the career on for size and determine whether you like it enough to actually pursue it. Second, you break out of the *degree with no experience* trap. Many college graduates say they cannot get a job because they have no experience. These training experiences give you the necessary skills and power to sell yourself when you do seek employment. Third, volunteering or interning provides you with valuable contacts.

Many people experience favorable results from their internships. John Singleton, the writer and director of *Higher Learning* and *Rosewood*, sold his first movie *Boyz 'n The Hood* while on an internship at a film studio. He was earning his Film degree at University of Southern California, and the internship was part of his degree requirements. While assisting on the set of a movie, he met some of the decision-makers in the business. This led him to the person who ultimately helped him sell his script. A friend of mine, Jack, started his career as a graphic artist by working for free. When a position became available, the manager hired Jack because he was trained and everyone in the office liked him and his work. Finding employment truly can be that simple!

PART-TIME WORK

Working part time in a field of interest also provides the opportunity for exploring while allowing time for additional investigation elsewhere. This experience offers some of the same benefits of interning and volunteering, with the added advantage of a paycheck. For instance, if owning a restaurant is one of your dreams, obtain a job now as a food server or manager in one of your favorite restaurants. This gives you the chance to test the waters before you write a business plan, obtain a loan, secure a restaurant, and invest a large portion of yourself into the project. If you don't have experience in the field you desire, start in an entry-level or support-staff position. You can still observe the workings of the job even though it's not the exact position you seek. Once you are trained and a better position is available, you may be one of the first candidates considered. Accept only offers that truly appeal to you and coincide with your career goals.

During your exploration time, write about your reactions to the options you're considering. Writing free-flow in a journal about various topics allows your mind to process the information you've discovered. Exposing your excitement, fears, and frustrations frees you up, allowing your intuition to make its way to the forefront of your mind, uncovering your soul's desires. Select some of these statements to write about for exploring your hopes, dreams, fears, and opinions:

- I need to spend more time researching careers.
- I know exactly what career I want.
- I will definitely have more than two careers during my life.
- My family is supportive towards me and my career choices.
- I would eventually like to have my own business.
- I feel confused about choosing my career.
- I feel excited about my choices.
- The careers I like require too much schooling.
- I would rather work part time and marry someone who has a good career.
- I have narrowed down my choices to three careers.
- Some of the careers I like have low salaries.
- I will get a part-time job in an area related to one of my career interests.
- I need to re-examine my results from the *YOU* chapter for more career ideas.
- I feel unsure about my ability to succeed in my careers of interest.
- I need to explore how I will juggle career, relationship, and family.
- I want to discover my priorities for my work and personal life.
- I need to become clear about my preferences for time, money, and security.

Let yourself drift into your intuitive mind and write with abandonment. Through the process of writing you will uncover your true feelings about your options and your future. Write about many of these topics. Write often. Writing brings you closer to a decision. Soon clarity arrives.

Speak candidly with someone you trust and admire. Share your thoughts and feelings about your research discoveries and your reactions to the statements above. Expressing your concerns and excitements out loud often brings clarity. Their comments and your processing of the information becomes a catalyst for discovery. Someone special to serve as a supportive sounding board helps you uncover your direction.

YOUR NEXT STEP

Learning as much as possible about the careers you like helps you make a decision about your future. The fear that we might not like the career we select is a major concern for a large percentage of people. Through your exploratory adventure, however, you will begin to feel more confident about knowing and selecting an option. You may have already eliminated some options. People often feel nervous about committing to a career when they don't really have an accurate understanding of the work and training required. Individuals feel nervous about their futures because they have neglected to spend time learning about their options and uncovering their purpose. In other words, take time to thoroughly investigate your options: *do not skimp on your research and discovery time*. Put your career choice in perspective with other major life choices by considering these questions: Would you get married to someone before dating and spending time with this person? Would you buy a house before carefully inspecting the inside? Would you purchase a car before taking it for a test drive? For most of us the answer to these questions is "No." Selecting a career deserves as much, if not more, attention and consideration as these major life choices. When you invest your time, thoughts, and feelings into examining the possibilities, you feel secure in making a decision for your future. As you come closer to a decision, keep in mind the following from Erica Jong:

> *Everyone has talent.*
> *What is rare is the courage to follow*
> *the talent to the dark place where it*
> *leads.*

Aspire to be honest and true to yourself as you uncover your talents. Savor and appreciate your time exploring. Your career search is like eating at a large buffet with endless tables of delicious food to sample. So it is with exploring careers: the sampling continues until it's time to select your main course. Once you've tasted enough options and have an understanding of each career you're considering, turn to Chapter Four - DECISIONS to discuss decision-making and to further explore how you will select a career (or careers) that fit with your purpose. In other words you will discover how you will actualize the question: *What's my purpose?*

I explore freely, willingly, with an open heart.

My mind rests as my heart feels its truest desires.

Worry escapes me as I trust the adventurous ride of exploring my passions.

Tenacity and commitment to life adds to my success.

Pre-judgement eludes me bringing greater security to the paradox of trusting.

I begin to understand this fabulous secret of life. Some how, some way, I am led to new heights.

Chapter Four

DECISIONS - Ask Your Genie

Have no fear of moving into the unknown.
Simply step out fearlessly knowing that I am with you,
 therefore no harm can befall you; all is very very well.
Do this in complete faith and confidence.

Eileen Caddy
Footprints On The Path

Minute by minute, we make decisions large and small, important and unimportant. There's no escaping. Free will remains our ultimate power. Although destiny plays a hand in our lives, for much of it, we decide when and where, how and why. We can explain ourselves. We can give no reason. Yet, with this power comes responsibility, often causing worry, anxiety, and sometimes regret. When deciding upon your career, steer clear of these negative emotions and instead focus on the joy, excitement, and anticipation of beginning a new journey. You are in the process of creating your life. At this point, you've hopefully narrowed down your possibilities to a few top careers. This chapter provides questions, exercises, and fresh perspectives to consider when making a decision. Through discussion, writing, pondering, and visualizing you will select the direction that's right for you!

A variety of possible career paths lie ahead, each one bringing different associations, life-styles, and encounters. Selecting a career leads to the thrilling adventure of change, mastery of new skills, and involvement with new people. Nevertheless, making a decision may feel like a dreadful step since it eliminates options and requires commitment.

As adults we don't always make choices so simply. Instead we analyze, ponder, discuss, and worry about what is right. Perhaps having a childlike outlook will make your decision easier. Allow yourself to be footloose-and-fancy-free, fresh and alive. Allow your truest desires to surface, trusting that you will select the choice that's best for you. With this attitude your intuition brings the choice loud and clear. After all, your intuition is *your* genie. It's not some magical figure that knows the answers; your genie is really *the knowing* inside of you. Continue to trust your deepest wisdom, giving your knowing the power it deserves.

Often children are more aware of their internal power, their natural knowing. Take for instance twelve-year-old Chip. This young guy entered his favorite hangout, the local bookstore, and started talking to his friend

Jackie, who worked in the store. Chip told Jackie that he was a little worried because he didn't know what to do: Should he join the soccer team or the school theater group? This was his big dilemma. The activities happened on the same days of the week and took a lot of time, so he had time for only one.

Jackie listened intently for a few minutes to Chip's desires and uncertainties.

Finally Jackie said, "Well, we can fix your problem." She took a nickel out of her pocket and said, "We'll flip this coin: heads will be for soccer and tails will be for theater."

"O.K.," Chip replied, feeling relieved that someone was finally helping him.

Jackie tossed the coin in the air and before taking her hand off the nickel, she said to Chip, "Now, which one do you want the most?"

"Heads," Chip said without skipping a beat.

Jackie didn't even bother to show Chip the coin. To play soccer was what he really wanted. Chip felt the most passionate about soccer even though he liked acting too. The decision was made almost effortlessly and that was the end of his problem. Chip won't feel the passion of emotional highs and lows through his characters or revel in applause after a performance. He will, however, feel the energy of competition and the exhilaration of running hard and winning games. He can, of course, pursue theater at another time.

Deciding between your many interests is your challenge. Certainly, there are situations in where you can have many wants satisfied. You may be able to experience a few careers throughout your life and/or combine interests to create a new possibility. Opting not to stay in one profession for 30-40 years is appealing to many of us. However, any decision involves a letting go of other dreams in order to fully commit to your choices. You may at first feel a sense of loss and sadness when you make a decision because you know you're saying good-bye to possibilities. The trick, of course, is to say good-bye to your secondary options, not to your dream!

Making a selection often feels uncomfortable. It's unknown. Journeying into alien territories may cause fear because we don't know what to expect. The road is foreign; we feel out of control and uncertain. We're anxiously anticipating; everything is fresh. Insecurities may surface. We wonder if we'll succeed. Nonetheless, we find our way. I encourage you to plunge bravely into uncharted lands and make your life fulfilling and thrilling. Your rebirth occurs when you follow the callings of your soul. This is living!

With this kind of living comes increased commitment to life. Your new path requires energy, effort, and time. You may begin to spend more time on your goals and less time playing. Your responsibilities may increase as you improve your skills through classes and practice. You may have less free time. Choose the career that's right for you so you'll *want to* dedicate your time to your new project. You'll *want to* stay up late to finish a paper, create something, prepare a resumé, or research an idea. The concept of sacrifice becomes foreign because you made the choice you desire — it's what you want. Resentment vanishes. You embrace your choice with enthusiasm and zest.

Consider your feelings as you eliminate options. Don't reject what you love. Accept any anxiety that comes with your selection as normal. You'll work it out as you go. Choose your commitment because you *want to* not because you *have to*. If your choice is right, you'll want to pursue that direction.

Your task now is to decide what suits you best. Now is the time to critique your options and be gut-wrenchingly honest with yourself. If you feel *somewhat* confused about your future, continue reading this chapter. If, however, you feel *totally* confused about your future, consider reviewing the two previous chapters and talking to more people working in the careers you like. Conducting informational interviews is *necessary* for your planning: it's not an optional item. For many of my students, these interviews became the turning point, leading them to their chosen career. If you haven't interviewed anyone, do so and *then* read this chapter. Also, spend time writing about your future in a journal. These two activities, writing and interviewing, will definitely move you to certainty.

If you have friends and family pressuring or asking you about your future and you would rather not give specific details about your path, prepare an answer. Politely say to someone asking a bit too much, "Thank you for asking. I'm in the process of exploring my options. How did you decide on your career path?" Now you're off the hook! If you get the same question again, simply repeat, "Oh, I'm in the process of exploring my options." Then excuse yourself or switch the subject. Resist any pressure to answer.

Another suggestion to follow when making decisions and setting goals is to be discreet about sharing them. Individuals and groups, from Zig Ziglar to *Science of the Mind* practitioners who live by the positive, self-fulfilling prophecy philosophy, actually recommend keeping goals private. They advocate revealing large personal goals *only* to one or two confidants. The more often you discuss what you might do or what you're going to do, you dissipate your energy. This reduces your power. Imagine that your dreams are like a balloon filled with helium. Every time you open your mouth to talk about what you're *going* to do you are letting helium out of your balloon. Soon your balloon, just like your goals, is empty and filled with nothing. Apply this talking energy to completing steps towards what you want. Use discretion when discussing your uncertainties and dreams as this preserves the energy surrounding your ideas.

THE TECHNIQUES -
Soul-Searching Exercises.

Thus far, you've discovered characteristics of yourself and gathered a list of potential career options. You've read about the possibilities and talked with people working in the jobs you like. Through the exercises and topics covered in this book, you may now already know what you want for your career. If so, skip to Chapter Five, GOALS. If not, continue reading as we uncover a variety of techniques designed to assist you in selecting your career.

The decision-making suggestions offered range from analytical, logical methods to intuitive, spiritual approaches. The best decisions incorporate all aspects of the self: your thoughts, feelings, and intuition. We will entwine these three aspects of you, finally revealing your decision.

The process of finding your niche involves uncertainty, often causing frustration and nervousness, so don't worry if you feel uncomfortable. It's very normal to still feel confused at this point — it's natural. *Stick with the process.* If you haven't investigated your options, return to the previous chapter. Once you've come this far in your planning, don't give up now. You're so close to making a decision; even if you don't feel like it, you are! The smart move is to continue forward, explore more, and soon a decision will be revealed, then you'll be ready to create a plan, and begin living your dreams!

If you feel anxious about moving forward, realize that going back to the old uncertainty will feel even worse. So, press on!

I've selected a variety of soul-searching exercises so you can address decision-making from several angles. When evaluating your options, use your *CAREER OPTIONS LIST, MAGICAL QUEST SUMMARY* from Chapter Two, *YOU*; and the information you obtained during your career research. Reflect on the themes that appear on your *SUMMARY*. Focus on your values and life purpose. What will motivate you to get out of bed and go to work? Use the information you gathered after reading Chapter Three, *CAREERS*, to consider your options. This knowledge brings a realistic perspective to your career interests. If a technique offered is not fruitful, then select another approach. Strive for open-minded perceptions as you examine your options. Be flexible, creative, and willing to discover interesting and unique combinations or alternatives. Stay true to your essence. Listen carefully and feel the rumbling inside your soul that speaks to you. Give credence to your passions.

> *By annihilating the desires, you annihilate the mind. Every man without passions has within him no principle of action, nor motive to act.*

Claude Adrien Helvetius

Certainly, making a decision calls for critical judgment; nevertheless, I encourage you to first address your situation by considering your feelings. Then view your options from a myriad of vantage points and make your selection.

The traditional way to make a decision involves learning about your options and then finding the good and bad aspects of each. Thousands of Americans, for example make appliance, stereo, computer, and automobile selections using *Consumer Reports*, which rates these products. But knowing only the facts about each career option limits your perspective. Likewise listening solely to feelings clouds reality. Gathering the facts and critiquing the possibilities using the rational, logical side of your brain provides a good foundation for uniting your feelings and intuition into the decision-making process. The best decisions involve a blending of thoughts, feelings, and intuition.

WEIGH THE PROS AND CONS

A rational and logical way to make decisions entails analyzing, evaluating, and critiquing each option. The process begins with stating your decision as a question, followed by gathering information, defining options, stating the good and bad side of each option, projecting possible outcomes, evaluating your assets and risk taking capabilities, waiting, and then making a selection. For example, if you decide you need a new car, you will determine which features you like, examine the characteristics of various models, test drive the cars, list the positive and negative aspects of each model, project how each vehicle will affect your lifestyle, and then finally come to a conclusion. Apply this same process to selecting your career. The following steps outline the process:

1. **STATE YOUR DECISION IN BROAD TERMS.** What is your decision about? Create an open-ended question, allowing for many outcomes. For example, if you are deciding which apartment to rent, don't say, "Should I rent the apartment on First Street or Orizaba Drive?" Say instead, "Where do I want to live?" This leaves many, many options, not just two. Now a myriad of possibilities come to mind, like renting an apartment, buying a house, living on a boat, housesitting, renting a room, or managing an apartment complex. You may decide, for example, between lots of different apartments or lots of different living arrangements. State your career question as, "What career will I select?" instead of "Should I be an astronomer or an artist?" The second example obviously leaves only two choices. By expressing the question broadly, entirely new ideas may emerge as you analyze and discuss your original options.

2. **DETERMINE WHEN YOU MUST MAKE YOUR DECISION.** When do you need to choose a career path? This date very much affects your analysis and outcome. If you're just beginning school, you may need time to take classes and explore your interests, not selecting a college major right away.

If you are in an enjoyable position at work or are a stay-at-home parent, you don't need to make a decision right away; there's time to explore. On the other hand, if you've completed at least 60 college units or you're in a dead end job or one you dislike, then it's time to take action. Decide when you realistically need to make a choice. Base your analysis on the facts. Don't hastily make a decision just because you're uncomfortable with having your life unplanned! Allow time for the exploring mode. Deciding too soon may limit options. Waiting too long may cause you to procrastinate. Assess your scenario honestly.

3. **SELECT YOUR OPTIONS AND ANALYZE THE POSITIVE AND NEGATIVE ASPECTS OF EACH CHOICE.** Weighing the pros and cons of each career gives you the opportunity to see the truth. List one career from your *CAREER OPTIONS LIST* at the top of a piece of paper. Fold the paper in half lengthwise to create a t-bar. Underneath the career write a plus in one column and a minus in the other. Then write the positives of the career in the plus column and the negatives of the career in the minus column. View the career realistically not just as a fantasy. Consider how the information on your *MAGICAL QUEST SUMMARY* relates to each career in question. How much do you *like* each option? Does the career fit with your values and skills? Do your *Elements* and *Work Personalities* fit with each option? Does the career fit you? List the aspects of your summary results in relation to your career as positive, negative, or neutral. Write neutral items in the middle on the t-bar line denoting neither positive nor negative. What will your days be like if you commit to an option? Include all angles when judging the different pieces of your options. State your opinion of the job duties, growth potential, salary, skills, training, personal commitment, and lifestyle for each career you're considering. What would your daily grind feel like? Use the information you gathered from researching your options. Think in new ways. Repeat this process for each career you're considering.

4. DETERMINE WHAT YOU ARE WILLING TO RISK AND WHAT MIGHT HAPPEN WITH EACH OPTION. Project what you are willing to handle and how you think *each* career option might affect your life. Answer the following questions for each option:

- Who would I associate with in this field?
- Does this career meet my monetary desires?
- Do I like the hours and work schedule this option demands?
- Am I willing to devote the time necessary to prepare for this option?
- Will this career fit with my lifestyle and family commitments?
- Can I handle the competition in this field?
- How will my life change if I enter this field?
- Does the personal satisfaction I would derive from this career outweigh frustrations I may experience from competition and preparation in the field?
- Do I *believe* that I will be successful in this career?

Note your answers and how you feel about them. Also, list these as positive and negatives on your t-bars. The information you uncover for steps three and four will lead you in the right direction. It may confirm a hunch or reveal something new.

5. WAIT A WHILE BEFORE ACTUALLY MAKING A SELECTION. After completing steps one through four and analyzing each option, stop thinking about your dilemma. For a while forget about your need to decide. Put your brain on restriction from analyzing! Apply some of the other decision-making suggestions in this chapter to your situation. Be creative and lighthearted. Then, *unwind.* Maybe go on a vacation, throw a party, watch movies all day — do anything to get your mind off your future. Just let go. Freedom from thought allows your subconscious and intuitive mind to gel with your conscious, rational mind. Waiting allows for your true desires to surface. A subtle confirmation will flow into your being. "YES, that's the answer!" may spontaneously pop into your psyche. Eventually an answer will come to you.

6. MAKE A DECISION AND TAKE ACTION. A decision without action remains a dream. Prepare to grow and change with your new commitment. The next two chapters offer guidelines for your planning.

Apply these steps to your career decision. If you're 100% committed to an option, move on to the next chapter, SET GOALS. If you're not exactly sure what you want, continue reading!

51/49% RULE

The 51/49% rule is helpful if you're one of those people who likes lots of things. In our fast paced, highly technological society so many options exist that we may feel overwhelmed. So the 51/49% rule offers structure to your situation. Many of your options suit you. The careers that match with your *SUMMARY* results are all good choices. Basically, the idea is to select the option you like 51% of the time, even though you like other options 49% of the time.

Often we like all of our choices; each alternative seems appealing. Your goal, of course, is to live your dreams; however, there may not be enough time in your life to pursue *everything* on your long list of passions. So say to yourself, "What can I live without?" In other words, select a few options you like just a bit less than the others. Letting go of anything interesting can be disappointing; you may feel mournful over this lost option — this is normal. Don't avoid your feelings because this may prevent you from actually making a decision. We may not be able to have everything, but we can have what we really want. If you feel torn between alternatives, know that when you select a "51% option," feelings of regret may creep into your being because "the 49% options" will not be a part of your life. Oh well! As simple as it sounds, this is life. Go for what you really want, the alternative that makes you feel alive!

Say to yourself, "What's my next right step? What feels right for now?" By moving in a *direction* you desire new ideas will be revealed. What you select now may not be what you'll do five years from now — that's O.K. If you are willing to spend time and energy learning the necessary skills and making the transitions, experiencing several careers during your lifetime makes for an interesting journey. Notice the variety of experiences of others. Former President Ronald Reagan, for instance, was a sports announcer, an actor, and then a politician. Dr. Seuss was originally a pediatrician before he became a well-known children's author. Similarly, Joseph Wambaugh was first a police officer, then an investigator, and now a writer. Gail, a close friend of mine, began her career as an elementary school teacher; then in her late twenties became a stock broker; a few years later she went on to work as a speech-communications consultant. Her latest adventure has been attending massage-therapy school. Several different career paths may suit you. There isn't necessarily just one option. And nothing is ever perfect — that's not life! Instead, there are *many great possibilities*.

PROCESS OF ELIMINATION

The process-of-elimination technique commonly proves helpful for decision-making. Many people use this technique in their daily lives, for example, when selecting a restaurant entree or clothes to buy. The technique can also be useful when deciding upon larger, more important issues. Simply examine each career option and rule out those that possess characteristics you find unacceptable. Begin by assessing the compatibility of your values with each career you're considering. Will your top five values be met? If a "no" answer appears for a possibility, explore your feelings about the issue and then determine if you want to eliminate it. Do the job duties of the choice fit with you and your personality? Determine if any alternatives possess traits you find undesirable. Assess your *Want* and *Don't Want* list and the other aspects of your *SUMMARY* with each career you're considering. Decide if there's compatibility. Then analyze the lifestyle associated with each career and determine if it fits with your needs. Are there any reasons not to keep a possibility? Glaring dichotomies between what you desire and the reality of the career may cause you to eliminate an option.

Jane, a young woman who came back to school after working for three years, was considering the following careers: public relations specialist, marriage-and-family counselor, and police officer. All of her alternatives sounded exciting and fit with her *SUMMARY* results. She really liked many of the activities of the public relations officer; however, the long hours and deadlines for planning events and writing press releases really bothered her. To Jane, the job felt high-pressure, even though she liked the excitement of the industry. Police work and counseling, on the other hand, seemed more flexible and less stressful because of the lack of deadlines. This young woman liked the idea of having to respond quickly, to the spur-of-the-moment calls or client needs. In addition, she liked the flexible hours and shifts of both jobs. Eventually, Jane eliminated public relations because of the deadlines and decided to pursue both police work and counseling. She liked work more than school, so her goal was to hire on with a police department as soon as she earned an associate of arts degree. Once she settled into her job, she planned to continue with school part time until she earned her bachelors degree. Then working as a police officer, Jane planned to save at least $500 a month so she could eventually afford to quit police work, work part time, and earn a masters degree in Counseling. By that time, she would be close to 30 years old and ready to start a family. Working as a marriage-and-family counselor would fit perfectly into her lifestyle as a working mother.

WORST CASE SCENARIO

Accentuating the positive has been our theme thus far. However, considering possible negative outcomes of careers may assist you in making a decision. Understanding the minimum you are willing to accept will help you discover your level of passion.

Visualize yourself for a moment experiencing one of your career options. Imagine the worst conceivable outcomes. Really dwell on potential negative conditions that might happen. For example, see yourself with negative co-workers, in unpleasant surroundings, experiencing difficulty being hired. Then ask yourself how you feel. Could you live with these possible outcomes? Would you still feel satisfied with your career choice? If you still feel positively about the career, then it is most likely a good choice for you. In other words, you like the option so much that you're willing to commit, in spite of the down side. If, on the other hand, your worst case scenario seems like an unbearable burden, then the option in question may not be ideal for you. George Burns summed it up best when he said, "I would rather be a flop in something I love than a success in felt hats."

A few years ago when I was in a quandary over which career to select, I used this technique. At the time I was leaning towards being a school counselor, yet I was not 100% certain that this was the right choice for me. I visualized myself in the worst case scenario: a low-paying counseling position, in a small, dingy office, with only a few people coming to me for help, at my old high school! Depressing? Yes. But when I imagined this sight, I still felt good about being a counselor. The field satisfied my basic desire to make a difference in society; I liked the idea of listening to people and guiding them along their personal-growth path. I didn't care where and with whom I did the work — just as long as I could counsel, then I was happy. Experiment with your options by imagining the worst case scenarios. Don't just choose any *felt hat,* select the hat that fits you!

In another case, I used this technique with Scott, a client in his late thirties with a wife and four daughters. He had been working as a repair person at a gas company for quite a few years. He was burned out. For years Scott dreamed of being a writer or doing some type of work in the entertainment industry that would use his creativity. We painted the worst case scenario for Scott: he would give up his secure job and work on TV or movie sets doing repair work, never developing the skills or contacts necessary to produce a movie or to sell his creative ideas. His family might be in a lower economic level, barely making it. There might be lean times when in between projects. Scott decided that, if necessary, he could live with this. He felt that at least he would be giving his best shot towards his desires. Scott also felt that setting an example for his daughters by creating a life worth living, instead of selling out to security and what he disliked, was an important lesson for them to learn. He wanted his family to see him happy about work, in spite of the potential monetary difficulties, rather than miserable at the end of the day. Fortunately his family was supportive of his dreams. Scott hungered for creative work; his desire exceeded his need for material comforts. Of course, he may eventually have both. Certainly Scott's values may be different than yours. Decide what piece of *your* equation will dictate your behavior. In other words when push comes to shove, which direction will you take?

By imagining a disastrous outcome, I am no means advocating negative thinking. On the contrary, visualizing the worst case scenario must only be a momentary exercise. Freely accepting a possible failure, however, reduces the pressure to be successful — it's all right to flop. In fact many successful people don't see mistakes as failure, instead, they view attempts at reaching goals as the basic steps necessary to achieving the goal. Learn to not judge the outcome. A shift in consciousness, toward not judging outcomes may reduce unnecessary stress. With the release of worrisome energy, the subconscious mind can work towards success without being burdened with the worry of failure. In our minds we've already accepted a possible terrible outcome, knowing that this is natural for the path to completion. The definition of terrible vanishes since we've decided that any outcome is O.K. Something that is O.K. is not terrible!

ROCKING CHAIR TEST

For this technique, to visualize many, many years into the future. Imagine yourself as a wise person who has lived a long, long delicious and satisfying life. Pretend that you are in your rocking chair or retirement perch, reflecting on your life, sharing your escapades of the good ol' days with a very dear friend or spouse. As you swap stories, you want no regrets. You want to have seized every opportunity that came your way and to not be saying, *I wish I would have...* or *If only I had...* You want to be saying, *I did ...! And it was fabulous!* What careers on your *CAREER OPTIONS LIST* call out to you? As people mature, their main regrets are not what they did, but what they *didn't* do. Don't be a *didn't do* kind of a person. You want to feel exhilarated about your life choices. Follow the words of Robin Williams from the movie *Dead Poet's Society*, "Carpe Diem — Seize the Day!" Apply this *test* to your life, projecting honestly how you might think and feel if you choose *such and such* or if you don't choose *such and such.* To ensure no regrets, what must you pursue *now*? What good ol' day stories do you want to tell about your life?

Pursuing our hearts' desires makes me think of a woman named Madeline, who worked as a CBS television executive, but years before had been an opera singer. She always loved singing, so she decided in her forties to once again compete and train as an opera singer. She could have easily talked herself out of the idea. Instead, Madeline, must have applied the rocking chair test and decided she wanted no regrets!

Undoubtedly, many people might say, "Oh, you're too old!" or "It's too late!" Is it really too late? I believe that it's almost never too late. A popular proverb states, "It's never too late to be what you could've been." It really doesn't matter if Madeline makes money as an opera singer. It really doesn't matter if she's successful. She still has a job to pay her bills. What matters most is that she is in the mix, in the ring, doing what she loves.

In contrast, I knew a woman who did have regrets about her life choices. One night in class we were covering decision-making by discussing a hypothetical example of a person who wanted to be a police officer, but whose spouse was against the idea. We came up with solutions as to how one might overcome this predicament such as educating the partner about the job, discussing the cause of opposition candidly with the spouse, and asking the spouse to accept a trial run of the career. Most of the class felt that a person in this situation should definitely pursue his or her dreams even at the cost of the marriage. I am not suggesting divorce, by any means, but merely recounting the story. My students felt that the only partner worth keeping would be the one who would support dreams, not stifle growth. Then one of the students, whom I'll call Barbara, around 55 years old, said that the exact scenario happened to her in the 1960s when she was first married. At that time, Barbara had applied to a police department, passed all the required written, oral, and physical tests, and was accepted to the department — an especially courageous feat to have achieved, since very few women were police officers during the 1960s. Then Barbara went on to say that she did not pursue this career because her husband felt jealous that she would be working with male officers. A student asked if she was still married to the same person. Barbara replied, "No." The room was silent. We all felt Barbara's deep sorrow as she was solemn and close to tears. The discussion had brought her broken dreams to the surface.

We never had a chance to talk about this painful loss and deal with letting it go, as she left quickly that night and never came back to class. Her pain was great and she needed to explore the pain so she could heal. At the time of that class, most police departments enforced an age limit, so becoming an officer was then not possible. At the very least she could come to peace with her experience and begin to focus on the future. Many more exciting options still exist for her. Dwelling on the past only causes bitterness and remorse. A new bright dawning always awaits, filled with a multitude of possibilities.

Consider how you might feel 10, 20 or 30 years from now if you decided against any of your options. Is there a career you will *regret* not having selected? You want no regrets; if you will lament over a missed experience, then you must select this option!

VISUALIZATION

Searching and seeking, moment by moment, leads you to your destiny, the path that's best for you. Visualizing what might become your direction gives you the opportunity to try the possibilities before actually committing. Imagining your ideal scenario transfers thoughts from your subconscious to your conscious mind. New ideas may spontaneously pop into your head as you visualize, providing a new perspective for your future.

Visualization can be a very powerful tool to augment change. Sometimes you discover new possibilities for your life. Other times you confirm what you want and program your mind with the goal you desire, which in turn stimulates you to take action. Many successful people, from athletes to performers, use visualization for decision-making and goal-setting. Shakti Gawain in her book *Reflections in the Light* explains the technique this way:

> *Creative visualization is magic in the truest and highest meaning of the word. It involves under-standing and aligning yourself with the natural principles that govern the workings of the universe and learning to use these principles in the most conscious and creative way.*

In other words, the energy you send towards a goal brings it closer into reality — this is a principle of the universe. The concept is similar to the old saying, "Be careful of what you ask for because you just might get it." What you think about most of the time often becomes your reality.

For the visualization exercise find a comfortable, quiet, and peaceful place to lie down and relax. Be open for anything your subconscious mind might reveal to you. The exercise works best if someone you trust slowly reads or paraphrases the next few paragraphs, guiding you through the narrative, pausing and giving you time to see yourself in your imagination. If this isn't possible, read the next few paragraphs and then direct yourself, perhaps taping your reading and then playing it back when you are ready.

To relax, close your eyes; breathe deeply and slowly. Take a deep breath, in and out, and begin to feel all tension and negativity leaving your body. You begin to feel very calm and peaceful. Then begin to slowly stretch your muscles. Start at the top of your body and gently move your head from side to side, from left to right, feeling tension releasing from your body and into the atmosphere. Next, flex, tighten, and release, one at a time, the muscles in each of your major body parts beginning with your fingers, then move to your hands, continuing through to your arms, shoulders, chest, stomach, buttocks, legs, feet, and finally your toes. Find an easy, slow rhythm, flexing and releasing each muscle area. Relax from head to toe.

You are feeling wonderful, calm and content. Now, take yourself to your favorite place in nature, such as the mountains, beach, or forest. In your mind, escape to this place with all of your senses. Feel a gentle breeze caressing your face, the glowing sun warming your body, and the security of the earth supporting your being. The soothing sounds of water from tumbling waves or a nearby stream comfort your soul. The setting is ever so peaceful. You feel in tune with the universe. The water, the sun, the earth, and the air all feel like lovely, caring friends. You feel wonderful. Envision yourself in complete harmony in this tranquil setting. Everything is the way it was meant to be.

Once you feel calm and peaceful, leave the nature scene and imagine that you are now in your room just waking from a very restful sleep. As you awake in your visualization, you realize that today is the day you begin your new career. You feel very happy and excited because you know the career you selected is right for you. You feel confident and enthusiastic.

In your visualization, imagine getting ready for work, showering, and dressing for your journey. As you prepare, notice where you live. Are you in your current home? Do you have a new bedroom? What are the colors and style of your room? Explore the details of your living space. Notice the time of day; is it morning, afternoon, or night? What time do you get up for work? Notice what you wear. What do you put on your body: a uniform, suit, jeans, or a dress perhaps? What type of

shoes do you select: loafers, work boots, tennis shoes, heels, wing-tips? What is the feel of your dress — casual, sporty, dressy? You feel confident and excited about your choices. You are heading in the right direction. Everything unfolds simply, easily. Throughout your visualization you have a calm sense of knowing you made the right choice.

Next, envision yourself beginning the journey to your new, fabulous place of employment. Explore how you get to work and where you go. Do you walk, take a subway, or drive? Do you work out of your home, close by, or far away? Do you take a freeway, side streets, or country highway? Are you in a big city or a small town? As you arrive at your place of employment, observe the location and environment. Where is it? What does it look like? Imagine your surroundings. What type of setting do you encounter? Do you envision a large office building, small shop, school, or hospital? Maybe you see a national park, construction site, or a television studio? What does your work setting look like? Discover the feel and image of your work place. Observe your surroundings in complete detail, the sights, sounds, and smells. What types of colors and furniture are in your setting? You feel confident and excited in this wonderful career that you created. You like your new environment. It feels right.

Now, imagine yourself working. Do you experience yourself conversing with clients or colleagues? If so, what do you discuss? What types of people are around you? Do you make telephone calls? If so, what do you discuss? Do you work on a computer or write at your desk? See if you can read the screen or paper. If you can, what you are reading? Perhaps you're fixing something, drawing, or operating a piece of machinery. Are you working outside in nature? Maybe you're building something or researching. What are you doing? Experience these activities in your visualization. Feel the purpose of your work. What do you create? Let your imagination and subconscious mind take you naturally to the workplace that is right for you. Again, notice your specific job duties and work environment. As you work, you feel confident and right about your choice.

Finally, imagine that you have concluded your work for the day. Finish any last minute things you must do before leaving. Put your project away and begin your journey home. Observe the time you leave. Again, notice the route you take on your way home. As you travel, what are the names of the streets? Are there lots of trees or high-rise buildings on your journey? You feel very pleased and confident with your choice. You feel calm, carefree, and assured. Up ahead you see the place where you live. What does it look like? Imagine that you arrive home from work and begin relaxing, feeling happy about your new career. When you're ready, open your eyes, and return to reality.

After your visualization experience, jot down in your journal how you felt and where you went. Write anything you remember, even if it's vague or strange. What you remember can be pieced together for clues that eventually lead to the discovery of your work. Did you go to the career you've been leaning towards? Were there any surprises? How did you feel? Visualization is a powerful tool. Sometimes exact answers emerge, while other times only small clues are revealed. Pictures, symbols, and colors can be interpreted literally or figuratively. For example, Rose, a student of mine, saw a briefcase throughout her visualization that symbolically meant power and success to her. Rose wanted a position of authority and responsibility. A few months after her session, she called to say that she had a management position with the type of job duties she had imagined.

Daniela, another student, experienced conflict in her pictures as she drove up to an elementary school in a brand new Porsche wearing flashy business clothes. Her flamboyant image didn't match the conservative feeling of the school. She couldn't begin teaching because she felt out of place! During her visualization Daniela left the classroom and saw herself conducting a business meeting for her own successful advertising agency. These images persuaded Daniela to pursue advertising, confirming her feelings to abandon the idea of teaching and proceed into a creative, business-type environment.

If you wish to learn more about using your subconscious mind for answers in your life, contact a professional hypnotherapist who can bring greater depth and meaning to your pictures. Pay attention to your dreams as well for clues to uncovering your desires. Consider repeating this visualization activity when the time seems right. You may receive different pictures and images each time you visualize.

FOLLOW YOUR INNER VOICE

Have you ever made a decision, but felt a nagging doubt that it was the right choice? Perhaps something inside you warned against it. Sometimes we hear a *voice* inside of us, an all-knowing guide that tells us the next right step to take. This voice inside is our intuition. Often carrying many names, such as a hunch, vibe, or gut feeling, intuition can be defined as *knowing the answer without knowing how you know it*. It may sound crazy, but we all possess a *little voice* inside of us. Making a decision based on intuition requires a leap of faith because the logical and factual information does not always support the choice. For some people intuition is connected to God or a Higher Power. By acting upon your intuition, you become God-dependent, or dependent on the collective life force energy. Pursuing a desire because you know it's right and you feel it in your gut, even though there are a million and one reasons not to pursue the desire — this is following your inner voice, your destiny, your intuition. When you act upon your natural spirit, life flows much, much easier. Listening to and acting upon your gut feelings for career decision-making can be very fruitful. Truly, your inner soul knows what's best for you.

Yet sometimes we are reluctant to trust our perceptive feelings because such trust requires a leap of faith, a risk into the unknown.

Making an intuitive decision may not be connected with logical proof. Of course, intuitive responses do not appear in a vacuum. Intuition is part of the process that occurs when we think and analyze, using our minds. As we gather information and consider the possible outcomes, a subtle knowing unfolds around this information. However, we often ignore these feelings because we're not always accustomed to valuing such sensitivity within our being. The Western world emphasizes logical and critical thinking, so support for this fine-tuned listening is often absent. Sometimes facts may not support the intuitive choice. Making a selection using your knowing psyche might mean pursuing a career with tons of competition and long hours, but inside that *little voice* calls. It might mean pursuing a career that is against your family's wishes or requires years of schooling, but you *know* the choice to be right. Clarissa Pinkola Estes, Ph.D., author of *Women Who Run With the Wolves*, teaches with stories and fables to confirm the power of intuition. She writes, "All these stories present the knife of insight, the flame of the passionate life, the breath to speak what one knows, the courage to stand what one sees without looking away, the fragrance of the wild soul (page 21)." With Spirit, take the path you know to be right. Follow your knowing.

By society's standards, taking action based on instinct may seem unintelligent, illogical, or silly. More logical, left-brained folks may view the approach as ridiculous. Intuition, however, offers a mighty power: it is always right. Receiving a gut feeling about something actually provides the inner strength and security you need to pursue your calling. Feel secure with an intuitive choice because it is never wrong! It is your mystical insurance if you will.

Of course, you must be sure that what you sense is truly intuition, not wishful thinking or over-analysis. The only problem lies in being able to hear and recognize your *knowing voice*. Sometimes we confuse our conscience or critical voice for our intuition. I believe that we all know deep within our soul what major life steps we should take, but we do not always hear the answer. It often becomes clouded with our own doubt and worry or negative opinions from others and society. You can, however, develop an awareness of your intuition. Spend time practicing your ability to hear and acknowledge a *hit*, a notion that comes from the very center of your being. Learn to rely on the insights you feel deep within your psyche. This is your power.

In our world, we are inundated by noise, rules, logical thinking and a barrage of responsibilities, and obligations. Stifled and repressed, our intuition remains lost in the commotion. We tune out the voice inside us, losing our ability to hear our ancient wisdom as the clamor of society becomes louder. To replenish your intuitive spirit, devote time to soul-building things you love, such as gardening, painting, singing, walking in nature, carving, or decorating. Also allow yourself to be frivolous and childlike as these experiences also nurture your soul. Time spent relaxing and meditating helps facilitate the development of these skills. Daily spend just a few minutes alone in a quiet place and your instinctual abilities will improve. Practice seeking intuitive answers in ordinary, unimportant situations, and then graduate to more significant happenings in life.

Intuitive answers appear more readily when you're relaxed and not focusing on your problem or situation. Rarely do we get what we want by using pressure and demands. Be gentle with yourself. Ask your subconscious mind for an answer to your question. You may receive an obvious answer, some type of image that provides a clue, or just a hunch to follow leading you to your next step. Any information will assist you in completing your goals.

Sometimes when we evaluate a career logically and rationally, a particular option appears as the *right* choice having heaps of positive aspects and only a few negative points. Something inside us, however, tells us not to choose that option even though logically it makes sense. Shari, a single mother in her thirties and a former student of mine, experienced this type of conflict between her rational and intuitive mind. Shari believed that her right career choice was to work in the field of personnel and earn a degree in business management. Her decision made perfect sense since she already had previous work experience in this area; it was a secure field and it paid well so she could support her two children. What more could she ask for? Shari was set. But there was little passion, delight, or spark in her eyes when she talked about her choice. She had mentioned, however, that her hobby was horses, so I suggested she investigate the equestrian major at a nearby university. At first she seemed doubtful about the idea since she believed that working in this field seemed unrealistic. I persuaded her to at least just investigate the option, not commit. When she reported her findings about classes and job possibilities such as stable management and public relations, she exuded enthusiasm. Shari's intuition spoke; she listened, accepted, and switched majors. She decided to take a leap of faith and forgo security for passion, trusting that with her strong love and belief in her dream she would create opportunities. About a year later, I saw Shari at the graduation ceremonies; she was radiant. Wearing cowboy boots and a stylish Western shirt with a glowing smile, Shari had found herself. She was a different, happier, vibrant person. Love for her new life shown in her eyes. Soon after earning her bachelor's degree in equine studies, she found a job in public relations for a national horse product supply company.

I believe that we all know intuitively when to wait and when to move forward. We know which door to open and which path to take. Yet we sometimes silence and confuse our intuition by over-analyzing and fearing that success isn't possible. Pursuing those *funny feelings*, however, makes life easier and simpler. Ultimately, you feel more confident and secure with your choices. You have that feeling of satisfaction, that "YES, I know this is right." Practice hearing your internal voice. Honor your intuitive gift when searching for answers.

THE WHAT IFS - Questions frequently asked

Sometimes we become overwhelmed with pressure to make a decision. Our internal worry voice becomes louder than our natural wisdom so we do not hear our true desires. As one of my friends said when he lamented over which career to choose, "I *created* a confusion in my own life." What a powerful statement! If you have the ability to create a confusion then you have the ability to create harmony.

During this uncertain time of turmoil, I often hear many of the same concerns from individuals struggling to make a decision. Below are answers to the commonly asked questions.

What if I still don't know what I want?

A variety of causes may contribute to your indecision. It may be too soon for you to make a decision. Perhaps you need to conduct more informational interviews, experience more job shadows, and attend classes and/or workshops related to your areas of interest. If you recently began college, you'll most likely need more time to explore. Learn more about your likes and dislikes and then return to this chapter. Lack of information, fear, self pressure and criticism, life transitions, indifference, and family expectations can all inhibit people from making decisions.

Worrying extensively about your future and fretting over what to choose puts a ton of pressure on your psyche. You can't function naturally and freely. Determine if you've carefully followed the steps in this book:

- adjusted your outlook, creating a positive attitude
- completed the exercises in the YOU chapter, fully pondering your life
- investigated your options thoroughly, reading and interviewing
- applied the decision-making strategies

If you've completed all of these steps and you still don't know what you want, then just relax. Stop wondering about what you should do with your life — you've done your part! Instead, entertain yourself. Read a good book. Go to the movies. Play with children. Goof-off! Do something fun that you don't normally do. Engage in enjoyable and relaxing activities. Releasing pressure from your mind provides freedom for your sub-conscious to reveal the right answer. Forget about making a decision. Simply loosen up!

In other scenarios, individuals haven't done their homework so they need more information. Remember our *Creative Career Planner*? Exploring self and careers are the first two steps before making a decision. Re-read chapters one through three, complete each activity, and follow through with your research and analysis. Examine your *SUMMARY* and *CAREER OPTIONS LIST* for themes, hints, or clues about what you can pursue. The answer may be right on the page. Conduct more informational interviews and job shadows. Volunteer in your areas of interest. Apply the decision-making techniques. Then forget about making a decision; the answer will come to you when you least expect it.

Sometimes fear may hinder an individual's ability to make a choice. Fear often immobilizes people. Some individuals fear loss or abandonment. They worry subconsciously that whatever they create may eventually be taken away from them, therefore they don't take action. They would rather do without than risk loss later down the road; thus, they give birth to very little.

Other people criticize themselves, which stifles their courage to take steps towards a career. The fear of failure (or success), petrifies them. Individuals afraid of failing don't try at all because they believe the mistakes they make will devastate their already tenuous self-esteem, causing them to feel even less worthy. The risk of trying is too great. People afraid of success also don't try because any degree of success would be too difficult to handle. Subconsciously, they feel unworthy of such greatness. If any of these characteristics describe you, practice achieving small victories and accepting the feelings that develop from these endeavors. You may also re-read Chapter One, BELIEF, read other self-help books, discuss your feelings with someone you trust, and/or seek counseling or therapy. You can learn to take action!

A word of caution, however, don't become fixated on labels or clichés like *fear of failure*, etc. Often our society uses these *catch-all* phrases to simplify and explain complicated human behavior by lumping people into general categories. You may have *tendencies* towards certain behaviors, but that doesn't necessarily put you into a particular category nor does it help you understand why you do what you do. It also doesn't help you make the changes you want. Nonetheless, if you desire, help is always available. Only you can assess your next right step by evaluating your situation with truthful compassion. Then make your next move.

Life transitions or commitments may prohibit decision-making because your focus is on these experiences, not on your career. For instance, if you are adjusting to college after recently graduating from high school, going through a divorce, entering a new relationship, reducing your child-raising responsibilities, mourning the death of a loved one, or experiencing a mid-life transition, consider revisiting career planning once you feel more settled with these new aspects of your life. Consider career when you feel more comfortable with your transition. Now may not be the time to make a decision. These other major life passages require your attention. You may need time to heal, rest, and adjust. You may need time to just be. Counseling and general self-searching may be in order, depending on your transition. Determine if it is right for you to focus on your career now. Evaluate the other happenings in your life. You have plenty of time to create. Remember, planning your career is a life-long process.

Some folks avoid making a decision about a career because they really don't want a new career! Some people are content with their current situation and not really interested in putting forth the effort to take a new avenue. Sure, individuals need to work, so they have a *job* (just something that pays the bills) or a career they're tired of, but they really don't want to commit to putting time and energy into preparing and pursuing something new. There's no sense of urgency to change. Some are waiting to get married so their spouse will support them. Some feel the effort to change isn't worth the benefits derived from the potential results. Others are satisfied with the status quo. When I trained to become a career counselor, one of my professors used to joke about this type of client. He called them the "Yes, but..." client. Every suggestion made by a counselor received a "Yes, that's an idea, but, I can't because, blah, blah, blah." My professor would say to that kind of a person; "Sounds like you're not miserable enough. Why don't you come back and see me in six months when you are *really* miserable." This may be a harsh way to address the situation, but being too comfortable is often a reason why people don't change. People playing the *yes, but* game have no motivation to change! If any of this describes you, just accept your position, explore why you feel uninterested, write in your journal, seek counseling, or wait until you have more desire. Maybe, after careful evalu-

ation, you realize that you like what you are doing. The only thing you'll change is your perception. Dr. Toni Grant, a well-known psychologist, believes that self-acceptance is one of the greatest determinants of happiness. It's O.K. to stay in your current position. Again, only you know what's best for you.

Sometimes family expectations, implied or blatant, can cause individuals to avoid their natural shining spirit. This often happens with creative souls who grew up in more traditional households, with intellectual types who grew up in working class families or vise-versa with both scenarios. Family climates can stifle any individual who feels different than their family culture. Unfortunately their true self has been covered and abandoned in an effort to follow the family norms and expectations. Explore your truest desires, revisiting the exercises in this book. Perhaps use Julia Cameron's book *The Artist's Way* if you feel stuck. Counseling can also help you find your true self.

What if I know what I want, but it requires too much schooling?

Frequently, I hear this question from individuals who don't really like college and are attending mainly to obtain the degree necessary for their career goal. Unfortunately, there really is no cure for this problem other than to grin and bear it or select a different goal. Attaining worthwhile things in life usually requires lots of effort. Other people feel frustrated about a time-consuming training period because it means delaying a new life style and an increased salary. They feel anxious because they want the changes now. These feelings are encouraged in today's fast-paced society by media messages showing the illusion of instant gratification. We rarely view the sweat and toil successful people invest. We see only the end result, never really comprehending the time and effort individuals in the limelight have put forth. Remember, the journey can be as joyous as the destination. When we truly live our passion, time presents no barrier. Time becomes meaningless because our attention centers on the process of living. So you must say to yourself, "How strongly do I desire my goal?" Re-evaluate your choice. Maybe it's not really what you want. Perhaps you're in love with the image of the career but not the actually job duties. Determine what you like about the career. Maybe these positive factors are enough to offset the effort of school. Most things worthwhile in life require considerable time and energy to achieve. If you really like the career, you'll pursue your vision with a burning desire, giving your goal a 100% commitment. Consider what you really want. When you truly love your work, you would do it for free. Mark Twain expressed this point very clearly by saying, "The secret of success is making your vocation your vacation." Your work becomes your life's passion.

To ease your frustration about years of school, consider setting short, medium, and long-term career goals for your path. If your dream is to be a psychologist, for example, you might first work as a teacher's aide (or select another decent paying job that requires a short amount of training) so you can pay your way through school. Then earn a teaching credential and a bachelor's degree. Upon graduating, work as a teacher and enroll in an evening doctoral program. Finally, you could conduct a chunk of your field hours during your summers off. Almost any career path can be put into manageable, realistic steps such as these. Be creative and flexible. If you really love the option, you will *want* to pursue your training to make it a reality.

What if I'm good at lots of things?

This is perhaps the most challenging question to address. If you're one of those lucky people blessed with many talents, it's often difficult to make a decision — you have so much to choose from! Be thankful for this dilemma, as it's better than the opposite alternative. To tackle your indecision, you might begin by addressing your life purpose. Select a specific reason for working. This will help you rule out options that don't fit with your purpose.

Another possibility is to choose what you like this moment, knowing that you can change and experience other options later in life. In other words, what's your next right step? Think of the big picture, your entire life. Perhaps you can select a career for each 10-, 15-, or 20-year period of your life. You might use the 51/49% rule to select the career you'll begin now.

You may also want to combine options. Consider careers that involve many of your passions. People with many interests are frequently integrated in their thinking and talents, being good at both right- and left-brain thinking. These folks may have learned a variety of things at an early age. For example, one parent who's an engineer (left-brained) and another who's an artist (right-brained) may expose children to a larger spectrum of experiences than parents that are more similar to each other. Often careers that require a great deal of responsibility entail a variety of skills and use of right- and left-brain thinking, e.g., entrepreneur, plastic surgeon, film director, corporate executive, architect, or CD-ROM designer. These careers have long learning curves since it takes a while before one becomes competent in the field. Re-examine your assessment results and career options lists. Perhaps you'll find new careers, or combinations of careers, that will suit you better than your original selection.

Consider pursuing two or more careers that work well together (or can both be done part-time). For example, you could be a teacher and a business owner, a flight attendant and a massage therapist, a per-diem nurse and a writer, an esthetician and an actor, a dog-groomer and a gardener, an electrician and a singer, or a graphic designer and an artist. These combinations of options have flexible hours, so it's possible to do both. Thousands more possibilities exist. Examine your situation and determine if more than one career works for you.

Similarly, consider pursuing careers that fall all in the same industry. You may have a group of preferences appropriately related. Passion for politics and the environment can bring endless entertaining options: research, writing, teaching, lobbying, speaking, managing, holding political office, and practicing law. Attraction towards teaching, writing, acting, and producing is suitable for a career in the film, television, and performing arts industries. Interest in science with a bachelor's degree in biology qualifies you for entry-level work in many science related fields. It would be relatively easy to make a switch from one career to another, from a research scientist, for example, to a forest ranger, to a biologist, and finally to a biology teacher. Again, so many combinations are possible, so explore your list of options. I know a gentleman who earned a bachelor's degree right after high school, worked as an aerospace engineer, took science courses at the local community college in his late 30's, and then finally went to medical school and became a doctor at the age of 43. Remember, anything's possible!

You might also create a new career. Recently, an actor started selling Tupperware using a song and comedy show during his Tupperware parties. He created his character: Pam Teflon, dressed in drag. Now *Pam's* the top Tupperware seller in the company and is known worldwide! In recent years, numerous new careers such as Web page designer, computer consultant, genetics advisor, cross-cultural communications consultant, and divorce mediator have sprung up based on need. During the past few years, businesses such as coffee houses, maid services, singles dating services, day-care centers, and employment out-placement offices have become popular because of changing societal demands. Explore and see what's missing in the world; people might pay money to fill this void. You may be just the one to provide this service or product.

Finally, some people don't find their niche until later in life. It takes some individuals a while to know their soul and determine their true passions. Often it is the accumulation of events and experiences that brings one to a career that seems complete and appropriate. An acquaintance of mine, Paul, tried many things in his life including graphic arts, public relations, teaching, and management, but never really found a place he could call his own. It wasn't until his 40's when he became the president of a liberal arts college that his skills gelled. The college was small so he was responsible for a little of everything: advertising, teaching, and of course, managing. He loved the position because it satisfied his eclectic combination of interests and his need for variety. Each and every one of Paul's life experiences led him to the position of president. Without all of his knowledge he would not have qualified for the position or had the right insight and finesse to do the job well. As a young man, the job of college president was not something he sought. Instead his life journey brought him to the right place. He pursued career interests that felt right at the time even though they didn't feel like life-long pursuits. For those of you with lots of interests, choosing a career *for the rest of your life* may not be a good idea. Make a selection you will be happy with in the short-run, perhaps for five years, knowing that later you can add to your skills and try something else.

What if my career choice is contrary to my family or spouse's wishes?

The only one who knows what's best for you is you. The issue to consider is *your* happiness, not the happiness of your loved ones. Clearly, family values and traditions influence behavior in many positive ways, but the danger occurs when you feel stifled and trapped. You don't want to be like Barbara, who wanted to be a police officer and never did. She regretted her past. If you will have doubts about a choice, then re-evaluate your decision. If family values greatly influence you, then you may need to let go of your top career desires and focus on your dedication to your family. There is no right or wrong path to take; however, you do want to feel good about your choice. You do not want nagging doubts. Honestly assess your feelings about your career goals and family commitments.

A very dear student of mine, Joselito, experienced just this conflict — a clash between his desires and his family's wish. Joselito wanted to pursue a career producing movies, yet his family, having conservative Filipino beliefs, wanted him to select nursing or computer programming since these were secure and respectable fields. Joselito wrote a letter to his parents expressing his feelings via the *Calendar* section of the *Los Angeles Times*. It was a bold move on his part; nevertheless, his inner turmoil was so great he was moved to write. His parents read the letter and some candid discussions followed. Ultimately, Joselito pursued his dream, and his parents began to alter their beliefs and accept his decision.

In another case, Jenny, a young student of Vietnamese heritage, gave up her desire to be a fashion designer in favor of her family's wish that she become a doctor. Jenny has little interest in medicine, but for her, pleasing her family was more important than being a designer. This was not, however, following the true desires of her soul. When she spoke to me about her decision a fine layer of tears always welled up in her eyes reflecting the turmoil between her essence and her family. I just hope she doesn't end up like Barbara, feeling regretful.

Most socioeconomic groups and families have their own beliefs and prejudices that dictate behavior. In some families blue collar occupations carry negative connotations while other families emphasize work over school. Some families value business and science related careers such as doctor, lawyer, and stock broker while discouraging creative careers such as designer or artist. There is no right or wrong choice, so become clear about your values, choosing what's right for you. The world needs a delicious blend of every occupation. You might have just the right spice to add new flavor to the world of work. Listen to your inner signals. Only you know what choice is best.

If we do not select what's best for ourselves, I believe we sell a piece of our soul and something inside us dies. No one can take away your freedom to choose the life you desire. If you feel compelled to pursue your passion, even in the face of opposition, stay strong in your own convictions, yet humble and tender in your communication with loved ones. Know that you cannot change the opinion of another, but you can always change your reaction to someone else's beliefs. Behave as a mature spirit, treating others with respect. A true test of love is the ability to accept the decisions of another, even if they are contrary to your beliefs. If you choose to live your dreams in the face of opposition, ask your family for their support. And if they are unable to provide you with the love you seek, go quietly down your own path knowing that support will come in other ways.

What if I can't make money with what I like?

This assumption just isn't true — almost all careers offer the *potential* for money to be made! The questions you really need to ask are "What amount of effort am I willing to put forth to be financially secure in a particular field?" and "How much financial risk am I willing to take?" For instance, if you want to enter a field with keen competition, countless training hours, and no set training path, you may want a back-up plan. Are you willing to take some risk, or will you feel better with a more secure option to accompany your more risky choice? You may want to have *Plan B* to support *Plan A,* your main objective. Plan B might be to train for a short vocational job, so you'll at least have a skill to make money while you continue pursuing your major goal. Plan B might also be to train for any type of secure career, and still, of course, also prepare for Plan A. Bill Cosby gave his children similar advice by telling them to pursue any career their hearts desired, such as acting or producing, but do so *after* earning a master's degree.

Everyone arranges their plans differently. Hung, a 19-year-old college freshman, for example, earned a certificate in medical assisting and works in the field; however, she's still in school working towards a bachelor's degree in chemistry as she wants to eventually become a medical doctor. Marco, a former student in his mid 30s, decided to train to be a tool and die maker while still pursuing his dream of becoming a professional golfer. An acquaintance of mine, Terry, supports himself as a hair stylist and is studying art so he can paint, and eventually sell his work and own an art gallery. Most of us need to earn money, so if necessary decide how you will make money while you prepare for your Plan A.

A former student of mine in her late forties, Evelyn, was laid off from a job she hadn't really enjoyed for some time. She also had recently received some inheritance money from the unexpected death of her mother and daughter. Being an only child and single at the time of these two emotionally tragic events, Evelyn was at a major crossroads in her life. She had no other family and felt strongly that it was time to contribute something meaningful to the world. Majoring in English in college, Evelyn always had a fascination with words, enjoying writing and editing. With some trepidation she decided to go after her life-long dream of becoming a writer. It was now or never! Although she was able to support herself for a short while with her inheritance money, she felt the more prudent choice would be to also earn money on a regular basis from another source, not relying on sporadic and unpredictable payments earned from her various writing projects. She conducted an informational interview with a woman who ran a private tutoring business for reading and writing out of her home. Evelyn found the woman's lifestyle very appealing so she decided to pursue both fields: writing and tutoring. This created just the right balance for her career by satisfying her needs for both security and passion.

Determine if the personal satisfaction derived from a particular occupation is worth the time and energy you will need to expend to make your dream a reality. You want no regrets. How passionately do you feel about your option? Remember, thousands of people *are* employed in the more competitive and unstable careers such as artist, writer, actor, musician, singer, dancer, newscaster, international journalist, talk show host, model, athlete, professional coach, politician, and movie producer. Other more secure positions such as FBI agent, physical therapist, foreign service officer, and fire fighter involve stiff competition, but they too hire new people into their ranks every year. One of these people could be you. Observe society; there are plenty of people in the fields you like, working and making money!

Pursue what you believe you have been called to do. Only you know whether this call is urging you into a competitive field. If your answer is "yes" — go for it! Re-reading Chapter One, BELIEF, provides encouragement and enthusiasm, reminding you to accept the notion that you do possess valuable skills that the world desires. If your faith wanes, consider the remarkable paths others have forged. Everyday heroes abound, from young individuals beginning in highly competitive fields to those re-training for new careers — all plugging along diligently toward their goals. Observe the multitude of individuals who *are* making money in the field you desire. Where there's a demand, there's a career. I know of an older gentleman who makes money repairing banjos! Boost your belief that you will be successful by interviewing folks pursuing tough paths. (If they did it, you can too!) Ask friends and family for contacts. Be aggressive when seeking candidates to interview. Read biographies about people you admire. Some of their courage may invigorate you to pursue your dreams.

In addition, assess your skill level and determine if you currently possess enough expertise to begin working now. If you need more time to prepare, determine when you will be marketable. Do you need to also prepare a back-up career? Arrange a plan that provides you with time to train, money to live, and flexibility to pursue your dream.

Finally, in all fairness I must address a cruel truth about the concept of living dreams: We are not always dealt the hand we desire. Sometimes we do not have enough God-given aptitudes to become skilled in a particular area. In other instances, we simply did not begin training early enough in life to accomplish a particular career goal. If, for example, I want to become a concert pianist at age 30 and I've never studied piano before, it's probably too late to become proficient. Similarly, if a 2.0 grade point average is the best I can earn, then it will probably be tough for me to get into medical school and become a doctor. *But there are always exceptions*; countless great men and women throughout history have defied the odds, eventually reaching their desired destination. Accurately assess yourself by neither selling yourself short nor inflating your talents.

Determine also the driving force underneath an option you desire. This motivation will lead you to a career that will satisfy you. In our pianist example, I would want to discover why I craved the path. Am I in love with music, its beauty and the chance to create? Perhaps my driving force is fame or maybe money. Once you know the reason for the passion, then you can select accordingly. If I am in love with music for music's sake, then I will learn to play the piano at all costs not caring whether I ever become a concert pianist. This may not be my career, but part of my life. If I desire fame and monetary benefits, then I can seek them with a different choice.

In many scenarios people underestimate their abilities, not seeing their potential to become skilled in a career of interest. Instead they pursue their second-choice major or career rather than their first because they think it will be easier. Often this becomes a bittersweet path. For after completing the training or major and working for a while, restlessness sets in. In hindsight, these people realize that, with all the time and energy they spent preparing for their second choice, they could have been just as successful, or more so, in their first choice career. Unfortunately, they neither understood the process of growth that occurs through training nor *believed* they could truly become good enough to work in their first choice career. In other words, the time spent completing a college major (or comparable schooling) you love can sharpen your skills, making you marketable!

If you're in doubt as to which direction to go, you might consider the *Plan A, Plan B* approach explained previously. Further explore your areas of interest through classes and interviews. Sometimes just studying what you love leads you to the right career. Kawanna, a friend I knew from work, found one of her career paths in that way. In college she majored in psychology but took dance classes every semester because this is what she loved. Toward the end of her junior year, Kawanna realized she was close to earning a minor in dance. She eventually graduated with a bachelors degree with a major in psychology and a minor in dance. Upon graduating, she learned of a dance troupe seeking new dancers. She auditioned and was accepted. Kawanna traveled and danced with the group. After two years, however, she tired of the lifestyle. She wanted to earn more money and live in one location so she began exploring other options. Kawanna is now teaching Pilates, a special exercise technique, in a studio of her own and going to graduate school to become a Physical Therapist.

I do believe, however, that 99% of the time the areas we desire to experience are the areas where we can excel. We are instinctively drawn to our greatest potentials. Usually we have the capability of becoming skilled and talented in our favorite areas of interest.

How can I pursue a career if I have to support a family or myself?

A transition from the old to the new involves a gradual shift. Change takes time. Create a plan that brings enough financial security for your tastes and allows time for you to train or seek employment in your new area of interest. A multitude of options exist. The three main ingredients necessary for a successful transition are commitment, flexibility, and desire. You must be willing to adjust and consider new ways of obtaining your goal. If you use family or monetary obligations as reasons not to pursue a passion, perhaps your interest in the idea is not as strong as you thought. Some folks work part-time, reduce their expenses, and prepare for a new full-time career. Some select a transitional job that offers hours conducive to going to school. What you select depends on your needs and your situation.

To make a transition, you will make trade-offs between money, time, and security. Suggestions for easing your transition into a new field of endeavor include the following:

- Save money to live off later (avoid unnecessary expenses, trim the fat).
- Obtain a loan so you can work less.
- Reduce your expenditures or sell assets, i.e. eliminate car payment, cable T.V.
- Seek family support: room and board, money, transportation, baby-sitting, etc.
- Work for a company that offers tuition assistance programs.
- Attend a college with weekend and accelerated programs for working adults.
- House-sit or manage apartments for free rent.
- Work and live in a college dorm as an RA (resident advisor), receiving free board.
- Rent just a room.
- Live in the YMCA or YWCA.

- Eat dinner at "happy hours" or eat at home.
- Swap services.
- Ride a bike.
- Put an ad in the newspaper, asking for support.
- Seek a sponsor.
- Keep your current job, but switch to part-time hours.

Think of unique combinations for your particular situation. Many career-changers simply work during the day and go to school at night. When I first began working as a community college counselor, a woman in her early fifties came in to apply for graduation. When we reviewed her transcript, I was surprised to see that she had taken one class every semester for the last ten years, finally completing her Associates of Arts degree! Your goal may not take this long, but the point is still the same — when you're committed to an outcome, it doesn't matter how long it will take. Allow yourself time to ease into the new direction you desire.

A couple I counseled supported themselves by working at the swap meet on the weekends selling Ginsu knives so they could go to school during the week. A lawyer I know, Richard, in his late 40s, with a family of five, always wanted to be an actor but never pursued his dream. Many people would say it's a too late to consider such an option. Regardless, Richard still yearned for the experience, so he began taking acting classes a couple of nights a week even though he had a family to support. After a couple of years of training, he had a head shot taken and obtained an agent. Eventually, he reduced his hours practicing law, cut some of the family's frivolous expenses, and began auditioning for parts. He incorporated his dreams with his responsibilities, honoring both aspects of himself. Certainly, this course is challenging, but Richard will likely have no regrets about his life, no matter the outcome. His satisfaction lies in the *pursuit* of his goal, not the *outcome*.

Hundreds of other people continue to experience career changes. Southern California Career Development Specialist, Arlene Levin, offers excellent examples of career changers in the *Gateway Magazine*. One of her clients asked, "When I get discouraged about changing careers, I try and remember that others have done it before me. Can you tell me about some people you know who have changed careers?" Ms. Levin answered with:

Sure! Starting with myself: I've been a dental hygienist, social worker, psychotherapist, management and marketing consultant, writer, editor, international lecturer and career counselor.

Among the many career changers I've worked with are: a wallpaper hanger who became a computer programmer; a clothing buyer who became a wallpaper hanger; a dentist who became a head hunter; a legal secretary who became a special events planner; a computer salesperson who became a lawyer and another who became a stockbroker; an engineer who became a dentist and is now becoming a patent lawyer; a lawyer who became an inventor/businessman; a secretary who became a sex therapist; a teacher who became a national sales trainer; a clerk who became a desktop publisher; a salesperson who became a nutritionist; an engineer who is becoming an animator; a restaurant manager who became an architect; a physician who became a bio-ethics administrator; and an interior designer who became a psychic.

Any of these people could be you! The possibilities abound. Use your creativity. Time passes anyway, so why not spend it preparing for a brighter day?

DECIDE AND GO

As you can see, making a major life decision brings a host of issues and factors to the forefront. You cannot escape yourself. The process takes time as you ponder, wrestle with your mind, and speculate future outcomes. Caring people can serve as sounding boards, listening to and supporting your thoughts, feelings, and revelations. Ultimately, however, the choice is yours. For it is you who must live and breathe the path you select. The paradox is great, for with this freedom to choose comes responsibility and effort. But the joys are limitless. Your career provides a rich life journey offering challenges,

excitement, and opportunities for growth. With each major life choice you embark on a new voyage to a delightful foreign land.

Continue exploring and questioning. Incorporate the techniques in this chapter into your decision-making process. Revisit the ideas that work best for you. Each new idea leads you closer to your ultimate decision. A small insight may seem insignificant, but with many stacked together, you soon know what makes you tick; you know what you can't live without. Your priorities emerge. If you are out in the world exploring, talking to people, reading, experiencing, analyzing your thoughts and feelings, asking yourself the tough life questions, and honoring your soul, an answer will appear!

Your career path is a journey, a magic carpet ride of trips to places unexplored, hidden highways and byways. Your career provides a framework from which to see life. You may stay on the straight and narrow path or you may veer onto unbeaten paths. Allow yourself the freedom to check out a new opportunity or a new version of an old idea. Open your mind to the possibilities. Become intimate with yourself. Discuss what you like about a choice. What holds you back from committing to an option? Go within. To make a thoughtful, deep personal decision you must be real and honest. You can't hide from yourself. State what you want. State why you can or cannot move in a certain direction. Do not judge your answers. Simply say, "This is me, I want to have such and such." Accept what is revealed. If necessary be willing to follow the road not taken.

You didn't think when you got up this morning that this would be the day your life would change, did you? But it's going to happen because the only thing that stands between you and grand success in living are these two things: Getting started and never quitting! You can solve your biggest problem by getting started, right here and now.

Robert H. Schuller

The Road Not Taken

by
Robert Frost

Two roads diverged in a yellow wood,
And sorry I could not travel both
And be one traveler, long I stood
and looked down one as far as I could
To where it bent in the undergrowth,

Then took the other, as just as fair,
And having perhaps the better claim,
Because it was grassy and wanted wear;
Though as for that the passing there
Had worn them really about the same,

And both that morning equally lay
In leaves no step had trodden black.

Oh, I kept the first for another day!
Yet knowing how way leads on to way,
I doubted if I should ever come back.

I shall be telling this with a sigh
Somewhere ages and ages hence.
Two roads diverged in a wood, and I -
I took the one less traveled by,
And that has made all the difference.

Chapter Five

GOALS - Look Into Your Crystal Ball

You will decide on a matter,
and it will be established for you,
and light will shine on your ways.

Job 22:28

Uncertainty about your future has begun to vanish and a clearer path emerges. Anticipation abounds. You know what you want, but you may wonder if you really have the power to make your career choice a reality. Can it really happen? The urge to seek answers for your future may cause you to look outside yourself for direction. The fortune teller with her forest green head wrap and fuchsia rhinestones smiles wryly, waiting to receive your wad of cash. You reluctantly hand over your money. But wait, is this necessary? Remember the *genie within*. Looking into your crystal ball is only *your* ability to create a reasonable plan for your future. Then you'll achieve your goals by completing the plan you've laid out. You own this power to succeed. Goal setting truly is that simple.

As you begin to carve your path and make commitments to yourself, expect that you will be provided with the things you need to fulfill your dreams. Know that resources, contacts, and experiences will come your way. Prepare to work diligently towards your dreams, not because you have to, but because you want to. As you put forth your best effort to be productive, Nature also puts forth her best effort for you.

Goals provide direction in your life. Developing a specific strategy helps you clarify how you will eventually live your life. You create your action steps, each scene of your life-movie.

In conjunction with developing an agenda and expecting positive outcomes, you must also exert energy and effort on actually completing your resolutions. A dream without action remains just an idea, but a dream with committed action eventually becomes reality.

Make space for your new goals by finding the necessary time. You may need to replace an old activity with a new one. Evaluate your current commitments to determine how you will fit your career goals into your daily activities.

The topic of goal setting is actually so simple that at times it seems unnecessary to discuss — just start completing steps towards your goal! However, we frequently feel overwhelmed with the task, and instead of taking action, we panic or procrastinate. We become overwhelmed, not knowing where to begin and what to do. Thus, it is crucial to evaluate specifically what, when, and how you will accomplish these goals. When you decide upon these steps, your future seems less mysterious. Your path seems clearer.

Trust that you will achieve your deepest desires. Whether you actually reach the height of your field is irrelevant; what's more important is the planning and doing. The experience continues to be more rewarding than the destination.

Through the previous chapters you decided what career(s) you want. Now you will write your life-movie script: a step-by-step plan of the action you will take to achieve your objectives. General information about goals including attitude, types, techniques, and suggestions for composing your goals will be given.

A BELIEF IS EVERYTHING

Adopt an optimistic attitude when writing your goals. Revisit the concepts discussed in the BELIEF chapter and know without a shadow of a doubt that you are capable of achieving what you want. Anything is possible. Visualize yourself experiencing and loving your new career. Believe 100% that you will receive the position you desire. If necessary, change negative thoughts to positive affirmations. If you project a negative outcome, this becomes your reality. Your thoughts have power, so retrain any unproductive thoughts into beliefs of confidence. Believe in what you want and this is what will come your way — expect something mediocre and *presto*, that's what you'll get. Exuding confidence sends a positive projection to the people you meet. They will feel your energy and treat you accordingly. People rise to the level of expectation. How you expect to be treated is what you will receive.

REJECTION IS LEARNING

Preparing mentally is also a crucial aspect of goal setting. Be ready for outcomes you may not like. This is just a part of the process. As the saying goes: *Expect the best, but plan for the worst.* Most achievements don't happen over night. Instead they require countless hours of preparation and follow through. Each *no* leads to the eventual *yes*, so prepare to accept all outcomes and still forge ahead. When you are challenged, face rejection, and experience disappointments, resiliently continue forward knowing that positive results await, just around the bend. Remember it's always darkest before the dawn. The moment you feel like giving up is precisely the time you must hold steadfast to your vision, persisting pas-

sionately as if you will never have another opportunity to pursue your goal. Consider all the great people in history and the number of times they failed:

> You've failed many times, although
> you may not remember.
> *You fell down the first time you tried*
> *to walk.*
> *You almost drowned the first time you*
> *tried to swim, didn't you?*
> *Did you hit the ball the first time you*
> *swung a bat?*
> *Heavy hitters, the ones who hit the*
> *most home runs, also strike out a lot.*
> *R.H. Macy failed seven times before*
> *his store in New York caught on.*
> *English novelist John Creasey got 753*
> *rejection slips before he published 564*
> *books.*
> *Babe Ruth struck out 1,330 times, but*
> *he also hit 714 home runs.*
> *Don't worry about failure.*
> *Worry about the chances you miss*
> *when you don't **even try**.*

Wall Street Journal, United
Technologies Corporation 1981

Give yourself the same gift of persistence — keep moving!

You are not a failure if you do not achieve your goals as planned. Plans serve merely as a blueprint, not a path set in stone. What you learn along the way provides insight and direction for future steps. Reflect on the following perspective:

> *There is no failure except in no longer*
> *trying.*
> *There is no defeat except from within,*
> *no really insurmountable barrier save*
> *our own inherent weakness of*
> *purpose.*
>
> Kim Hubbard

Hold your course with dignity, fueling your vision with strong unrelenting power deep from within your soul. You help to shape your destiny, inventing what's in your crystal ball. Remember you are your own *genie*. Honor your ability to create the life you desire.

USE YOUR CREATIVITY

To your belief and endurance, add imagination. Your life is your own vision. To accomplish your goals, experiment with new and different ways of seeking solutions. See infinite, limitless possibilities. Your life is your work of art, original and unique. Freely make choices that fit you and your life. Trust your instincts. Trust your ability to creatively support yourself and plan for your new career.

Often lack of money and time can be a stumbling block. Do not allow these excuses to prevent you from pursuing your goals. Believing in scarcity creates limits. Believing in abundance allows your mind the freedom to process unique ways to have more money and time. Learning about someone else's good fortune causes us to increase our belief that we too will soon experience similar positive results. A couple in Hollywood, California, for example, wanted their movie script to be purchased and made into a movie. Tired of the rejection they received from submitting their script the usual route via agents and producers, the couple stood at Hollywood and Vine with a huge sign and a telephone number asking for help. They received offers, about 15 calls in all! Last I knew, the couple was negotiating a contract for their script and for acting roles in the movie as well. Don't think these things only happen in California! Other individuals have obtained sponsors or received gifts from caring individuals. Sometimes all you have to do is ask. Perhaps what we receive as gifts is limited only by the expectations we believe possible.

STAY FOCUSED

Every day accomplish something that moves you in the direction of your dreams. Your something may take just five minutes — you might write a letter or make a phone call. Other days you may spend eight hours on a goal — perhaps rehearsing for a performance or attending classes. As long as you take some type of action towards your goals, perhaps weekly or daily, no matter how large or small, you are a success. I believe success is measured not by how much you accomplish, but rather by the effort you put towards your desires. No one except you can measure how much effort you are capable of giving. Challenge yourself. When you feel like quitting a task, hang in there a bit longer and continue working. Tell yourself to increase the time you spend on a task. At first you may work only 10 minutes longer than

usual, and then the next time work 15 minutes more, gradually increasing your productivity. Soon you'll be pursuing your goal an hour longer than you anticipated! Goals are completed step-by- step, day-by-day, requiring effort and commitment. Build your stamina. Say *no* to frivolous requests for your time; instead use the time to accomplish your dreams. You may want to reduce the length of your telephone conversations or the time you spend watching television. In the end, with enough passion and perseverance you will arrive at your destination. Remember, however, that your journey, not the end result, remains your prize.

BE FLEXIBLE

Remember that your plan serves only as a guide. Most proposals need revisions and reworking once begun. As you acquire more information and complete some of your objectives, you may alter your direction, adapting to fit your needs. Your circumstances and desires may change. You may not accomplish your goals exactly as planned. Adjust and modify with the flow of life. Timing is everything. Something you want to complete *now* may not be possible until you accomplish something else. You may need to wait or learn a new lesson. Your timing may be off, but your goal right. We don't always know the reasons why our desires don't evolve according to *our* plans, but life usually unfolds just perfectly. As long as we do our part to facilitate the development of our goals, then we can rest assured that everything else will fall into place.

One of my dear friend's grandmother used to tell him, "It might not come when you want it, but it always comes on time." This seems to the ebb and flow of life. I remember my own painful career struggles after graduating from college. For three years I tried unsuccessfully (or so I thought) to find my niche. I worked in management, sales, administration, public speaking, and finally collections. I took classes and sought help from counselors. The counseling I received was poor. Nothing clicked. During this time I would say to my mom, "When am I going to find my career? I can't stand this!" She would listen supportively, not really knowing how to help me. Finally a friend referred me to Ardeth Miller, an excellent career counselor. Ardeth taught me many of the concepts in this book. After researching many options, I decided career counseling was for me. Looking back, I know that my frustrating years of feeling lost were really a blessing in disguise. Without my experience, I would never have been able to relate as well to my students and clients. I know the frustration of indecision. I know the pain of feeling lost. Pondering that time in my life still brings deep sadness because I was so very lost and unhappy. All the while, however, that I thought things were taking too long, everything was really happening perfectly! Often we don't know the reasons for things. So you must trust. Pay attention to the signals and clues that come your way. Follow your intuition. When it's time to wait, be patient. When it's time to move, take a step. An opportunity for something may arise when you least expect it — gratefully accept the gift, even if it's not according to *your* plan. Be flexible. A step you selected for the later may be for now. Something you tossed may be your next right step. Feel the natural rhythms humming inside you and in the world. When you complete tasks easily you're on the right track. When many mishaps occur, it can be a signal that you're a bit out of sinc or as in my case, and most cases, everything is unfolding perfectly. Relax and assess the situation, making adjustments. Adapt as necessary. Stay true to yourself and trust your instincts.

DEFINING GOALS

Goals include anything you want to have, own, become, or experience in life. Without goals your life becomes stagnant, lacking direction and purpose. Only you put a limit on what is possible for your life. Specifically defining what you will accomplish gives you a guide from which to measure your progress by comparing your goal to your end result. Projecting a completion date provides a time mark to move towards.

Include each small step necessary to take in order to make your career and educational dreams a reality. Include steps like save money, obtain a loan, apply for an internship, make contacts, write a resumé, buy work clothes, etc. The examples and directions in this section will provide you with ideas, stimulating you to create your own plan. After you write your plan, you may want someone in your field to evaluate your plan. Your contact may offer valuable suggestions that end up saving you time, money, and heartache.

Depending on your objective, the steps you take may be specific and required or varied and optional. Some career goals involve direct routes. For example, to become a hair stylist, radiology technician, massage therapist, or medical assistant usually requires completion of appropriate course work, an internship or apprenticeship, and an exam for a license or credential. Similarly, occupations such as a teacher, dietitian, occupational therapist, or accountant (CPA) require a bachelor's degree, internship, and state license. Many occupations, such as these mentioned, have training guidelines decided upon by the state and the professional associations governing the particular career.

Other careers have less defined paths. Public relations specialist, sports caster, writer, fashion designer, radio producer, singer, actor, artist, or politician, for example, can be attained a variety of ways. There is no clear-cut path. State law rarely requires a particular license for these more creative careers. Numerous possibilities for training exist. If you seek careers with varied training options, develop a flexible attitude. While traveling toward your destination, you may wind and swerve in unexpected directions. You may need a bachelor's degree, you may not. You may work for a variety of organizations before you reach your goal; you may not. You may achieve a high level of skill and recognition quickly, or it may take years until you reach success.

If you are considering a career with a loose career path, still *be specific* in stating your plans, but leave room for variation, flexibility, and maneuvering. Continue taking small steps towards your desired goal.

DEVELOP CONTACTS

Contacts are essential. Almost no one achieves their goals without the help of other people, so nurture relationships with people who can help you. When pursuing a career in a competitive industry, knowing people is especially necessary. You can create those *lucky breaks* people talk about by creating opportunities to meet possible contacts. As Benjamin Franklin said, "Diligence is the mother of good luck." Go to places and events where you can meet people with goals and ideas similar to yours, such as seminars, fund raisers, alumni gatherings, and parties. Be friendly and genuine when establishing relationships; contact those individuals with whom you feel a rapport. Follow up initial meetings with a telephone call or letter. Continue communication. Call or write periodically, creating a reason for interaction, such as to share an interesting story, ask a question, or express a concern about your field. Soon you will have a list of contacts to call on for jobs, referrals, and information.

THE OUTLINE

Counselors, teachers, self-help authors, and motivational speakers offer different suggestions about setting goals. No right way exists; many techniques work.

One way to outline goals is by major time groupings. Below are the categories I like to use when writing my goals by time:

- **long-term goals:** lifelong pursuits
- **medium-term goals:** one to five years
- **short-term goals**: one month to one year
- **mini-goals**: daily and weekly activities

Long-term goals are general statements, such as to be the world's best teacher, to have a happy family, or to travel the world. It is best to state these aspirations in large, limitless terms. For example, the goal *to be the world's best photographer* allows for more growth and continuous learning than the goal *to be a photographer*. To be *the world's best* is a continuous life journey, never completed; thus it never becomes boring. Once a goal is reached, the satisfaction derived from the accomplishment soon diminishes — we become anxious, stagnate, and desire to seek new horizons once again. By making goals endless, you always have a new frontier to conquer. Long-range goals satisfy this need.

Medium-, short-term and mini-goals, however, should be *specific* and *measurable*. These goals support our lifelong goals. When writing these goals, specify the *who, what, where,* and *when* of the goal. For instance, the short-term goal *I want to get good grades* does not meet the criteria. We don't know when this goal will happen and it's not measurable. To make this goal more precise, change it to, *Next semester I will earn a 3.5 grade point average (g.p.a.)*. This goal meets the criteria: who, what, where, and when. At the end of the semester we can measure if the goal has been met. For each of your medium and short-term goals include the mini-goals or action steps you will take to complete the goal:

short-term goal
- Next semester I will earn a 3.5 g.p.a.

mini-goals -
- I will study at least ten hours per week.
- I will meet with a tutor once a week, if my work becomes too difficult for me.
- I will reduce my work hours by 15% to allow for more study time.
- I will watch T.V. only two nights a week.

Your mini-goals become a big part of your life; they represent your street map while you travel on earth. They provide you with direction so you won't wander aimlessly. With a specific course to follow, you can measure where you began and when you have moved to a new place.

Select your long- and medium-term career goals first, and then make them more manageable by choosing short-term goals and mini-goals. Break each goal into small measurable steps. Basically, list everything you need to do to make your desires reality. Brainstorm when writing your goals. List every idea that comes to your mind and use the career research materials and other knowledge you gathered during your informational interviews. Talk to many successful people working in the areas you seek. Most career goals will include steps regarding education, internship or volunteer work, money, contacts, and job search.

These examples include the who, what, where, and when each goal will be accomplished. The individual accomplishing any aspect of these examples will know when an item is complete. Each action item is detailed and specific, yet flexible enough to allow for change if necessary. Remember, any plan is only a blue-print, a guide; and you might change your course of action depending on outcomes. Write goals that fit for you and your career desires. Use the examples as guidelines when writing your guide.

The following examples illustrate *THE OUTLINE* format using the long-, medium-, and short-term and mini-goal categories:

OUTLINE EXAMPLE

long-term - To be the world's best pilot.

medium-term - To become a pilot working for a major airline by Spring 2010.

- Finish a Bachelor of Science degree in Aeronautics from Emery-Riddle Aeronautical Univer -sity at Dayton, Florida by Spring 2005.
- Finish required number of flight hours for commercial pilot licenses.
- Teach beginning students how to fly at least 20 hours per week.

short-term -

- Log in 150 hours of flight time during Fall 2003 semester.
- Complete Fall 2003 semester with at least a 3.8 g.p.a.
- Save $1,000 by the end of Fall 2003 semester.

mini-goals -

- Fly at least 10 hours per week.
- *(for one week)* Study at least 10 hours per week.
- Meet with department advisor as soon as possible.
- Select classes for each semester five days after meeting with advisor.
- Interview a national airline pilot within the next two weeks.
- Continue to work out at least three times a week.
- Deposit $50 into savings account every Friday.

OUTLINE EXAMPLE

long-term - To be an expert radiology technician in the health care industry.

medium-term -

- Complete a Radiological Technician (R.T.) program from a local community college by June 2003.
- Have a full-time position as a radiological technician at an HMO at least six months after graduation.

short-term -

- Volunteer in a hospital during Fall 2002.
- Complete Spring 2002 semester with at least a 3.0 g.p.a.
- Research hospitals and clinics in my area of choice by the end of Spring '02.
- Subscribe to a health care journal.
- Reduce credit card debt by $2000 within two years: pay $100 monthly.
- Complete prerequisites for R.T. program.

mini-goals - *(weekly)*

- Volunteer in a hospital every Thursday from 1-4 p.m.
- Go to class Monday - Friday from 8 a.m. to 12 noon.
- Study every Monday, Wednesday, and Friday from 7-10 p.m.
- Read a health care journal once a week for two hours.
- Save $100 every paycheck.

THE SPIDER

The *SPIDER* technique works great for brainstorming. It provides a format to spontaneously conceive the pieces of your goal, without restriction. I suggest applying this technique before you list your goals by time because it offers you notes to use for forming your action steps.

On a sheet of paper write your main goal in the center of the page and circle it. Draw a line branching off this goal and write a step you can take to complete your main goal. Circle this step. Then draw a short line from this new circle and list another step. Circle this new step. Continue branching and circling from each step until the circles on the edge of the page are small, mini-goals that can be completed in an hour or a day. Evaluate your circles, breaking these down by adding mini-goals to any goal that takes more than a day to complete. The *SPIDER* makes a great visual picture of the action steps needed to achieve your ultimate goal. It is an appropriate format for creative, intuitive thinkers. *FIRE, WATER, MYSTIC, EXPLORER, ARTISAN, HEALER,* and *RULER* types will also find this technique useful.

SPIDER EXAMPLE

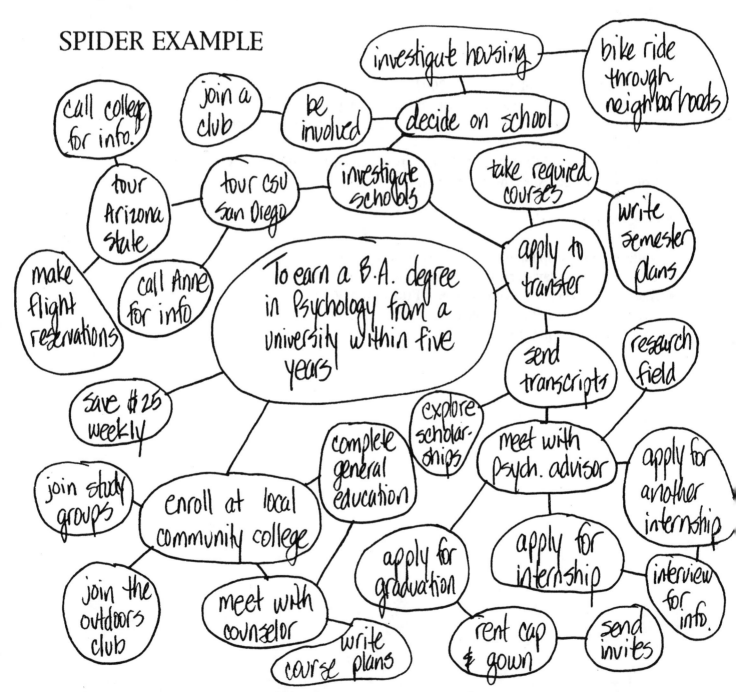

SPIDER EXAMPLE

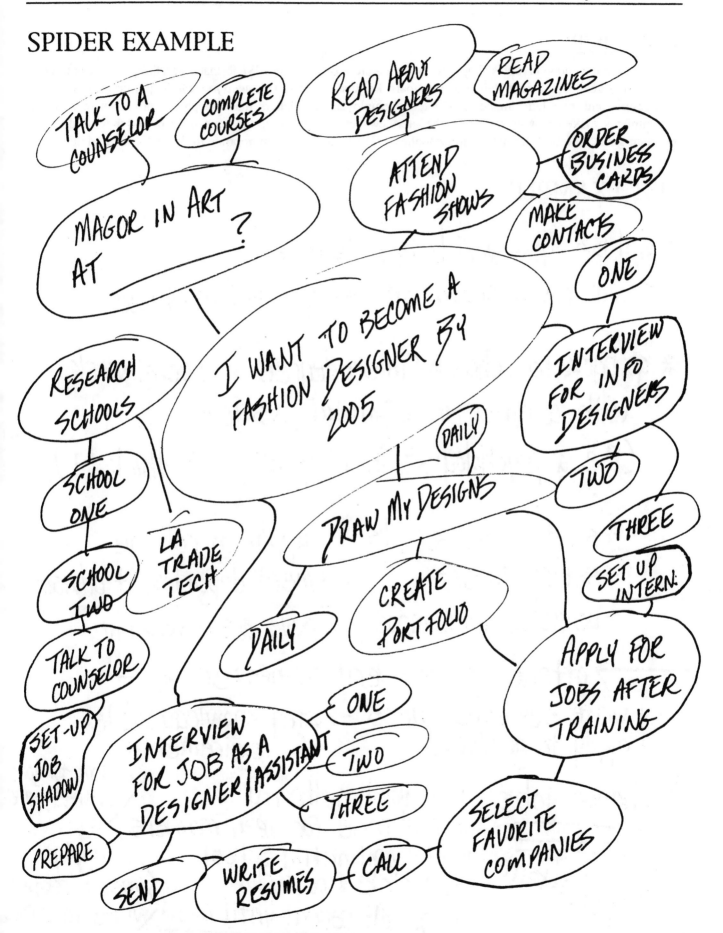

THE LIST

Another technique involves simply writing on a piece of paper, in *LIST* format, everything you need to do to achieve your goal. Break each step into mini-goals. For instance, the step, *get a job*, can be put into smaller steps: write resumé and cover letter, make list of potential employers, mail letters, make telephone calls to set up interview appointments, make follow-up calls after the interviews, etc. After writing the steps, determine if they need to split into mini-goals. The *LIST* format is similar to the *SPIDER,* but is more appropriate for linear, structured thinkers.

LIST EXAMPLE

I will be the world's best helper:
  I will be a probation officer within 3 years

* go back to school & finish degree in social work,
   with a minor in criminal justice.
   (Be a psychologist in 10 years - I think !?)

+ send for transcripts   + apply to college
+ select classes   + meet department advisor
+ be active on campus   + save $30 - weekly

——→ attend school every semester ←——
+ write semester plans → stay knowledgeable
+ apply to graduate   of requirements

* change jobs : tour youth authority
                 tour a home for teen mothers
                 visit a contination school
                 visit girls & boys club
                 * call repeat until hired

look for jobs in these area
↓
apply
meet people
write resume

be persistent

THE ACTION PLAN

After you've completed an *OUTLINE, SPIDER* and/or *LIST* plan for each of your main goals, review your work. Check to see that you've included every piece needed to complete your goal and that you've made every step as small as possible. Your mini-goals, remember, are tasks you can complete in a day or less. Put any medium- and short-term goals into mini-goals if necessary.

Create your *ACTION PLAN* by organizing each small step chronologically. Use weekly or monthly headings, continuing as far into the future that's comfortable for you. Use your *OUTLINE, SPIDER,* or *LIST* information to outline your *ACTION PLAN*. After each goal add completion dates. The steps you list under each heading should be manageable, small things you can complete in a few minutes or hours. Your *ACTION PLAN* becomes your *to do* list, consisting of months of mini-goals. Revise your list as you complete various phases of your goal and as your situation changes. Your *OUTLINE, SPIDER* or *LIST* delineates the big picture while your *ACTION PLAN* shows the nuts-and-bolts, the daily activities of your plan. Both are necessary. The first reminds you of your purpose. The second offers a daily map.

Use the time categories that fit you best. Some individuals prefer monthly or quarterly headings, allowing for flexibility in completion of their activities. Many times what they intend to work on for a particular day doesn't fit their mood, so they select a different activity from their monthly selection. Within this relaxed structure, they still complete their goals as close as possible to the deadline date. Other people, however, prefer specific daily steps that they complete weekly. Arrange your goals in the fashion you like. Many notebooks, day-timers, and organizers are available for purchase to also assist with creating your schedule. You might want to get creative by writing and drawing colorful poster size charts with pictures and quotes. Select the format and style that's best for you.

GOAL SETTING EXAMPLES

The following pages illustrate goals diagrammed using the *OUTLINE, SPIDER,* and *LIST* formats with corresponding *ACTION PLANS.* Remember that *ACTION PLANS* are mini-goals with completion dates that are organized by time.

WORKSHEETS

The pages after the examples offer worksheets for you to list your goals. Use the pages to diagram and categorize by time your medium- and long-term goals. Experiment with the different formats to decide which fits you best. You may want to outline the same goal using the three different formats: *THE OUTLINE, LIST,* or *SPIDER,* testing which style you like. An *ACTION PLAN* accompanies each *OUTLINE, LIST,* or *SPIDER.*

Study the previous examples in this section. Look for similarities between your goals and the examples. Notice the specific steps listed for each goal and decide which pieces you need for your particular goals. Depending on the depth of preparation for your career, you may benefit from having two separate plans: one for education and one for career.

If you are still undecided about your future, your career goal could be: to make a career decision by *such and such* date. Your short-term and mini-goals would include exploratory activities that you will do to bring you closer to a decision. They could include conducting two informational interviews with *so and so* by this summer and volunteering to work at *such and such* by this fall.

After you diagram your goals, update your mini-goals as necessary. Extract new mini-goals from your other goal categories as needed. The creation of your mini-goals depends on your productivity and the nature of your career. Your mini-goals, remember, become your daily *to do* list.

OUTLINE EXAMPLE

long term - To be the world's best pop singer.

medium-term -
- Sign a record deal with a reputable company within five years.
- Cultivate contacts in the music industry by taking classes, attending music production conventions, and meeting other motivated singers and musicians (ongoing).
- Produce a demo tape within the next year.
- Produce another demo tape the following year.
- Update head shot and sales package when necessary.
- Continue studying vocal technique and writing songs (daily).
- Make at least $2000 per month giving karaoke shows at clubs and private parties within a year.
- Continue to believe that I have the skills, talent, and confidence to create and sell CDs. Know that I am enough!
- Save at least $4000 for demo tape and recording studio fees within three years.

short term -
- Evaluate for six months: solo versus band singing.
- Choose a path: solo or band after the sixth month.
- Fine-tune singing style A.S.A.P. and ongoing.
- Create a karaoke show, party demo tapes, brochure, and business cards within eight months.
- Get head shot and develop a sales package within six months.
- Advertise to friends, acquaintances, and social organizations one month after advertising materials are ready.
- Write follow-up letters to clients one week after successful gigs.
- Write at least 10 new songs within one year.
- Attend an event at least once a month (class, performance, industry party, etc.).
- Make follow-up calls three days after meeting new people in the music industry.
- Evaluate singing in a night club within two months. If idea sounds good, create show and send promotional materials to clubs within six months.
- Investigate the benefits of having an agent during the year. If having an agent seems right, find out how to get one.
- Read at least three books about singing, performance, and marketing this year.
- Save $300 per month.

mini-goals (for one week) -
- Read at least two music related publications weekly.
- Sing daily.
- Work out at least three times a week.
- Write in journal at least twice a week.
- Talk to two respectable singers about their careers by next week.
- Re-write one song by next week.
- Brainstorm for pamphlet ideas for karaoke show by next week.
- Get a list of night clubs. Call about gigs by this week
- Buy a book about marketing myself as a singer tomorrow.

OUTLINE ACTION PLAN EXAMPLE

January
- practice daily
- take music classes
- write two new songs
- save # 200 dollars
- organize songs

February
- practice daily
- interview for info two successful singers
- read a book related to goal - save #200 bucks

March
- practice daily
- tape back-up music
- get business cards
- write promotion brochure

April
- practice daily
- get head shot
- solicit businesses for shows
- write 3 new songs

May
- practice daily
- write at least 4 new songs
- continue soliciting businesses
- investigate agents?

June
- practice daily
- call around for info about demo tape
- arrange shows

July
- practice daily
- practice / polish songs
- make demo tape
- attend awards show, to "schmooz"

August
- practice daily
- send out demo tapes w/ promotional material
- audition for "star search"

September
- practice daily
- continue writing songs
- follow up on promos

October
- practice daily
- search for new ways to get signed
- continue to believe!

November
- practice daily
- submit demo tape again & again
- continue saving #100-

December
- practice, but go on holiday!
- send follow-up notices to contacts

SPIDER EXAMPLE

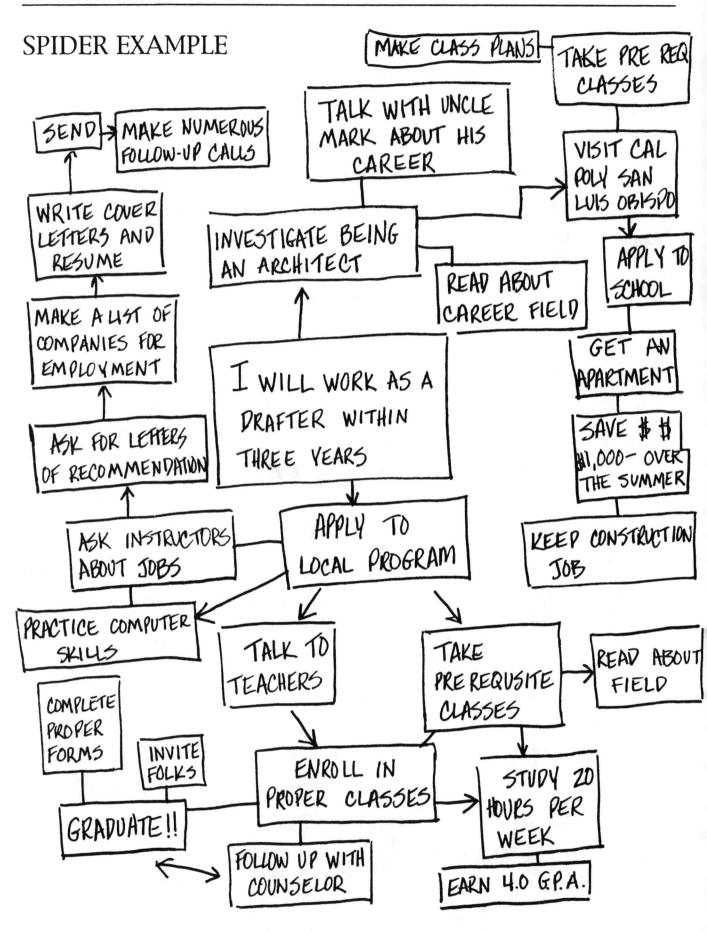

SPIDER ACTION PLAN EXAMPLE

January
- SEARCH THE WEB FOR INFO ABOUT DRAFTERS & ARCHITECTS
- SIGN UP FOR CLASSES
- MAP OUT COURSE PLAN
- STUDY 20 HOURS PER WEEK

February
- VISIT CAL POLY
- TALK TO UNCLE ABOUT HIS CAREER
- KEEP STUDYING 20 HOURS PER WEEK

March
- START SAVING $150 PER MONTH
- MEET WITH COUNSELOR
- STAY FOCUSSED
- GET TO KNOW INSTRUCTORS

April
- INTERVIEW FOR INFO A DRAFTER & AN ARCHITECT
- SUBSCRIBE TO DRAFTING JOURNAL
- STUDY

May
- ASK INSTRUCTOR FOR LETTER OF RECOMMENDATION
- LOOK FOR INTERNSHIP
- ASK INSTRUCTORS FOR CONTACTS

June
- CONTINUE CONSTRUCTION JOB
- TAKE SUMMER SCHOOL CLASSES
- SAVE $150 PER MONTH

July
- REGISTER FOR FALL CLASSES
- LOOK INTO PLACES TO WORK
- RELAX

August
- BEGIN CLASSES
- BUY BOOKS
- STUDY DAILY
- WRITE RESUME
- ASK INSTRUCTORS FOR JOB LEADS

September
- MEET WITH COUNSELOR
- MAKE PLAN FOR CSU SAN LUIS
- KEEP STUDYING

October
- APPLY FOR JOBS AS AN ASSISTANT DRAFTER
- PRACTICE CAD

November
- FOLLOW UP ON JOB LEADS
- GET JOB
- LEARN ALL I CAN

December
- DO WELL ON FINALS
- START TO DRAFT/ DESIGN DREAM HOME
- RELAX

LIST EXAMPLE

To Become A Buyer For Major Department Store in 5 Years

- interview for information buyers at Macey's, Nordstroms and Robinsons May
- write resume & cover letter
- write list of target stores and departments
- buy new clothes
- save ~~# $~~ → $100 per month
- read VOGUE
- take some business classes
- become top sales person → listen to sales tapes
    -use ideas
- learn management duties
- volunteer for extra jobs
- apply for department manager
- change hairstyle → have "colors" done
    ↘ update wardrobe
- learn business meeting procedures
- talk to the "right" people
- don't gossip!

→ send resume & make call backs

send thank you letters

continue until hired

LIST ACTION PLAN EXAMPLE

January

- interview for information 3 different buyers
- write resume for sales job and assistant manager
- make "target" list

February

- send resumes & complete applications - 20 stores
- make follow-up calls
- read trade magazines
- continue saving $150 monthly

March

- buy new suit
- have "colors" done
- continue job search until hired
- send thank yous

April

- buy new outfit
- land new job ??!
- learn as much as possible
- attend sales seminar

May

- be top sales person
- ask manager for advancement advice
- meet other department managers

June

- buy another outfit
- have the best displays
- read a book on management

July

- look out for management positions → apply?
- listen to sales tapes
- practice assertive communication

August

- buy new outfit
- arrange a job shadow with 2 buyers
- stay abreast of company happenings

September

- learn more about being a buyer
- keep on the look-out for new positions

October

- begin reading more magazines, etc.
- get involved in store events

November

- change "look" - update!
- continue cultivating business relationships
- stay positive

December

- evaluate goals & update
- relax - don't get caught in "holiday trap"

MY OUTLINE

MY ACTION PLAN
(Using the OUTLINE format)

January   *February*   *March*

April   *May*   *June*

July   *August*   *September*

October   *November*   *December*

MY SPIDER

MY ACTION PLAN
(Using the SPIDER format)

January

February

March

April

May

June

July

August

September

October

November

December

MY LIST

MY ACTION PLAN
(Using the LIST format)

January

February

March

April

May

June

July

August

September

October

November

December

Review your *ACTION PLANS* and adjust if necessary. By committing to completion times you create a desire in your mind to reach this programmed action — a positive self-fulfilling prophecy for change. Your commitment fosters action towards solidifying your goals. By committing to completion dates, you create momentum which spurs you towards your destination. Without a timeline, we subconsciously think we have forever to reach the goal. With a date, however, we feel obligated to take action. Believe it or not, most people do not attain their goals by the projected date. If you do not reach your goals by the date you have set, don't worry. Simply make a new timeline and continue along your journey, knowing that your initial projection date served its purpose: to move you in the *direction* of your dreams. Movement is the key.

Do notice, however, if you do not have movement towards your goals. Needing additional time because something took longer than you thought is different than delays due to procrastination. If failure to attain goals becomes a pattern, have a talk with yourself to determine the cause of your inaction. You might want to read applicable self-help books, talk with people who care about you, and/or reevaluate your objective. In some circumstances it's just not the right time to pursue career goals — other life issues may be taking precedence. Other times the goal you've selected just isn't the right one and that's why it's difficult for you to complete tasks. Selecting a different course of action may cause you to feel more motivated and committed. There are other ways to overcome procrastination, if that applies to you. Make a stronger promise to yourself, change your self-talk, evaluate your motivators, work with a goal setting partner, and/or go to counseling to assist with increasing your progress. Fear and love also motivate people — fear that you'll be in the same place that you are now, if you don't take action. Love for your goal that you can't help yourself from pursuing your desire. Being in love also motivates people to make progress towards attaining goals. You are the best judge of your reasons for delaying your achievements, so evaluate your situation, if necessary.

Regardless of your personality style, it is very beneficial to *write down your goals*! On the surface this may feel redundant. We logically tell ourselves that we already know in our minds what we want to achieve, so why write it down? Writing intentions on paper, however, solidifies our ideas in our mind. The impressions in our head are just dreams. Dreams become real with an actual guide and follow through. With a concrete direction, your brain begins to work on these new ideas. Complete this vital step of career planning by committing your mental images to paper!

TRANSITIONS - Adjusting Your Choices

Preparing for a career requires time and money. Create space in your life for your new destination, perhaps rearranging and reshaping your current lifestyle with new habits. This may mean working fewer hours, socializing less, and cutting out wasted time, such as idly talking on the telephone, watching television, or surfing the internet. You may naturally stop unproductive behaviors and begin new worthwhile activities. If you are pursuing a goal that you truly desire and you've made the decision to live this dream, change often occurs naturally. If not, make a conscious effort to fit your new commitments into your life.

The changes you make will affect the people around you. Communicate clearly and tenderly your plans to loved ones. Explain your new commitments and how these will affect your current lifestyle. For example, if you will be graduating soon, you may want to take on an internship which may change your income and your available time for pleasure. Or, if you currently work from 9 a.m. - 5 p.m., cook dinner for your family, read the paper, and garden on the weekends and you now want to finish your degree by taking two night classes every semester, other people within the family or hired help may need to take on some of your responsibilities. You'll need time to go to class and study. Most likely your goals will lead you to new people with similar interests and goals — changing your lifestyle as well. Brainstorm for solutions to make your situation enjoyable. Possibilities abound. Be flexible, open, willing, and enthusiastic while you work towards the fulfillment of your dreams and you will experience satisfaction.

If you're a young adult (or older for that matter!) and are still very much influenced by your family, you might need to develop more independence so you won't take a direction based on your parents' or society's biases for or against a path. Stay tuned into your intuitive spirit. Express yourself confidently, giving value to *your* desires. If you need more support or freedom from your family, ask for it. Selecting a career and pursuing it often affects your relationships with others, so strive to communicate clearly your feelings, desires, and concerns to the people around you.

In addition, determine what type of resources you need. If money for school, a new job, a new apartment, or support from friends is necessary, creatively consider all the options available to you. Money can be obtained in a variety of ways, as we covered in *Chapter Four*. Adjust easily. Ask for assistance from loved ones. Change is exciting. Change keeps you alive, young, and vibrant. You will grow in a positive direction!

In spite of your enthusiasm, resistance from friends and family may occur. Some people close to you may subtly sabotage your efforts to change. This type of behavior may manifest in conversations where your opinions and feelings are invalidated; i.e., questioning why you want to do *such and such*. Other times individuals close to you may make your life difficult by failing to help, by making unreasonable requests, or making promises they don't fulfill. Observe your situation and your feelings. Realize that some people are envious of others making positive change. Consider how you might address jealousy from any less secure people you know. Some individuals will grow with you, while others will not, so be willing to let go of relationships that no longer serve as positive influences. Do not subject yourself to negative comments and energy. Decide which relationships add to your life positively. You may phase out old relationships and create new ones, determining that some folks in your life bring too much negativity and strife. If you begin to feel that people close to you consistently take unsupportive actions against you, consciously or unconsciously, then avoid as much as possible interacting with these individuals. If this seems too harsh, then at least insist that conversations and unsolicited opinions about your future are off limits. You cannot afford this type of negative energy in your life, especially as you progress towards your desires.

Once you begin your quest, you will never be the same. Familiar ways of dealing with life that once were effective may no longer work. New priorities and communication skills may emerge. Accept these willingly. One of my clients, Anthony, a freeway construction worker living in Southern California, decided that he wanted to complete his bachelor of science degree in forestry from California State University, Humboldt, in Northern California. He also wanted to incorporate writing into his new career, eventually move to Wyoming to live in the wilderness, and begin a family of his own.

However, Anthony had a conflict: Robert, his brother-in-law, wanted him to work in his newly formed freeway construction company. Anthony strongly valued his family and believed in supporting family members. He wanted to follow his own plan *and* help Robert. Anthony approached Robert with his concerns. Together they decided that while Anthony finished a few more prerequisite classes at the local community college, he would work for Robert for at least six months and then move to Humboldt. With this short-range plan, Anthony would be working towards his bachelor's degree and also have time to research employment opportunities before moving. This arrangement gave Anthony time to solidify his medium-term goals and to honor his value for family and it gave Robert time to seek a permanent work partner. This conflict could easily have been a family disaster. Fortunately, Anthony addressed the issues firmly, tactfully, and honestly. Together, he and Robert created a workable solution.

Assess your lifestyle. Determine your priorities. Consider how you might handle changes at home, work, and school. Decide how you will address requests for your time from others. Preparing for a career is time-consuming, so be ready to say *no* if people request too much of your time and it hinders preparations for your career. Loretta, a neighbor of mine, decided to enter college after having worked 10 years full time as a telephone operator. She decided to keep her job, take two classes per semester, and look for a more flexible job. She wasn't really sure what to choose for her new career, she just knew that it was time to explore new options, so she enrolled in college. Loretta, a very socially active person, soon realized that she would have to turn down some of the invitations she received, such as going to concerts or the river, to make time for studying. This was a new concept for her. However, Loretta was willing to make the adjustment because she desperately wanted out of her position as a telephone operator. You, too, may need to make similar choices. Ask loved ones for support, help, and understanding. Decide how you can communicate your needs, spend time with people you care about, *and* pursue your career goals. Do not let yourself down. Make a space for your new endeavors.

CREATING BALANCE -
Life Is For The Tasting

While our focus has been on your career goals, consider incorporating general life goals into your plan as well. Balance is a key ingredient to a successful life. Your life is much more than just your career. After all, if you are your career, then who are you when you are not working? The most interesting and successful individuals have interests and passions other than their careers. Complete goal setting include activities other than career activities. In addition, many people *like*, not love, their careers, but it is not their main focus. It may be a means to an end. Even those of you who feel completely ecstatic about work, you too need outside stimulants. Enjoy and explore life! Treasure the beautiful pieces it offers. Thousands of exciting and interesting activities wait for your attention. Well-balanced people immerse themselves in a myriad of experiences throughout their lives, rarely becoming stagnant.

Ideally, your life goals will cover many areas of your spirit. Life goals can be put into five main categories: intellectual, social, physical, emotional, and spiritual. Selecting and experiencing goals from each of these groups helps to create balance in your life, reducing the risk of job burn-out and life crisis. If you experience unsatisfactory results in a particular area, you'll still have success in the remaining areas. The next few pages outline the five categories of *Dimensions of Optimal Health* through a diagram and explanations.

Dancing, laughing, riding
Surfing, swimming, running
Weaving through the choices, the
life banquet overflows.

Work a little, play a little enjoying
the feast, still honoring the inner
compass.

Learning, growing, creating adds
to the depth of character.
Expressions of the mind, heart, and
soul satisfies hunger, curtails
boredom.

The adventure of life, its
cornucopia forever abundant
entices, challenges, comforts.

Traveling to new places and
spaces entertains, offers wisdom.
Customs and mores show the
grand scheme in action.

Your way, his way, my way — all
ways valid bring a humbling awe
to appreciating the intricate
connection of plentiful options.

A thousand thank-yous offered.

Dimensions of Optimal Health

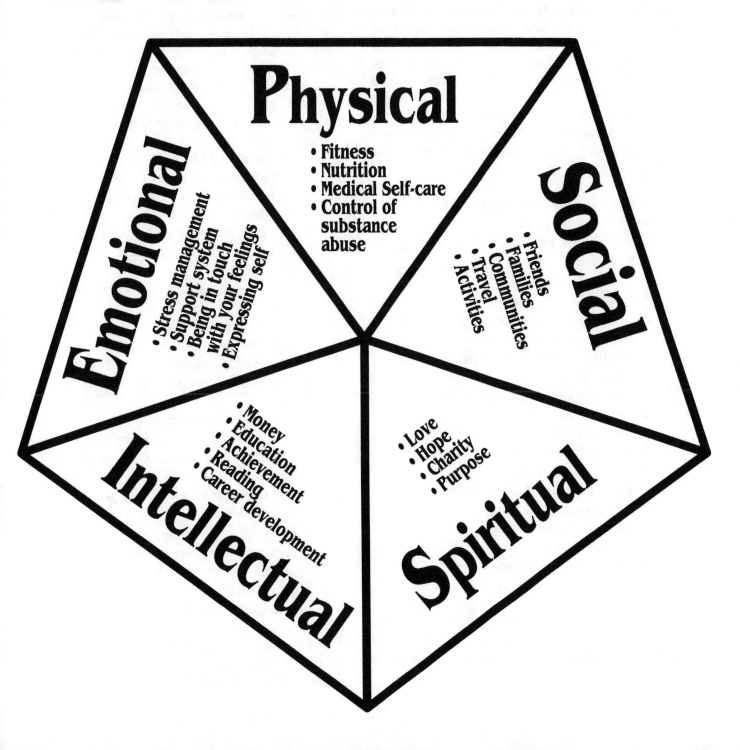

Physical
- Fitness
- Nutrition
- Medical Self-care
- Control of substance abuse

Social
- Friends
- Families
- Communities
- Travel
- Activities

Emotional
- Stress management
- Support system
- Being in touch with your feelings
- Expressing self

Intellectual
- Money
- Education
- Achievement
- Reading
- Career development

Spiritual
- Love
- Hope
- Charity
- Purpose

INTELLECTUAL GOALS
Exercise Your Mind

The intellectual group includes goals that stimulate your mind, including education, career, and money. Investing $2000 in stocks, reading the newspaper daily, and attending a seminar related to your career are examples of intellectual goals.

American culture places a high value on intellectual ambitions, so it often becomes the dominant force in our lives. Through the media and our socialization process we learn to emphasize career achievement, monetary success, status, education, and intellect. To have a prestigious career, own a nice home, drive a new car, and pay for our children's education all enter into the American dream. While intellectual goals are worthwhile, do not let peer pressure and the values of others influence your selection. Choose goals based on *your* values and beliefs. Below are examples of intellectual goals:

- Learn about the stock market.
- Earn a college degree.
- Read *Newsweek* once a week.
- Buy a vacation home.
- Read the Classics.
- Secure $25,000 in the bank.
- Learn how to speak a new language.
- Go on an archeological dig.
- Buy life insurance for your family.
- Earn a doctorate.
- Read *National Geographic* magazine, monthly.
- Buy a sail boat.
- Watch *Discovery* channel.
- Save $500, monthly.
- Take a class related to your career.
- Earn a promotion at work.
- Buy a new stereo system.
- Earn a 4.0 g.p.a.
- Read one novel, monthly.
- Learn how to play chess.

Hundreds more intellectual goals exist. What other types of intellectual pursuits interest you? Evaluate your current development in this area, and then decide what new things you would like to experience in your life. Select intellectual goals you can experience throughout life.

SOCIAL GOALS -
Let's Have Fun

Without fun and recreation, life loses its spice, excitement, and vigor. When our lives are over we won't say, "I wish I had worked more." Instead many say, "I wish I had spent more time with my spouse," or "Why didn't I take my spouse on that surprise trip to the Florida Keys?" Social goals include spending time with family, relatives, and friends; socializing, and traveling. Doing fun things, such as having a BBQ, going to an amusement park, or visiting a museum are examples of social goals. Following are more suggestions for social goals:

- Give a dinner party.
- Plan a camping trip to the Ozark area.
- Arrange for a hot air balloon ride with some friends.
- Attend a ballet or musical, twice a year.
- Pitch a tent in the backyard with my family or lover.
- Cook a special birthday meal for my sweet heart.
- Go on a safari in Africa.
- Travel throughout Europe.
- Plan a family reunion.
- Take ballroom dance lessons with my honey.
- Look at old photo albums.
- Have a murder mystery dinner party.
- Travel in a motor home to the United States national parks.
- Go to a play, twice a year.
- Go to Greece.
- Plan a 4th of July party.
- See my favorite group in concert.
- Go on a one-day road trip.
- Go wine tasting.
- Tour Washington, D.C.

What other social activities appeal to you? Make a list of places that you would like to travel and/or live during your life. Consider new activities that you would like to try. Explore your current social life. Typically, teenagers and people in their early twenties spend more time socializing than those 25 or older. Young adults may sacrifice their career and educational goals for parties and ski trips, while older adults focus more on work and running a household, forgetting to take time to play. Honestly assess how you spend your time and create a healthy balance. Decide what social goals you would like to experience in your life.

PHYSICAL GOALS -
Use It So You Won't Lose It

Physical goals sometimes overlap with social goals; however, physical goals focus more on maintaining and improving health. Eating a well-balanced diet and exercising three times a week are two worthwhile physical goals. The expression, *A sound body helps make for a sound mind* definitely brings positive results. Perhaps some of the physical goals listed below are things you would like to incorporate into your life:

- Learn how to water ski.
- Obtain training in *CPR* and basic medical care.
- Quit smoking.
- Go to the gym three times a week, an hour before work.
- Go sky diving.
- Eat two servings of vegetables, daily.
- Reduce *fast food* intake by 50%.
- Join an intramural sports team.
- Learn how to play golf.
- Take tap dancing lessons.
- Get eight hours of sleep per night.
- Go skiing at least twice a season.
- Go roller-blading.
- Workout with a personal trainer.
- Meet with a nutritionist and follow suggested program.
- Do 100 sit-ups and 25 push-ups before bed.
- Take a yoga class.
- Take vitamins daily.
- Lose 10 lbs. within three months.
- Eat 50% fewer sweets.

Decide if you want to adjust your current physical commitments. If you already live a fairly healthy lifestyle, consider trying something new, such as learning a new sport, entering a competition, or attending a weekend health camp for some pampering. Again assess your situation and think of what you would like to experience throughout your life.

EMOTIONAL GOALS -
Oh, I Feel Joyful

An often overlooked category involves emotional well being. As a society we ignore our emotional health, expecting it to be rosy, while putting little or no attention towards the care of our soul. Poor and undeveloped emotional health can make our lives unbearable and is often the cause of illness, divorce, and work stress. It's common to see people with lots of success in their lives, but still they remain dissatisfied because of inadequate emotional care. Emotional health basically involves loving ourselves and others and knowing how to understand and effectively deal with our emotions constructively. Emotional growth includes stress management, expressing yourself honestly and tactfully, knowing how to handle conflict, and having high self-esteem. It also involves wrestling with and moving past childhood issues that may encumber our growth as adults. With a mature mental attitude the rest of life falls into place naturally.

If emotional health is intact, we are content the majority of the time. Observe the many rich and successful people who remain unhappy — this is proof that emotional well-being greatly influences life. Quite often these people haven't addressed their own psychological needs; thus they feel despondent in spite of their abundance of material wealth. Below are some examples of emotional goals:

- Express to your partner how you feel about your relationship.
- Make amends with someone with whom you had a falling out.
- Say *I love you* to your mother.
- Seek counseling for at least six months.
- Express your feelings to the people close to you.
- Change one internal dialogue statement from negative to positive.
- Pamper yourself when necessary with a

bath or massage.
- Leave an unsatisfactory relationship.
- Join a support group.
- Resist saying, *I told you so.*
- Compliment yourself and others.
- Accept people as they are.
- Send cards and letters to the people you love.
- Learn to be more assertive.
- Create a comforting living environment.
- Hug and kiss frequently the people you adore.
- Say *I'm sorry* when you make a mistake.
- Be honest about your life.
- Read a self-help book.
- Be flexible and true to yourself.

Numerous other emotional goals exist. Spend some quiet time pondering your emotional health. Assess your communication and stress management skills. Decide what you would like to add or change in your life. Risk just a little, then risk a lot. Be generous with your emotions and feelings. Give up the need to control others and engage in power plays just to keep yourself in control. Expand yourself and experience new emotional behaviors, showing your vulnerabilities, and life will feel much more rich, full, and meaningful. Laugh and cry often, knowing that these are gifts from the heavens!

SPIRITUAL GOALS - What's Life About?

Spirituality has often been expressed through organized religion, although there are many, many other options for spiritual enlightenment. Spiritual goals include activities relating to love, charity, peace, and hope. These types of goals help provide meaning in our lives. Without some type of spiritual belief, life can feel bewildering. The fulfillment of your spirituality is very personal. Finding solace with a particular congregation is an outstanding way to address spiritual needs. For others, meditating and reading about healers throughout history may bring spiritual satisfaction. Still others volunteer their time performing charity activities. The following serve as examples of spiritual goals:

- Study different religions.
- Adopt a *little sister* or *little brother*.
- Donate food and clothes to a charity.
- Be the first to smile at ten people every day.
- Be a courteous and patient driver.
- Meditate daily for 15 minutes.
- Visit a convalescent hospital once a month.
- Give 10% of your income to charity.
- Send love to people you normally ignore.
- Instead of judging others, see the divine love.
- Write a page in a journal, daily.
- Sing songs.
- Learn about people different from you.
- Volunteer in a soup kitchen.
- Express your dislike of racist remarks.
- Read biographies about people you admire.
- Don't litter.
- Be more patient.
- Write poetry.
- Attend church weekly.
- Read the *Koran* or *Bible* daily.

So many spiritual tasks await us that would take more than a lifetime to conquer. We are all immortal human beings with flaws and shortcomings, so unlimited options abound. The task of spiritual enlightenment never ends. Be gentle with yourself. Consider what aspect of spirituality you would like to change or improve in your life. Select ideas that fit you. The examples listed above serve only as samples — create your own.

Ideally, your spiritual beliefs and life purpose should be in harmony with your career goals; if not, conflict may emerge. My spiritual, life, and career purposes are the same: *To make positive social change through creative projects.* This broad statement allows me the freedom to tackle any creative project that I feel benefits humanity. If a career opportunity comes my way that doesn't meet the criteria I've set for myself, I decline. Consider how you will create your personal spiritual life.

LIVE LIFE FULLY

Create your life the way you envision, not a life defined by society's standards. A family of four I know wanted to live in a more rural, slow-paced environment. They sold their home in Los Angeles and moved to a small town on the East Coast, without employment secured. People they knew cautioned against such a move, proclaiming that it was "too risky and a bad career move. You may not be able to find a new job." Blah, blah, blah. Yes, anything is possible. They may get laid off or die in an earthquake if they stay in Los Angeles! With this type of attitude no one would ever want to leave their homes in the morning. Life has many twists and turns, so too many negatively skewed *what if* speculations are just a waste of time. Live life with no regrets. Live life to its fullest. Listen to your intuition: *You* know what's best for you. Don't let other people negatively influence your decisions. If you want to quit your job, put your belongings in storage, and travel to South America on some of your savings — do it! If you're in college living on a small budget and you've spotted an exciting business venture that seems reasonable — go for it! If you're over thirty, supporting a family with a mortgage payment, and you believe that finding a different type of job (or going back to school), living a simpler life, and starting a small service business feels right — begin now! As long as your choices are legal and don't harm other human beings, explore and change! Begin now to step towards your new vision.

Make your life journey enjoyable, exciting, and worthwhile. Don't make reading about someone else's life your passion. *Make your life your passion.* You're the hero in your life, it's your movie, so make your scenes imaginative, spectacular, fantastic, riveting, extraordinary, sensational, and outstanding.

Select goals from all the optimal health categories. Think of the person who focuses mainly on one area in his or her life, for example, a high-powered businessman who strictly works and neglects the other areas in his life. He doesn't even know his family. He experiences very little real joy. His life becomes one dimensional. It's no wonder many businessmen have heart attacks — they've squeezed the joy from their lives! Conversely, think of the people who always play and party and focus solely on the social side of life. These individuals accomplish very little. They shirk their responsibilities as adults, even abandoning their children. We don't count on them to follow through with anything.

You, however, want a rich, meaningful life with depth and passion, so experience all aspects of your spirit creating a soulful life.

The next page provides a worksheet on which to write your life goals. Select at least five goals for each dimension, from the examples on the previous pages. If you don't like the offerings, make up your own! Then select at least one goal from each category to pursue within the next three to four months. Decide when you will complete this goal. If the goal is too large to achieve within this time frame, such as *buy a house*, then complete one small step towards the direction of completion. Your goal might be to set up a savings plan for buying a house. You may also want to diagram the goal using the *OUTLINE, SPIDER,* or *LIST* format and then create an *ACTION PLAN.* Mini-goals, such as *write one page in my journal, daily* do not, of course, need to be diagrammed. Be realistic with your commitments. Choose the type and number of goals that suit your lifestyle. No rules exist for goal setting. You make your own guidelines.

Far better it is to dare mighty things, to win glorious triumphs, even checkered by failure, than to take rank with those poor spirits who neither enjoy much nor suffer much, because they live in the grey twilight that knows not victory nor defeat.

Theodore Roosevelt

MY LIFE GOALS

INTELLECTUAL GOALS - Exercise Your Mind

SOCIAL GOALS - Let's Have Fun

PHYSICAL GOALS - Use It So You Won't Lose It

EMOTIONAL GOALS - Oh, I Feel Happy

SPIRITUAL GOALS - What's Life About

YOUR LIFE LINE

Another clever way to outline your future life accomplishments is with a *LIFE LINE*. Include in your *LINE* the major life events you've already experienced and the ones you would like to experience. Write these major goals in a time-line format. If you have a significant other, make a *LINE* with your partner. You might like to enlarge your *LINES*. Use a bulletin board or wall to develop and display your *LIFE LINES*. You might also create three *LIFE LINES*: one for you, one for your partner, and one for both of you. Put the *partner line* in-between your two individual lines. When major life events involve both of you, curve your two individual lines and connect both of them to the partner *LIFE LINE*. Be fun, crazy, and carefree when developing your *LIFE LINES*. Use colored paper, poster board, or make a scroll. Use paints and markers. Add pictures and symbols. The next two pages illustrates examples of *LIFE LINES*.

LIFE LINE EXAMPLE

add more! ?

have children 32 buy a house 33

learn spanish   get hired w/ cool firm   28   30   get married?

go to Europe   begin law school   27   keep playing drums   Age 25

traveled across country on motorcycle   age 20 began college   worked, saved $

graduate from highschool   age 18

won state championships

age 16 moved in w/Dad

parents divorced   age 15 - got first job   camped a lot

fun kids stuff   age 14 - joined sv/varsity football team   delivering assistant

moved to AZ   age 13 - started playing drums

age 12

played first football game   age 10 - traveled to Hawaii   age 40 → visit China

age 5 - meet Daniel - best friend   age 45 → visit Africa

Born May 1 in Boston Mass. - Mark Jameson   age 46 - start own firm

LIFE LINE EXAMPLE

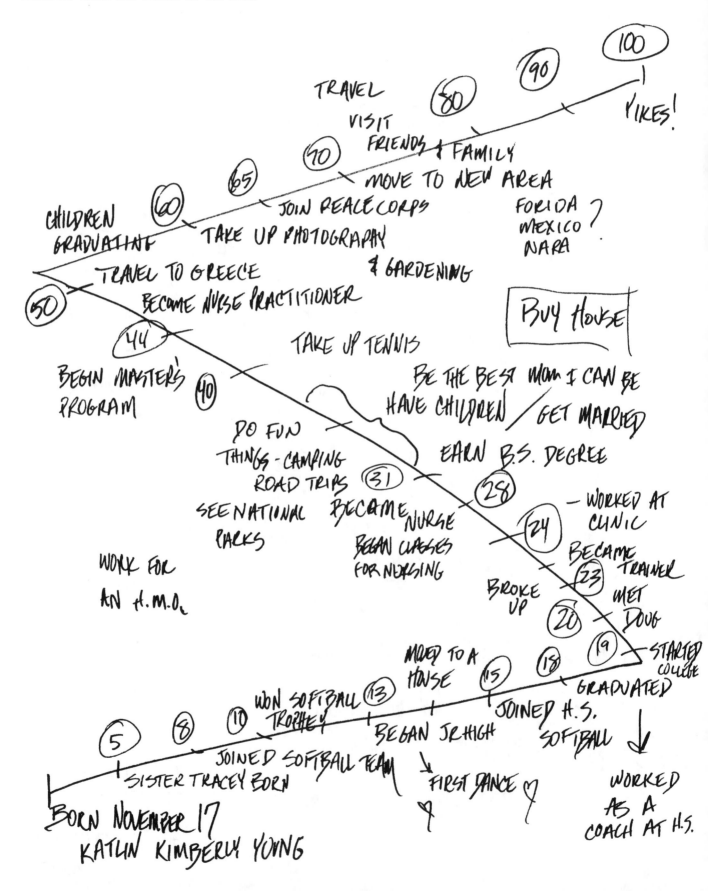

A DREAM BOOK

Designing a *DREAM BOOK* (or poster) also helps cultivate the completion of your goals. The *DREAM BOOK* includes all the things you want to have, experience, and become throughout your life. Purchase an artist's pad of unlined paper (any size) and fill the book with pictures and slogans that represent the things you want for your life. Include goals for career, education, family, travel, hobbies, personal development, and material desires. Cut pictures, words, slogans, and designs from old magazines. Use photos or draw your own pictures. Glue the pictures, words, and designs into your book. Arrange in collage style, tell a story, or separate your pictures into general categories, perhaps using the dimensions of optimal health. If you need ideas for your book, answer the following questions with pictures:

- What type of degrees and/or training do I want to have?
- What top five cities would I like to live in?
- How many children would I like to have?
- What does my ideal home look like?
- Where might my vacation home be located?
- What ten places do I want to visit within my life?
- What three hobbies will I develop?
- What new sports would I like to try?
- What second (or third) language would I like to learn?
- What causes will I support?

The *DREAM BOOK* serves as a wonderful creative exercise providing a tangible place for your conscious and subconscious mind to commune. Create a vision that feels magnificent!

> *If I do not dare to dream, then I do not dare to live.*
> *For life without dreams is like breath without air.*
> *A dream not attained is far better than no dream at all.*

FORGE AHEAD

With a plan in hand, you are now prepared to move in the direction of your dreams. Anxiety has subsided because you know your purpose. Anxiety has subsided because you know your next right step. You see the big picture and know how to get there. Feelings of indecisiveness have been replaced with feelings of excitement! You are ready to start completing your goals. Success is no longer out of reach because you know where you're headed. Your goal setting plans provide a framework for action for your working life. Your blueprint, however, is pliable and flexible, designed for change if necessary. The poem below provides a worthwhile guideline to live by:

> *What is Success?*
>
> *Setting goals, but not in concrete.*
> *Staying focused, but turning aside to help someone.*
> *Following a plan, but remaining flexible.*
> *Climbing the ladder, but not stepping on toes.*
> *Fighting to the finish, but choosing your battles.*
> *Taking a bow, but applauding those who had a part in your success.*
> *You are a success.*
>
> *Positively Greeting Card*

Your success is not measured by the amount of money you make or the type of car you drive. Success comes from using your gifts and talents to their fullest potential. The United States Army says it best, "Be all that you can be!" As corny as that sounds, it's a great mantra. Continue to cultivate balance in your life, accomplishing goals and nurturing yourself and loved ones daily.

The last chapter, ACTION, provides you with some final pieces of advice for effective career planning. We will continue to answer our last important question: *How will I get there?*

Oh success, so many ways to measure, so many choices to make. But in the end it's how you conduct yourself along the journey, not what you earn, not what you own.

A successful person knows the "right" choice is probably harder and takes more time.

A successful person has empathy, reserves judgment, accepts and admits mistakes with heartfelt apology.

He or she is someone you want to sit next to at dinner, to dance and laugh with.

A successful person sees life as an experience to enjoy and cherish, continuously growing, accepting change gracefully and with enthusiasm.

A successful person risks once, then twice, and again and again — never giving up.

A successful person seeks answers, asks for help, freely reveals an open heart.

A successful person loves romantically far better than the movie screen.

A successful person laughs and smiles and jokes and cries, and laughs again because he or she knows that life is a trip designed for Goodness.

A successful person is free.

Chapter Six

ACTION - Make It Happen!

Until one is committed, there is hesitancy, the chance to draw back, always ineffectiveness.
Concerning all acts of initiative (and creation), there is one elementary truth, the ignorance of which kills countless ideas and splendid plans: that the moment one definitely commits oneself, then Providence moves too.

All sorts of things occur to help one that would never otherwise have occurred.
A whole stream of events issues from the decision, raising in one's favor all manner of unforeseen incidents and meetings and material assistance, which no man could have dreamed would have come his way.

Scottish Himalayan Expedition

With confidence, you begin now to make your dreams a reality. You are prepared mentally, physically, and emotionally to tackle the tasks required for the fulfillment of your dreams. The screening of your life-movie is scheduled for release! You, the number one star on your magic carpet, willingly agree to participate in the highs and lows, the good and bad of your show. New sights and sounds, experiences, and relationships are all part of your ride. Excitedly you anticipate the beauty of the days to come.

As the sun consistently rises and sets, you too must approach your goals with the same commitment and steadiness. Every day, like nature, you will contribute to the world by passionately living your purpose. Some days you may toil and sweat; other days you carry a lighter load, finally basking in the fulfillment of your dreams. You make a contribution to life. You find yourself living in harmony with the seasons, knowing your mission is right. The cycle of life continues; you move within the cycle.

Through the BELIEF chapter, you learned the power of motivation, visualization, and expectations. Learning to trust in universal power revealed your unlimited potential. You began to expose your true essence, allowing the real *you* to emerge. You now understand how your beliefs affect your future. You have cultivated and nurtured a belief in victory. You know without a doubt that you will be successful on your new journey. Through Chapter Two, YOU, you came to know yourself better, discovering and confirming your preferences and personality characteristics. You uncovered new work options. You fantasized and imagined yourself in different scenarios, dreaming of the possibilities. Your journey continued. In Chapters Three and Four, CAREERS and DECISIONS, you learned how to explore, ponder, and visualize your options. Combining your head and your heart, and using your intuition, you selected the path you want. You've decided upon the trip best for you. Through Chapter Five, GOALS, you created your road map. Now the work and effort begin to make your dreams reality.

Perhaps you decided to change your college major and explore internships and part-time jobs related to your new area of interest. You may have decided to go for a risky, not so secure career dream. Maybe you'll leave your current career and retrain for a new field. Or you may have discovered that you feel content with your current path, having renewed your appreciation for your original choice. All you changed was your perception. Maybe you've selected a short-term *and* long-term career goal (for example, to become a medical assistant, then a teacher, and eventually a business owner). You may still be exploring your options, knowing that at some point you will make a decision. For now you're satisfied with just taking the next right step.

As you prepare to take action towards accomplishing your desired goals, remember your decision may not be for the rest of your life. So don't put too much pressure on yourself in making sure your choice is right. There are many right choices. As you travel through life, you will change and grow; thus, it's reasonable to believe that your career desires will also change. Be open to the opportunities that come your way. Shaping your career is a lifelong quest.

In this last chapter we will explore ways to obtain employment and overcome obstacles, discovering more facets of our last question: *How will I get there?*

EMPLOYMENT - Putting It All Together

No one likes to look for a job. In fact, employers probably find the task even more tedious than job seekers; so your job is to be totally prepared, making the process as easy as possible for everyone involved. You've already completed the first step: knowing specifically what career you want. Unfortunately, people often look for work without a clear objective in mind. I've heard individuals make vague comments like, "Oh, I'm looking for anything that pays well." This is the worst approach possible! It's an absolutely ridiculous statement. First, most of us won't accept *just anything*. Second, employers do not have time to do your career planning. You are in charge of knowing precisely what you want. Of course, this lack of clarity will not happen to you because you already know what you want — you've done your career planning! With specific career goals, seeking employment is much, much simpler.

In addition to knowing your goal, decide upon the other factors you want for your work.

Even though your purpose remains a top priority, consider what type of environment and life-style suits you best. Examine your values and personality when selecting where you'll work. Evaluate the many facets of work environments. With most occupations a variety of settings are available. You've selected your career field; however, now you must also select the specifics of *where* and *for whom* you'll do your work. Explore the various options, selecting the ones that fit you best. Determine your answers to the following questions within the context of your field:

- How much money do I want to make?
- How much flexibility and freedom do I want?
- What type of security do I want?
- Is interaction with colleagues important to me?
- Do I have the discipline and temperament to work out of my home?
- What's the minimum salary I will accept?
- How far am I willing to drive for work?
- What type of leader do I want?
- What size company do I want to work in?
- What type of environment do I want, i.e., own office, quiet, friendly, etc.?

- Do I have any special needs, i.e., flex time to care for children?
- Am I willing to travel for my work?
- What type of work schedule do I want?
- How many hours per week am I willing to work?
- What type of people do I want to work with?
- What things I will not accept in my work?

Answering these questions will help you select the appropriate work setting. If you have answers for these items, then, when you begin interviewing, you will know which positions to eliminate. If a position does not meet most of your criteria or at least your most important ones, then you may want to continue your search. Be reasonable in determining your criteria. Talk to people in your field of interest to determine what employers want and how you fit with the environment of the industry. If you are entering a new field with very little experience, then you most likely will accept entry level or part-time work; however, do not let employers or stiff competition intimidate you into settling for something you do not want. Do your homework so you will have an accurate picture of what is realistic, yet satisfying. There are many, many jobs available. The right place for you may not be available today; however, it may be right around the corner. Be patient and trust that you will find the position that suits you.

If you are considering being a consultant or starting a business, read additional materials targeted for this avenue as the necessary information is too much to cover in this one chapter.

Similarly, for those of you seeking work in a competitive, less traditional career, for example, as a musician, actor, or dancer, the employment process is a bit different from what's outlined in this section. You'll need a performing style resumé, a head shot, and possibly a tape of your work. Often it's common practice to obtain an agent for these talent driven professions. In addition to getting an agent, you will want to market yourself. Talk with people in your profession for suggestions on materials such as books, and papers, such as *Backstage West*, that offer employment opportunities and explain how to obtain employment in your particular profession.

Seeking employment involves the following steps: select desired environment, prepare a resumé and cover letter, gather a list of employers, send resumé and cover letter to employers, solicit and prepare for interviews, complete interviews, send thank-you letters, and make follow-up phone calls. Continue the process until you are hired. In the next few sections we will cover all of these pieces of the employment process in more detail.

TYPES OF JOBS - Where Do I Fit?

During the last 40 years, work environments have changed drastically. The expansion of a highly-technological economy, competition from foreign markets, increase in the numbers of women working, and development of the information superhighway have caused company down-sizing and changes in the types and availability of jobs. Some people will still choose the traditional career path and work for a large company for a lifetime, but the majority of people will work in a variety of settings and for smaller companies. Changing jobs and careers has become the norm. Many workers will have two part-time jobs; others will freelance or consult. Aside from being skilled in your field, you want to be self-promoting, creative, flexible, and good at communicating in order to obtain employment.

Working long-term for a large company and expecting them to nurture and provide for your future are now the exception, not the rule. Decisions companies make may not be best for you and your future; therefore, you must do your own planning. You are responsible for marketing yourself. Do not trust a company to provide you with job security. The best security available is for you to create your own. Continuously improve your skills and attributes making yourself an outstanding candidate for a variety of positions. Take classes, attend seminars, read trade journals, and stay informed in your career field. Regardless of where you earn your living, you're in charge of your employment and your destiny. Remain focused on your mission, your purpose, and you will select the right path. If you're living your purpose, the *where* you make money becomes less significant. Instead, the *work* becomes your emphasis.

THE TRADITIONAL CHOICE

The typical career path of earning a college degree, working for a large corporation and then moving up the corporate ladder, might fit you and your needs. This choice is exceptionally appropriate if you're interested in management and other business related careers. A large company offers a sense of security, a variety of positions, advancement opportunities, stock options, bonuses, and excellent insurance and retirement benefits. They also tend to be conservative, often operating like a slow-moving machine. In many large organizations, procedures are bureaucratic and decisions are made slowly, often not allowing for much creativity and personal expression. Evaluate your needs. Compare your personality and values with the style of potential employers. Determine if you might fit well in a corporate environment, perhaps by conducting informational interviews. Books that evaluate corporations may help you as well: *The 100 Best Companies To Work For In America* by Robert Levering and Milton Moskowitz; and *Hoover's Handbook of Emerging Companies 1996: Profiles of America's Most Exciting Growth Enterprises,* edited by Patrick J. Span and James R. Talbot.

SMALL COMPANIES

You might also consider working for a small business. In a smaller setting, you have the opportunity to be responsible for a wide variety of job duties, often making your position more interesting. In turn, you increase your repertoire of skills, becoming more marketable for future employment. A company with fewer employees often offers a more relaxed atmosphere than a larger corporation. There can be a greater willingness to accommodate your personal needs by offering special bonuses or flexible hours to take care of family needs, for example. Knowing company owners and being part of decision-making and company growth are other benefits of working for a less bureaucratic organization. The trade-off for this type of atmosphere is, of course, less security and possibly less room for advancement, depending on the expansion and management style of the business owners. In Orange County, California, two owners of a medium sized computer company gave each of their employees an average $300,000 bonus check after the company earned millions in profits. The own-

ers felt their employees really deserved to share in the money they received, since the company would not have been successful without the skills and dedication of each worker. In another situation, a restaurant owner, who broke away from a corporate group of restaurateurs because he wanted to retain the intimacy of a small organization, gives his employees special celebrations from time to time. On one occasion, this gentleman arranged a surprise weekend getaway for his employees, flying them to a nearby resort for fun and frolic. These situations may seem rare; however, entrepreneurs with true spirit and good hearts reward their employees more often than we realize.

SEEK VARIETY

Working part time or as a temporary employee offers versatility, freedom, and flexibility. Part-time positions provide free time that can be used towards the fulfillment of personal goals and other career interests. This is especially helpful for those individuals acquiring training for a new career or transitioning from one career to another. Two part-time positions can provide a full-time income and still offer flexibility. In some cases you may be able to negotiate part-time work with either your current or new employer. Working less gives you time to go back to school or gain experience in your new field of interest.

Job sharing is another popular option, offering the same benefits as part-time work. People going to school, changing careers, transitioning, and wanting to spend more time with their children find this option beneficial. Not everyone wants to spend 40-plus hours a week working. Some people want more free time in exchange for less income. The trade-off is tough: time versus money. You can have an exciting, rewarding career working only 30 hours or less per week. For example, Karen, a wife and mother of two, initially worked full time as a high school French teacher; however, after her first child was born, she began teaching part time. Her husband, William, works full time in the evenings and watches the children during the day while Karen teaches. For this couple it's important for them to care for their children instead of relying on child care. Many careers can be arranged with part-time hours; the choice is yours.

Temporary services supply another option for part-time opportunities. Such services often specialize in particular career areas such as accounting, nursing, or other health related careers. Various agencies accept qualified applicants to work for them on an as needed basis. If a company has peak work times or absent employees, they call the appropriate agency to fill the need with a substitute. A professional affiliated with a temporary agency has the option to accept or decline the assignment offered for that day. A friend of mine, Roland, in his mid-thirties, is a physical therapist who owned a clinic for 10 years. Recently he sold his business to pursue acting, and now he is represented by a theatrical agent. Roland auditions for acting roles, works as a physical therapist for a health registry, and, in addition, sells vitamins. These three areas provide flexibility, variety, and a decent salary while he transitions into his long-term goal of becoming an actor full-time. Investigate options by calling your professional association and businesses in your career area, creating your own network of employers who can call on you for temporary work. Use the internet, business yellow pages, Chamber of Commerce directory, or library to locate names and addresses of temporary organizations that seek people in your area of expertise.

If you're a college student, instead of choosing a basic student type job, such as retail or restaurant work, seek positions in fields related to your career interests. This gives you new experiences and skills. John, a superb athlete and former student, selected professional coaching as his career goal. While in school, he decided to became a personal trainer by using his current athletic skills, completing a short certification program, and making contacts at various gyms to obtain clients. Now he works as a personal trainer and takes classes towards a degree in physical education and business. Review your career research and talk to knowledgeable people to determine the steps you may take to find entry level employment within your field.

The downside of part-time work is possible loss of health and retirement benefits, stock options, and paid vacation time. Consider how important these items are to your lifestyle and financial needs. You may be willing to forgo many of these perks for a short while. Some health care providers are beginning to sell insurance and medical benefits to individuals at reasonable rates. Investigate the options in your community by contacting your personnel office, professional association, health care provider, or Chamber of Commerce. If you are a college student, low-cost student health insurance and the student health center are both available. Check with student services on your college campus for options.

BE AN EXPERT

Working as a consultant also offers variety, flexibility, and interaction with new people. The special skills you possess or will develop could possibly be offered as a service. Similar to starting a business, marketing yourself and developing a clientele are the two biggest challenges of becoming a consultant. It often takes years of experience in a particular field before one attains the appropriate expertise and contacts necessary to become a consultant. In some instances individuals naturally progress into consulting as it develops from their work. In other scenarios, would-be consultants create brochures and materials describing their services and then diligently network and market themselves aggressively. If you are seriously considering this route, speak with other consultants, attend professional seminars in your field, and read books that outline how to begin a consulting business.

A college professor I know teaches speech communications classes and has an ongoing communications consulting contract with a major corporation. His consulting position brings him sporadic, lucrative checks, while the teaching provides a smaller, yet regular, income and personal satisfaction. Not having a regular 40-hour work week offers a lifestyle that gives this professor time to enjoy his new-found interest in photography.

Sandy, a former student who had a profitable position as a financial planner for a real estate company, decided to pursue her lifelong dream of becoming an attorney. Now, at age 40, Sandy is in school to earn first her bachelor's degree and then her law degree. Being the major breadwinner in the family, her two children and husband count on her income. Sandy needed to work fewer hours, so she could take nine units per semester and care for her family. She quit her job, sold her Lexus, became president of a professional association for financial planners, and started working as a consultant. Being president of the association has given Sandy the contacts and leads she needs to obtain consulting contracts.

Consulting work, similar to part-time work, has less security and usually no health and insurance benefits. It does, however, provide flexibility in work hours and the potential for earning large sums of money. Again consider how you feel about the trade-off of time, money, and security.

WORK FROM HOME

For many people working at home would be a dream come true. This option is ideal for individuals who are independent, disciplined, and self-motivated; and it is especially convenient for people with children. Some careers fit especially well with this option. If you like interaction with co-workers and the office environment, working from home, however, may feel oppressive. Again, evaluate your preferences and your career choice to determine if a fit exists.

In the past, workers needed to go into work because many positions required interaction with individuals and the use of materials and machines. Now, many of these restraints have vanished due to the exceptional growth of communication systems. Set up a computer, modem, and FAX machine in your home and you're ready to work! The challenge may lie in persuading an employer to agree to the arrangement. If an employer is not agreeable to the idea, consider negotiating one or two days at home and the rest at the office.

You might also consider starting a business from home. Perhaps your career choice fits well with a home business. The book *The Best Home Business For The 90's* by Paul and Sarah Edwards may offer helpful information for working at home.

FREELANCE

Some career fields naturally fit into the freelance category. Freelancers are self-employed and sell something they do or create, i.e., a performance or a book. Creative careers, such as a writer, photographer, actor, or artist, are often performed on a freelance basis. This option is similar to being self-employed. Many creative people prefer to work on their own, liking the freedom and flexibility. Similar to consulting, free-lancing requires discipline and tenacity, as time must be dedicated to creating and practicing or preparing, as well as marketing and selling. Even people with agents still spend time promoting themselves in addition to working with their agents. Often individuals have a steady, part-time position in conjunction with their freelance work as the latter does not always provide a consistent income.

RUN YOUR OWN SHOW

Owning a business is another viable choice — a very attractive alternative for the creative, independent, hard-working, and motivated individual. The path requires an incredible amount of time, energy, and risk, but, in the end, most business owners report that it was worth it. The extensive hours and relentless responsibility may seem like a good trade-off because of the personal freedom and potential for monetary success. If self-employment feels right, interview a variety of business owners, read business magazines, attend seminars and workshops geared for business owners (these are often publicized in the business section of the newspaper), read books on self-employment, and contact your local Chamber of Commerce. After you've acquired enough information, write a business plan and begin seeking funding. Ideally, before venturing out on your own, it's best to work for someone else in the setting you desire. You acquire *risk-free* experience, hopefully reducing the possibility of costly mistakes once you've begun your business. An acquaintance of mine earned a bachelor of science degree, worked for a large cellular telephone company, learned how the business was operated, and then began his own company with his newly acquired skills. Starting a business involves lots of planning and preparation, so do your homework.

RESUMÉS -
Your Ticket In The Door

For most employment situations you will need a resumé. A resumé is a summary on paper of your work history including your areas of expertise, skills, education, and previous positions. Your resumé is an advertisement of you — selling you to a potential employer. It should highlight your best qualities, be easy to read, free of errors, and motivate the employer to call you.

Different styles of resumés reflect your image. As an advertisement represents the image of a business, your resumé represents you. A *chronological* resumé emphasizes your previous positions and duties listed in reverse chronological order. A *skills* resumé, on the other hand, includes abilities acquired from work and *personal experience*, and relates these to the position you seek. You may want to use a combination of a chronological and skills resumé.

The skills resumé is perfect for people who do not have a consistent work history, who have had many different jobs, or who are changing jobs. It is also fits well for people with very little work experience in a particular field. The skills format provides a structure that allows people with less traditional work histories to shine, whereas the chronological format is better for individuals with consistent experience in just one (or two) field(s).

With your resumé include a *cover letter* — a letter that briefly explains your career goals and why you are submitting your resumé. Employers may ask for your resumé via FAX, internet, or computer disk. It's possible, in the future, e-mail and CD-ROMS may take the place of a hard copy resumé. Determine what format the companies you apply to would like. Keep abreast of employment trends as they change.

If you send your resumé via FAX or e-mail also include a cover letter using standard, easy-to-read fonts compatible with most computer systems. Use a minimal amount of italicizing, underlining, and bold lettering as these may not transfer to the sender in an eye-appealing fashion. You may prefer to send an original copy on resumé paper as a follow-up to your electronic copy.

Your resumé should fit with the style of the company you are soliciting. Research the industry and organization to determine if its *feel* — climate and style — match with you and your desires. Talk to people you know, and research the businesses on your employment list in the library or on the internet. Contact the personnel department, a receptionist, or a secretary to give you information about an organization. Request written materials about the company, its services, products, size, and goals and review them before your interview. If you're still not sure of its style, be somewhat conservative. It's better to error on the side of *too formal* than *too casual*. However, don't assume anything about an organization — do your homework.

WHAT TO INCLUDE

Make your resumé detailed, but brief; accurate, eye-appealing, and grammatically correct. List the most important information about you first. Highlight your assets and skills. Regardless of the style you select, most resumés usually include the following sections:

- your name, address, and telephone number
- your objective
- highlights of qualifications
- education and training
- experience
- special skills and experiences
- awards and publications
- professional affiliations
- hobbies (optional)

The order and amount of information listed in each category depends on your experience and goals. Usually it's best to list your most important areas of expertise first. If you are just out of college with little or no work experience, for example, then list your education first and emphasize the relevant information you learned in your classes. If, on the other hand, you have experience in a particular area, but little or no formal schooling after high school, then leave the education and training section out all together. Your resumé should ordinarily be from one to two pages in length, depending on your work history. If you have years of experience it may be appropriate to have a longer resumé or a separate supplement of more detailed information, such as publications, research studies, or special projects. Submit the supplement if appropriate. *If you are seeking employment in a variety of different positions, tailor a separate resumé for each position, emphasizing your skills that correspond best to the skills required for the work being sought. Don't send a generic resumé.* Lastly, print your resumé on high quality resumé paper and send with a cover letter in a matching envelope. In this section we will explore further how to construct each of these items.

WHAT NOT TO INCLUDE

Eliminating the unwanted information is as important as including the right information on your resumé. Just the smallest piece of unnecessary information, could cost you a first or second interview invitation. Do *not* include:

- gender or ethnic background
- religious preference and affiliations
- social security number
- political affiliations
- age, birth date, & marital status
- height & weight (unless in entertainment)
- first person pronouns
- previous employers' addresses & phone numbers

The following guidelines and examples will help to clarify how to construct a resumé.

CHRONOLOGICAL RESUMÉ

The *chronological* resumé best suits the person who has worked in one career field, has a stable employment history, and will continue to stay in the same field. Below are the standard headings to include in a *chronological* resumé:

- name, address, telephone and FAX
- education & training
- objective
- awards & affiliations
- special skills
- publications & research
- work experience

With this format, your work experience is listed in reverse chronological order beginning with your most recent position and ending with your earlier positions.

In your *objective*, state specifically the position and environment you desire. Always include an objective. Employers do not have time to do your career planning. Examples might be:

- Position as an electrician
- Assistant fashion designer for children's clothing
- To develop new, exciting programs for a progressive CD ROM organization.
- Seeking a position as an obstetrics nurse in an HMO.

Write separate objectives and resumés if you seek different types of positions.

The *special skills* category gives you the opportunity to list qualities about yourself that you would like to emphasize. Include for example, knowledge of languages and computer programs, positive personality traits, licenses, strength in a particular work area and important accomplishments from previous work. Also include years of experience in a particular area — anything you feel makes you marketable. Below are some examples of special skills:

- Excellent ability to read, write, and speak in French
- CPA license, earned 1996.
- Able to quickly and efficiently handle multi-tasks.
- Enthusiastic and caring when meeting customer needs.
- Successful in promoting a business and creating funding.
- Exceptional expertise in computer programs: Word, Amni Pro, and Page Maker.

The *special skills* section is similar to the *highlights of qualifications* section explained in the directions for the *skills* resumé.

In the *work experience* category, include your current or most recent job title with relevant duties conducted for that position. Continue this process for each position you've worked. Include accomplishments and contributions you made to each organization, such as the number of people supervised, reduction in office expenditures implemented, positive effects of creative ideas, percentage increase in sales, style and abilities in communicating, projects developed and/or organized, positive customer feedback, etc. Leave out activities that don't relate to the position you seek. If you're having difficulty remembering what you actually did at a job, begin by visualizing yourself in that position; then write a play-by-play account of these pictures in your head. Jot everything down, even activities that you judge as irrelevant or unimportant. Once you have a list of job duties, then begin to edit and arrange appropriately. After the accounts of one position are in order, move to your next previous job, visualize, jot, and edit. Continue in this same manner until you've described your experiences for each position. If your resumé becomes too long, eliminate the least important items. Sell yourself, yet be honest.

The *education and training* section includes your experiences from colleges, vocational schools, courses, seminars, and private lessons or coaching. List degree(s) and major(s), certificates, and special training you earned. If you earned a 3.8 grade point average or higher, graduated with honors, or were valedictorian, list this information after your degree. If you attended a college, but did not earn a degree, list just the name of the institution. List your units completed or class standing if it's at least at the junior level. If you are currently attending a particular institution, state your program of study and projected graduation date. Unrelated special training that does not apply to the position you seek can be left off your resumé, although you may want to include this experience, as it shows your accomplishments. Listing dates of graduation are optional. In most cases it is not necessary to list your high school graduation.

In the *awards and affiliations* section, list your involvement with charity, cultural, educational, professional, and social organizations (exclude religious organizations). The awards and affiliations you list might be related to community, work, school, sports, or hobbies. You might list experiences such as:

- *employee of the month* - XYZ company
- *football player* - Garfield High School
- *member* - Key Club
- *troop leader* - Boy Scouts of America
- *vice-president* - Alpha Delta Phi Sorority
- *writer* - Phoenix Paper at ABC University

Dig deep to find your accomplishments. Then decide if each experience is noteworthy enough to place as an award or affiliation. If you do not have these experiences, then leave this section out.

Research projects, professional presentations, and writings in articles, papers, and books should all be listed under a separate category: *publications and presentations.* If you have just one or two entries for this grouping then place them under a section mentioned previously. If you have at least three items, then create a publications and presentations heading. Contributions in this section show your motivation and commitment to your field. Again, if you do not have these experiences, then leave this section out.

Decide which categories you want to list first. Usually it's best to list the sections from most to least important. For instance, if you have lots of work experience, but very little education then list work before education, perhaps leaving out the education section. Decide which areas of your background are most noteworthy and then place them accordingly. Your resumé reflects you, so design it carefully. You want to feel good about giving it to potential employers or clients. Put yourself in the employers' shoes and create a resumé that shines! The examples listed after the skills resumé section offer an idea of how to organize your resumé.

SKILLS RESUMÉ

A *skills* resumé is similar to the chronological format, however, it focuses more on skills acquired rather than past work history. This style works well for people who have worked in a variety of jobs, have very little experience in the field they desire, left the job market and are now returning to work, have a sporadic work history, or are changing or entering a career for the first time. A person who has not officially held the type of position being sought, but has experiences related to that career, can show this fact with a skills resumé. An individual without a formal position in a particular career can show his or her related skills. A student who worked as an intern at a radio station, for example, can list, on the *skills* resumé, his experience on the air and in selecting music even though he never officially held the positions of disc jockey or program manager. You can include knowledge learned through classes, volunteer work, and general life experience on the *skills* resumé. I will summarize how to create a skills resumé.

The *skills* resumé headings are similar to the *chronological* resumé.

- name, address, telephone, FAX, and e-mail
- job history
- objective
- education and training
- experience - skill headings
- highlights of qualifications

Again the placement of these categories on your resumé depends on your personal preference and work history. Usually it's best to list the most important categories first.

Create your *objective* in the same fashion as described under the *chronological* resumé. Refer to that section for examples.

The *highlights of qualification* section is your opportunity to advertise yourself; it is a summary of you and your best experiences related to the position you seek. Include special skills, highlights of your work history, unpaid applicable experiences, achievements, awards, positive personality characteristics, exceptional work habits, and years of expertise. This category is almost identical to the *special skills* section as explained for the *chronological* resumé. Refer to this section for more examples of *highlights*. The entry below offers an example of an objective and highlights:

Objective: Position with an HMO in medical billing.

HIGHLIGHTS OF QUALIFICATIONS

- Experience in medical billing in a variety of health care settings.
- Exceptionally skilled in several word processing programs.
- Flexible, friendly, and detail oriented; learn new systems quickly.
- Able to professionally and efficiently handle patients' needs and complaints.

Under the *experience* section list specific duties and accomplishments of your work background, as well as *other experiences* — paid or not. You might call this heading *Relevant Skills & Experience, Professional Experience,* or *Related Experience*. Include knowledge from hobbies, volunteer work, paid employment, class-room instruction, private instruction, traveling, and general life experiences. Begin by following the directions given under the experience section for the *chronological* resumé: list all previous work experience and everything you did in these positions. Then list other life experiences, such as volunteer work at church, a hobby refinishing furniture, officer in an organization, a fund-raiser you managed, girl scout cookies you sold door-to-door, etc. If you have lots of life experience, edit your choices by including those most meaningful and related to your career goal. If you are younger or less experienced, include even those items you deem unimportant, i.e. student council, baby-sitting, P.T.A. member.

Now that you have a list of life experiences, brainstorm for everything you did when you were involved in the particular activity. Again, include even the smallest description, such as *called members to inform about upcoming fund-raiser, created fun play activities for children.* Don't worry about the importance of an item, just write it down. Don't spend time selecting the right words, just describe the activity. Your goal is to assess and describe your experiences.

Next, analyze your list and compare it to the career you desire. Determine which experiences relate to the job duties of the career you want. Focus mainly on the skill, not where you did the activity. You may have skills necessary for the work even though you never worked in the industry. Include the items that fit with your career goal, exclude those that don't.

After you have listed all the things you've done in your work, volunteer, and life experiences, select two to four main skill headings that relate directly to the position you seek. Put yourself in the shoes of the employer, tailoring your resumé to match what is requested for the position. Review your career research information or a job advertisement to assist you in determining the *skill headings*. Use all of this information to create your headings. Next, review the skills you've acquired from your life experiences. Categorize your experiences according to the *skill headings* you've selected. Place each experience that relates to your *skill headings* under the appropriate heading. Leave out experiences that do not fit with the job you want. For the position of Public Relations Assistant, for example, the *skill headings* might be *Communications - Writing & Speaking, Customer Relations,* and *Research.* If you were on the debate team in school, then you might write, *Experienced at fielding questions about controversial topics* under the *Writing*

& Speaking heading. If you had a job in school answering telephones, you might list, *answered telephones and took accurate messages for 20 employees,* under the *Customer Relations* heading in our example.

In the *Job History* section simply list in reverse chronological order, your job titles, company names, and dates of previous jobs. The specific job duties of these positions are listed under the *Experience* heading.

Write the *Education and Training* section as you would for the chronological resumé.

The examples at the end of this section will assist you in creating your own resumé. In addition, Yana Parker in her book, *The Damn Good Resumé Guide,* gives detailed instructions on how to construct a skills resumé or as she calls it, "a damn good resumé." For more specific information, refer to Ms. Parker's book and her sequel book, *200 Examples of Damn Good Resumés.*

HOW TO CONSTRUCT YOUR SKILLS RESUMÉ

To write your skills resumé list the following information:

- your objective (based on your career exploration and specific to the job you seek)
- previous jobs (no job is too small, even include short one day experiences)
- volunteer or life experiences (i.e. being a scout leader, Sunday school teacher, Red Cross volunteer, extensive traveler, guitar player, wine connoisseur, etc.)
- brainstorm for skills experienced from these jobs and life experiences. (nothing is too small to include during brainstorming)

Next, organize your information using the guidelines below:

- List your name, address, and telephone number at the top of page.
- Analyze the position you desire and create your *highlights of qualifications* category using the information on your brain storm sheet.
- Arrange *highlights of qualifications* items by listing your most important highlight first.
- Select two to four skill headings that relate to your objective.
- Arrange your past experiences under the appropriate skill headings.
- Edit and rearrange (take out experiences unrelated to the job you seek).
- List your awards and education.
- List your past job titles, companies, and dates employed.
- Edit, proofread, edit, and proofread.

Finally, ask a creative person to critique your resumé for style and eye-appeal. Ask a detail-oriented person to proofread your resumé for punctuation, grammar, and readability. Your resumé must be easy to read, esthetically pleasing, and free from spelling and grammatical errors. Remember it represents you and your image!

Following are examples of skill and chronological resumés.

CHRONOLOGICAL RESUMÉ EXAMPLE

SUSAN LYNN HUNT - 620 Rosarita Drive, Fullerton, CA 92635; (714) 879-2245

CAREER OBJECTIVE -Physical Therapist Assistant

EDUCATION

University of the Pacific, Stockton, CA
MS Physical Therapy, expected May 2002
University of California, Berkeley
BA Physiology, May 1998

STUDENT CLINICAL AFFILIATIONS

one week
3/01	Sequoia Hospital, Redwood City - out patient
7/01	St. Jude Hospital, Fullerton - rehabilitation
10/01	ACSF Medical Center, San Francisco - out patient

six week
1/99-2/02	Saddleback Community Hospital, Laguna Hills - acute care
2/99-3/02	Naval Regional Medical Center, Oakland - out-patient
4/99-5/02	Hospital of The Good Samaritan, Los Angeles - rehabilitation

WORK EXPERIENCE

1/00-8/00	Susan Woods P.T. Services, Pasadena; *Physical Therapy Aide*
1/00-12/00	Ralph K. Davies Medical Center, San Francisco; *Physical Therapy Technician*
4/99-6/99	Ross General Hospital, Ross, CA; *Physical Therapy Aide*
Fall 1997	University of California, Berkeley; Exercise Physiology Lab, *Student Researcher*
Fall 1996	Children's Hospital of Oakland; *Emergency Room Aide*

HONORS &
ACTIVITIES

California Physical Therapy Fund Scholarship Recipient
National AMBUCS Living Endowment Fund Scholarship Recipient
American Physical Therapy Association Member
Delta Delta Delta Sorority
Alumni Scholar's Club, UC Berkeley

CHRONOLOGICAL RESUMÉ EXAMPLE

Peter Nguyen
4621 Union Street
San Diego, CA 92103
(619) 298-2234

Objective: Position as a Graphic Designer within an established design firm with a strong reputation in both two and tree dimensional design projects.

EDUCATION & AWARDS

B.A., Graphic Design with Honors, UCLA School of Design, 1995
Senior Graduate Graphic Design Award - recipient

PROFESSIONAL EXPERIENCE

1998-now **Graphic Designer,** Freelance, San Diego CA
Direct client experience in two and three dimensional design with an emphasis in trade show publications and packaging. Skilled in industry graphic design software such as *Adobe Shop & Illustrator.*

1995-98 **Graphic Designer,** Floppy Copy, San Diego CA
Created and implemented a myriad of projects for large corporations such as Lexus, Warner Brothers, MGM Grand, Coca Cola. Innovative designs included brochures, large scale advertisements, packaging, and trade show publications. Received numer ous accolades from clients for original concepts, client communications, and project management.

1995 **Intern & Assistant to Creative Director,** RT Advertising, Los Angeles, CA
Assisted the creative director in market research, concept development, print and me dia presentations and commercial production for their national accounts. Interfaced with clients in various capacities.

1994-95 **Sales Representative & Assistant Manager,** The Gap, Los Angeles, CA
Worked with a variety of customers suggesting merchandise, fitting, and styling out fits and gifts. Supervised a staff of 15 people, developing schedules and interfacing with employees on all personnel matters. Created concepts for window displays and floor layouts.

CHRONOLOGICAL RESUMÉ EXAMPLE

LACEY M. HARRIS
6200 Dundee Drive
Huntington Beach, CA 92647
(714) 892-5821

Objective: To work as a biological researcher with an innovative company.

HIGHLIGHTS OF QUALIFICATIONS

- Motivated, intelligent, prudent, and dedicated
- Well versed in biological terminology and research
- Reliable and adaptable; quick at learning new systems
- Knowledge of Spanish and 3.85 college g.p.a.

RELEVANT EXPERIENCE

1999-now **Biological Research Assistant,** UC Irvine Medical Hospital
Participates in various research projects exploring the effects of the e-coli virus in various environments. Collects pertinent data and documentation recording in computer system for analysis. Oversees two assistants and interfaces with a team of internal medicine physicians keeping them abreast of project results as well as determining new direction for study.

1998-99 **Biology Teaching Assistant,** UC Irvine, Biology Department
Facilitated discussions about relevant science principles for labs, mid-terms, and final exams. Explained concepts and experiments to students, fielding a plethora of questions. Met weekly with professor for class update and discussion.

1997-98 **Lab Assistant,** Citrus College, Science Department
Assisted students in Biology and Chemistry labs. Worked with professors conducting experiments related to medical biology. Prepared labs by cleaning and arranging equipment for lab classes.

EDUCATION

B.S., Biology, UC Irvine, Irvine CA, 1999

SKILLS RESUMÉ EXAMPLE

NADINE ELIZABETH THOMPSON
2833 East First Street, Corona Del Mar, CA 92662; (714) 759-8878

Objective: *To be a full-time counselor in a community college.*

HIGHLIGHTS OF QUALIFICATIONS

- Experience counseling and teaching in various colleges
- Extensive counseling with a variety of populations
- Talented with people of diverse backgrounds
- Enthusiastic, dynamic, compassionate, creative

PROFESSIONAL EXPERIENCE

Counseling & Teaching
- Provides academic, career, and personal counseling to students of various backgrounds including ethnic minorities, disabled, hearing impaired, and single parents.
- Teaches and develops career and orientation classes for diverse student populations.
- Teaches and counsels Single Parent population through special grant program.
- Familiar with special needs of ethnic minorities, single parents, and recent immigrants.
- Educates students on computerized guidance systems: EUREKA & SIGI.
- Receives excellent ratings from students and workshop participants.

Program Development & Presentations
- Increased student enrollment in counseling classes by 20%.
- Developed and implemented specialized programs: Career Fair, Career Panel for Re-Latino Student Groups, Non-traditional Career Panel, Personal Growth Seminars.
- Purchased, updated, and wrote educational and career materials.
- Asilomar Research Conference Presenter. 1995.

EMPLOYMENT HISTORY

1996 - present	*Counselor (part-time)*	Irvine Valley College, CA
1995	*Vocational Counselor*	Bellflower Unified School District, CA
1991- 94	*Hair Stylist*	Styles One, Cerritos, CA

EDUCATION & CREDENTIALS

M.S. Career Counseling - California State University, Long Beach
B.A. English - California State University, San Diego

SKILLS RESUMÉ EXAMPLE

SIBYL BEDFORD
200 Carmen Plaza, PH 11, Newport Beach, CA 92663; (949)646-3144

CAREER OBJECTIVE:
Seeking a position in public relations with an organization that fosters innovation, individual excellence, creativity, and advancement.

SUMMARY OF QUALIFICATIONS:
Excellent skills in journalism, public relations, creative writing, communications, informational interviewing, researching, and editing.

EXPERIENCE:

Communications
- Media liaison and public relations coordinator with local television, magazines, and newspapers.
- Seminar leader of workshops for adults and students in human development.
- Handled life-threatening emergencies (such as attempted suicides, drug and alcohol abuse, runaways, date rape, domestic violence) and evacuation planning and procedures.
- Developed publicity campaigns, wrote and distributed news releases and wrote articles for the monthly newsletter; created program and handout materials.
- Wrote and edited institutional documents, accreditation reports, administrative manuals, activity guides, handbooks, and college preparatory workbooks.
- Creatively wrote speeches, press releases, newsletters, ads, brochures, and featured articles in community publications. (Personal writings include anecdotes, poetry, songs and narratives in a 7 year collection of over 20 journals.)

Event Planning
- Coordinated fund-raisers, patient activities, school programs, open houses, religious service, graduations, installations, and dedications.
- Planned career and college day fairs, sports banquets, award ceremonies, graduations, and formal dinner dances.
- Excellent ability in creating artistic themes and decors, producing commemorative videos, designing original handmade greeting cards and gift books, and performing stand-up comedy.

EMPLOYMENT HISTORY & EDUCATION

Director of Community Affairs, Caring Convalescents, Tustin, CA (1997-99)
High School Teacher, Jeffrey's High School   Tustin, CA (1996-97)
Substitute Teacher, Various Schools, K-12   Orange, CA (1994-96)

Bachelor of Arts, Sociology - CSU, Fullerton, CA
College Courses in Public Relations, Journalism, Creative Writing, and Advertising Design

SKILLS RESUMÉ EXAMPLE
(*Format for Performing Arts Resumé*)

Andrew Stockton

Height:	6' 2"	**Hair:**	Blond/Brown
Weight:	185 lb.	**Eyes:**	Green

Representation

Universal Talent	Manager	(310) 433-2535

Film & Television

Bull Worth	Campaign Manager	Sunset Casting
Shakespeare In Love	Tavern Boy	Susan Wyat Casting
ER	Car Accident Victim	Unlimited Requests

Commercials

(available upon request)

Theater

Death of A Salesman	Biff	CSU Long Beach
Raised In Captivity	Kip	Paulino Play House
Blood Wedding	Leonardo	Costa Mesa Theater
Romeo & Juliet	Romeo	Hawthorn Theater
Fabulous Baker Boys	Jack	Cypress College

Training

Theater Arts, Bachelors of Art; CSU Long Beach
D.W. Brown Studio, Commercial; Santa Monica
Greg Watkins, Improvisation; Costa Mesa
Sonja Smith, Vocal; Los Angeles

Special Skills

Dialects - Southern, English, German
Musicianship - Vocal, Baritone & Guitar
Dance - Swing, Cha-Cha, Tango; Modern & Ballet
Sports - Surfing, Motorcycle Riding, Kick Boxing, Scuba Diving, Baseball, Tennis, Golf

COVER LETTERS -
Your Introduction

Include a cover letter with your resumé. The cover letter is a business letter that accompanies your resumé. Explain in the letter briefly why you are writing, why you want the job, and why you are the best candidate for the position. In the closing paragraph state the date *you will telephone* to arrange an interview. Do not wait for the employer to call you. Your letter should be professional and brief. It can be personal and intriguing if you have something interesting to add, such as an inspiring quote, an article about the industry, or a relevant story. A friend of mine, Carla, included a picture of her favorite bed frame when she applied for a sales and management position at a furniture store. The bed frame was a style that fit well in this particular store. The employer/owner was intrigued with her request for employment as the bed frame in the picture was his favorite too! And, yes, she ended up getting the job!

Write your cover letter in business letter format. Again, ask someone skilled at proofreading to edit your letter for proper grammar, punctuation, spelling, and flow. Print both your cover letter and resumé on high quality business paper and put in a matching envelope. Do not staple your cover letter to your resumé; simply place your letter on top of your resumé and fold in thirds.

Following are examples of cover letters.

I stand tall, walking with grace and confidence.
Greeting with a smile, I offer my abilites to serve the world.
A cheerful countenance and a willing attitude carry me towards my destiny.
Humility and openmindedness are my gatekeepers for truth.

Guided by Love, I observe carefully, accurately, intuitively.
Choices unfold naturally as my heart leads the way.
I know when to say yes and when to move on.

Worry eludes my search, as I naturally step to the rhythm of my soul, the beating within my being, and the dance of the earth.

Each stride takes me to greater heights and deeper valleys that teach and guide.

I fear not.
I relax easily.
I am free.

COVER LETTER EXAMPLE

NADINE E. THOMPSON
2833 East First Street
Corona Del Mar, CA
(714) 759-8878

March 1, 2003

Personnel Office, Search Committee
Westside Community College
15551 Main Street
San Diego, CA 92881

Dear Search Committee:

It is with pleasure I submit my application for the position of Counselor (one year replacement). I have been serving as a part-time counselor at two community colleges in Orange County and am highly qualified to work in a full-time counseling position. I will be re-locating to the San Diego area shortly so your offering is perfect!

I greatly enjoy working with students and have served a variety of populations from single parents to recent immigrants. I am well versed in career planning and academic advisement and have taught counseling related courses and workshops.

You will see from my resumé that I have also written and presented professionally. I would like to contribute to your staff by creating and writing appropriate handbooks, brochures and manuals as the need arises.

I am hopeful that we can meet and discuss this employment opportunity in more detail. Please contact me at the address or phone number listed above. I thank you in advance for your time.

With respect,

Nadine Thompson

COVER LETTER EXAMPLE

SIBYL BEDFORD
200 Carmen Plaza, PH 11
Newport Beach, CA 92663
(949) 646-3144

September 9, 2003

Mary Stevens
Shore House Travel
P.O. Box 97264
Beverly Hills, CA 90211

Dear Ms. Stevens:

I was interested to learn of your opening for the position of Public Relations & Events Coordinator. I have planned and organized parties and events for various charities, employers, personal friends, and acquaintances. I have over five years' experience in public relations, in all styles of writing and formats from press releases to brochures to articles. I am eager to put my best skills and abilities to work in public relations and event planning within the private sector.

My experience working with charity and educational event planning has caused me to "roll up my sleeves" and get into everything from designing invitations, hiring entertainment, communicating with the media, setting up and tearing down events, to ensuring that the necessary audio-visual equipment was available and operative. I have often emceed events and served as the main hostess or social director. In short, I am comfortable with all phases of event planning.

I have heard many positive comments about your company from my friend Tanya Avery who works in customer service, so I decided to apply immediately. Enclosed is my resumé. I will follow up with you next week to arrange a meeting to discuss employment possibilities.

Most sincerely,

Sibyl Bedford

COVER LETTER EXAMPLE

LACEY M. HARRIS
6200 Dundee Drive
Huntington Beach, CA 92647
(714) 892-5821

June 23, 2002

Jack Richards
TVI Diagnostics Inc.
2184 Main Street
Orange, CA 92640

Dear Mr. Richards:

I am applying for the Biological Researcher position available with your firm because of my high regard for your work and my passion for scientific investigation. Being a motivated and creative scientist, I would contribute positively to your organization and would find it very stimulating.

I have training and experience in various laboratory and research settings and am knowledgeable about a variety of research procedures and techniques. At UCI Medical Hospital I worked with a team of physicians where I learned the importance of collaborative efforts when creating a quality product within a scheduled time period: I'm a great team player.

I would greatly enjoy working with your firm as medicine is one of my passions. I will call you within the next two weeks to schedule an interview appointment. Please feel free to contact me at your convenience.

Best regards,

Lacey M. Harris

JOB SEARCH -
I'm The One You Want

Assertive, persistent, determined — you are on a mission. Pursue with enthusiasm and tenacity the position you desire. Avoid settling for second best. H. Jackson Brown, Jr. in his *Life's Little Treasure Book On Success* writes, "Remember that just the moment you say, 'I give up,' someone else seeing the same situation is saying, 'My what a great opportunity.'" Conducting a job search is like being a sales person: you receive far more no's than yes's. Yet each no brings you closer to the eventual yes. Be prepared to face rejection and still continue pursuing your goal. You are responsible for creating contacts, submitting your resumé, arranging interviews, making follow-up calls, and ultimately receiving an employment offer. Be persistent, but not annoying, with a relaxed confidence. If you become anxious, employers subconsciously feel your needy energy. The old cliché, *It'll come when you least expect it,* is true for this very reason. Human beings generally don't want to be around people who feel anxious or desperate. This is one of the reasons why it's often easier to get a new job when you're still employed. The particulars of your situation are irrelevant, the important thing is to be confident and self-assured. You probably have already cultivated this state of mind; after all the guidelines are offered in the first chapter! You know yourself; you have a purpose; you're on the way to getting there! Visualize yourself successfully working in the position you desire — the job is yours, it's just a matter of time until you begin.

Typically, people think of using the classified section of the newspaper when looking for a job, although only about 10% of jobs are found using this method. The most successful job search involves direct contact with employers. It's those person-to-person and friend-of-a-friend relationships that lead to a job. If you don't know people in your field, then make cold-calls to create these relationships. Soon you'll have a host of contacts. The most comprehensive job search campaign includes all methods: direct contact, the Internet, classified ads, professional association publications, employment centers, and placement firms.

DIRECT CONTACT

The majority of jobs are found by directly contacting a potential employer either by submitting to an actual job opening or by soliciting an organization even when no opening exists. Contact the organizations for which you would like to work, *even if there are no positions offered at the time you inquire.* Answer the questions listed at the beginning of this chapter to help you decide your ideal job setting and organization. Search for a position with your job blueprint in hand, being adamant and flexible at the same time. The best job search involves targeting specific places you would like to work, sending your resumé, and continuously speaking to these potential employers until you secure employment.

Perhaps you've heard the term *the hidden job market.* Nothing is hidden! It's just a fancy way to talk about job hunting. The phrase really refers to using the direct contact strategy. Finding the hidden job market means calling employers directly and selling yourself and your assets, whether there's a position available or not. I strongly urge you to use this approach because it is the most productive method. Reach employers through the yellow pages, Chamber of Commerce, internet, business directories (available in your public library), and professional associations. Check your local library for books that give information about companies. Many large organizations, such as school districts, hospitals, HMOs, government agencies; city facilities, i.e. police and fire departments; and large corporations post job openings via the internet and in their personnel offices.

Ask anyone you know: friends, friends-of-friends, relatives, neighbors, work colleagues, classmates, instructors, and service professionals such as your hair stylist, dentist, etc. for job leads. If you recently attended school, keep close tabs with your professors or instructors for possible opportunities; call weekly. School departments and career centers often post openings; check these out. Contact your previous supervisors from internship and volunteer experiences. Contact the people whom you interviewed for information — they may offer a lead or a suggestion. The squeaky wheel does get the oil! Be the person on everyone's mind.

THE INTERNET

Using the Internet is another great way to search for job leads. Many companies list positions available and others offer information about their organization. Log on to any network by using key words related to your career goals. Each Web site offers numerous links making the places to explore almost endless. The magnitude of information available is mind-boggling. Resources and information change and grow daily; therefore, an accurate assessment of the possibilities is very difficult. Following are some internet sites that were available at the time of printing:

Career Builder -
http://www.CareerBuilder.com/
More than 60,000 job postings.

The Federal Government's Official Job Site -
http://www.usajobs.opm.gov/

Jobs for Firefighting & Law Enforcement -
http://www.911hotjobs.com/

Hot International Jobs -
http://www.internationaljobs.org/hotjobs.html

Jobs for Musicians -
http://www.careersformusicians.com/

Monster Board! -
http://www.monster.com/
Enormous database of job listings, searchable by geographic location, industry, contract jobs, or keywords.

Jobs for Scientists-
http://www.sciencejobs.com/

Top 100 Electronic Recruiters -
http://www.interbiznet.com/eeri/
As a part of the 1997 Electronic Recruiting Index, over 3,500 recruiting web sites were evaluated and reviewed in detail. These are the Top 100.

Additional sites include:

http://www.jobhunt.org/

http://www.myfuture.com/career.html

http://www.jobweb.org

http://www.ushotjobs.com/front_2.html

http://www.jobsmart.org/

http://hotjobs.yahoo.com/

http://www.careerone.com.au/

http://www-1.ibm.com/employment/

http://www.summerjobs.com/

THE CLASSIFIED ADS

Another resource for job openings is, of course, the classified section of the newspaper; however, most job openings are not advertised in the newspaper, especially more competitive positions in fields such as fashion designer or cruise ship director. If ads for your career are placed in the want ads, then definitely apply for these positions; but don't rely on this avenue as your only strategy for seeking employment. Use this in conjunction with other methods. Respond to the ad by simply sending your resumé and cover letter to the address given. Tailor your resumé to fit with the skills and experience they request. Paraphrase and/or use some of the phrases they used in their ad when listing your relevant experience (make sure you truly have the experience you claim!).

JOB FAIRS

Most major cities and colleges offer job fairs which often specialize in particular industries, i.e. computer job fair. Check your newspaper for events that may occur in your community. The internet may also have information as well; try http://jobsmart.org/resource/fairs/jobfairs.htm for a particular site. When attending a fair, bring ample copies of your resumé, dress appropriately for the positions you seek, and be open and friendly. Network by asking questions in a personable and upbeat manner, gathering as much information as possible about openings and the industry itself. Be assertive. After the event, follow up with telephone calls to the contacts that you make.

ASSOCIATIONS & PUBLICATIONS

The majority of professional associations publish a weekly or monthly newspaper, magazine, or journal available with membership or by purchase in a bookstore or newsstand. The publication keeps professionals abreast of their field by covering upcoming conventions, on-the-job events, new research findings, and industry trends. Often they offer an employment section in each issue. Sending your resumé and cover letter to an opening in one of these publications is another excellent way to secure a position.

EMPLOYMENT DEVELOPMENT CENTERS

Various government offices post jobs and offer employment programs. Employment services may be located in city hall, welfare offices, job training programs, and employment development departments. Check in the front of the white pages of your local telephone book for services in your area. Contact the mayor's office, the local library, your city councilman, or the Chamber of Commerce for further assistance. If you are a student in a college or university, check the job placement office on your campus for further job listings. Send your resumé and cover letter to any appropriate leads.

PLACEMENT FIRMS & EMPLOYMENT SERVICES

Placement firms and temporary employment services offer job seekers some relief from the stress of job hunting. Depending on your career goal and work history a placement firm may be able to arrange appropriate interviews for you. Do not pay a fee for these services. The company seeking employees hires the placement firm to find applicants for the position available. When the appropriate candidate is found, the placement firm receives a commission from the company. This is usually a percentage of the applicant's first year's salary. Some placement firms specialize in certain career areas while other fields are rarely represented by a placement firm. Check your yellow pages under *employment agencies* and *employment-technical* for companies in your area.

Temporary services provide a quick opportunity for you to work. Often you will be called to fill an assignment the day you register with an agency. You can accept or decline assignments depending on your schedule. This is often an ideal set-up for job hunters. Sometimes temporary positions turn into full-time permanent assignments or provide a foot in the door. Many of these positions are office related, but provide a starting place within a company. Like a placement firm, some agencies do specialize in particular fields, such as health related careers. Check your yellow pages under *employment-temporary* for services in your area.

INTERVIEWING - Sell Yourself

An interview gives you and the employer an opportunity to learn about each other. It helps you determine whether you like the atmosphere and people in this particular organization. *So often we worry if the employer will like us, instead of deciding if we like them.* Evaluate the position and employer during your interview. Ask questions, covering areas such as performance expectations, department goals, and management style. Talk about yourself easily and naturally when answering questions.

The length and type of interviews you experience will vary as much as personalities. Some interviews will be very informal and relaxed, while others will be more structured with set questions. Some interviews will be with one person, while others will involve a panel of three to six people. You may be hired on the spot, or you may be called back for more interviews and never hired. Your challenge is to remain calm, natural, and flexible in any setting. Do not let yourself become intimidated by the interviewer. Confidence is everything.

A woman I knew, Teresa, after a fairly lengthy interview process was selected as one of the top three candidates for a teaching position. Her last phase was to interview with the president of the college and two administrators. Teresa told me she sat in the president's reception room waiting calmly for her appointment. Then this tall, striking, confident women in four inch high-heels entered the room. The president smiled warmly and said, "Come on in." For an instant, Teresa felt intimidated by this woman's stature and worried that she wouldn't measure up. In the next second, Teresa firmly shook the president's hand, smiled, looked her in the eye and said, confidently, "Hello." At that moment, Teresa decided that she would get the teaching job, she had the right stuff; and she wanted to work for a strong woman. And yes, she got the job!

Preparation helps to make your interview flow. When your nerves kick in, your preparation will carry you through. You won't be worried about what to say or how to act because your responses will be in your mind. Prepare answers to typical interview questions, learn about the organization before interviewing, dress appropriately, and arrive on time.

GUIDELINES FOR INTERVIEWING

Participating in an interview is a very personal experience; however, following general guidelines will benefit any interview. These suggestions include:

- Before interviewing, learn about the company, including its products or services, and competition.
- Prepare your answers to typical interviewing questions. Role-play with someone you trust.
- Dress appropriately.
- Determine the directions to your interview the day before.
- Arrive 5-10 minutes early.
- Bring a copy of your resumé (even if you've already sent one) and reference letters.
- Prepare questions to ask about the position and organization.
- Be courteous and polite.
- Be yourself — it's OK to laugh and smile; be natural.
- Afterwards send a thank you letter to your interviewer.

As you interview, remember that an employer needs you just as much as you need him or her, so do not give the interviewer all the power. You are in the driver's seat as well! An interview is your chance to gather information about the potential employer and position. Notice the environment, meet people in the organization, and learn about the company's philosophy and goals. Can you be happy at this place? Be selective. Compare and contrast what you learn in your interview with the items on your blue-print list. Does this particular position and setting fit with your purpose and career goals? Take time to make your decision, considering your dreams and desires.

TYPICAL INTERVIEW QUESTIONS

To ensure a smooth and successful interview, decide how you will answer possible questions before you interview. There are no right or wrong answers; nevertheless, there are better ways to answer questions. Your goal is to sell yourself to the employer, to show the best possible you. Write and rehearse what you will say before you interview, perhaps by role-playing with someone you trust. Below are suggestions for answers to some typical interview questions:

1. Tell me about yourself.

Give information about your work history, skills, and education that relate to the position you seek. Be brief, but complete. Elaborate when appropriate with examples from your experiences that illustrate your abilities. If your direct experience is minimal for this job, explain how your skills from other areas of your life, including life experience, hobbies, volunteer work, and previous jobs can be applied to the position you desire. Never say, "I have no experience."

2. Why do you want to work here?

Explain how your personality, interests, and values fit with the position you seek. Also, mention what you like about the organization, such as "It's a leader in the industry," or "I've heard very positive reports about the management in your organization". Tell the truth; don't make up something you don't believe! Be prepared to back up your answers in case you are asked specific questions.

3. What are your strengths?

Relate your strengths to the position you seek. You might describe some of your positive personality traits that you discovered in the *YOU* chapter. You might bring up contributions you made in previous positions. You might describe some of your work or skills. You might mention some of the positive comments managers and customers have said about you. Give examples to validate your points.

4. What are your weaknesses?

When discussing your weaknesses be honest, but not too frank. Don't really admit your negative habits and qualities! Instead turn a strength into a weaknesses, i.e. "I tend to be an over achiever, but I'm usually able to keep a healthy balance of work and play." If you're creative, you may be able to answer with a cute quip and avoid answering the question altogether, yet still be respectful. Lastly, never say, "I don't have any weaknesses." This just isn't true; we are all humans — imperfect!

5. Why should we hire you instead of someone else?

This question is similar to *What are your strengths?* just put in a different form. Relate your experiences to the position you are seeking. Cite specific accomplishments that suggest you are the ideal candidate — make yourself stand out! Explain your uniqueness. Perhaps you have an interesting combination of skills and experiences, speak another language, know particular computer programs, received some awards, or possess specialized training. Don't be shy about answering this question. Be forthright, complete with a dash of humility.

6. What contributions can you make to our organization?

Summarize your answer from the previous question and explain how your knowledge, creativity, and ideas will benefit the company. Mention your career goals and ideas you would like to implement if hired.

7. Where do you see yourself five years from now?

Simply state your career goals and relate them to the organization. Your goals might include additional training, advancement within the organization, or development of a special project. You do not have to be on the management track. Your goals may be more related to your development within your career. If your five-year plan does not include the organization, avoid stating this; describe how you would like to develop within your field.

8. What are your major accomplishments?

State examples that relate to the position you are seeking, and perhaps others that illustrate your development as a person. You might mention educational, athletic, and/or work accomplishments. A high grade-point average, development of skills, exceptional customer feedback, management of a special project, or advances within a company are examples of ideas you might give. Also, state experiences that show your initiative, enthusiasm, creativity, and intelligence.

9. What type of salary are you seeking?

Do not state a specific dollar amount. Wait for the employer to give the salary range. Instead you can say, "What type of salary do people in this position usually earn?" or "What salary range were you considering?" or "I am open to discussing an appropriate salary." The problem with stating an amount is that once a figure is on the table, you've now set a limit. The employer may have been willing to go higher than the amount you give, or she may decide that you are too costly. Before your interview, research salary ranges of people in the position you seek. Call other organizations to determine salary ranges. Avoid at all costs saying a dollar amount. Give vague yet polite answers, or answer the interviewer's question with a question. Ultimately, you want the interviewer to give the first number. Salary discussion can move from that point. Consider researching further negotiating tips and techniques as your lack of skills in this area could really cost you!

During your interview, give answers that feel comfortable and natural. Be yourself. Employers may ask you situational questions related to your field, so you may want to anticipate these types of questions. Other questions may address philosophy, theory, techniques, or industry trends. Sometimes an interview may ask for a demonstration of some kind that relates to the job duties of the particular position. Know your profession and you'll know how to answer these types of questions. Additional interview questions will usually be similar to the questions 1-8 just couched in different phrases. An interview might ask, "If your clients were standing around talking about you, what might they be saying?" This question is basically the same as "What are your strengths?" The employer wants to see how you handle yourself, your level of confidence, and your type of communication style. What type of attitude do you exude? Will you fit with their organization? More advice about job hunting can be found in books on job search.

Preparation is key. Prepare and you will be a success. An interview is your chance to sell yourself and explore the organization. Let your personality shine. Show your strengths and special skills. Many opportunities will eventually be available, so avoid settling for a position based on fear. Remember that you can accept or reject a job offer. Your intuition will guide you; be prepared to heed the call.

YOUR LOOK

The old adage, *You never get a second chance to make a first impression, applies* perfectly to interviewing. Look the part you seek. Dress and groom yourself appropriately. Your dress says something about you, so you'll want to be stylish, color coordinated, and neat as a pin. Sloppy, out-of-style clothes tell the employer that you don't care about yourself and your future. Money is not an issue for finding appropriate clothes because enough discount and second-hand clothing stores are available to meet any budget. You only need one or two outfits, and when you do get that third interview, just buy a different shirt, tie, or scarf to change your look a bit.

A general rule of thumb to use when selecting clothes for your interview is to dress at the level of the position you seek or one step above. For example, if you were interviewing for a position as a sales manager you would most likely wear business attire such as a suit or blazer, since most sales managers dress in business clothes. On the other hand, if you were interviewing for a position as a construction fore-person, you would not wear a suit or work clothes. Instead you would dress a bit nicer than work clothes, perhaps casual pants and a button-down or polo-type shirt.

If in doubt as to what type of clothes to wear, investigate. Call the personnel department and ask about the position and the type of dress of their employees. Talk to people in similar jobs in different companies. Another possibility is to visit the place of employment. Use your own judgment, however. A neighbor of mine, for example, works as a computer programmer and wears shorts and T-shirts to work most of the time. On an interview, this type of attire would not be appropriate, since computer programmer is a more professional position.

In another scenario, a young woman interviewed for a position with MTV. She dressed in a funky style, appropriate to the style of the show. Failing to do her homework, she did not know that the company had very conservative management. She lost the employment opportunity because she did not fit the image of the organization. Do your homework, use your best judgment, and follow your intuition.

Look in fashion magazines and talk to personal shoppers in reputable department stores for clothing ideas. You're not obligated to buy the items you are shown. Use the experience to determine your best style. Select simple clean lines that are not too ostentatious. Avoid loud prints. For men, avoid short-sleeved dress shirts, boring ties, out-of-date lapel and tie size, and too-tight pants and shirts. For women, avoid big earrings, frills, busy looking clothes, low-cut necklines, night club type shoes, too-tight skirts, and large cumbersome handbags. The theme for any career is *professional* within the style of the career field.

Good grooming is another important aspect of interviewing. Take care of yourself. Be showered, shaved, clipped, groomed, lotioned, and styled for your interview. Get a fresh hair cut a few days before your interview. Do not wear perfume or cologne. Get a good night's rest and work-out before your interview. You want to be at your best.

THANK YOU LETTERS

Send a thank you letter within one week after your interview. A simple thank you letter shows the employer your genuine interest in the position being offered. It also lets the employer know that you are a professional — polite, detail-oriented, and conscientious. In your letter thank the employer for spending time with you and considering you for the position. Reiterate why you are the right candidate for the job.

JOB SEARCH -
Summarizing The Steps

Below are the basic steps to follow when seeking employment using the direct contact method or any of the other suggestions covered, e.g., classified ads, internet:

1. Decide specifically what you want: *What* do you want to be paid for, *where* do you want to do this work, with *whom* do you want to work? *How much* money do you want to be paid? You may decide to create a new job; if you see a need — fill it! Sell yourself to the employer letting him or her know why you are needed.

2. Select from 10-20 places of employment where you prefer to work. Use sources from the areas mentioned previously, e.g. direct contact, professional association publications.

3. Prepare your resumé and cover letter to fit each position you seek.

4. Send your resumé to the address given on the advertisement. If you're using the direct contact method, telephone each organization you selected and ask for the name of the decision-maker of the department that interests you. Send resumés directly to these decision-makers (even if they are not hiring).

5. Telephone each potential employer about a week or two after your letter and resumé were received. Introduce yourself, discuss your strengths, and set up an appointment to discuss employment opportunities. If the de-cision-maker prefers not to meet, then ask if you can check back in a week or two to see if their employment needs have changed. (Mark on your calendar the date to make your follow-up telephone call.) Ask the potential employer to refer you to another organization that might be seeking someone with your qualifications. Complete this process with each employer, calling every week or so, until you secure the job you want.

6. *Repeat the above steps (1-5) with many organizations, sending resumés and setting up interviews, until you have the job you want. Be persistent!*

7. Prepare answers to typical interview questions. Research the organization you will be interviewing with. Think of interesting questions to ask during the interview, such as questions about the company's goals, services or products, or management style. Rehearse and role-play interviewing with someone you trust.

8. Select appropriate interview clothes. Know exactly how to get to the interview site the day before your appointment. Ask for directions and where you can park. Ask for a telephone number to call in case you run into problems. Carry a map with you. Arrive a bit early.

9. Send a thank you letter to the interviewer. Reiterate why you are the best person to be hired.

10. Telephone within one to two weeks (or less, use your judgment) to determine the next step, i.e. a second interview or employment.

11. After a second interview, send another thank you letter. *REPEAT steps 3-11 until you are hired.*

Apply these steps when seeking any type of work. Decide where you want to work. Determine what skills and benefits you offer an organization. Keep in mind that an attitude is crucial.

> *It's a funny thing about life;*
> *if you refuse to accept anything but*
> *the best,*
> *You very often get it.*

> W. Somerset Maugham

Stay focused and positive and vow to accept only the best. Realize, however, that you may need to secure a lower-level, entry-level, or part-time position first in order to gain the necessary experience for a position you really want. Determine what you can reasonably accept today in order to move to what you would like in the future. Take a job that fits with your skill level. Don't be grandiose, but don't be meek. Follow your dream, while adding a dash of realism.

Finally, remember you won't get a job by *waiting* for them to call you, *you must call them.* Continue to telephone the decision-makers of the organizations you prefer until you meet your goal. You will obtain the position you desire. Keep the faith. Believe in yourself and your potential, letting nothing stop you!

OVERCOMING CHALLENGES

As you move into the action phase of your career expect the best. I am confident that you will have bountiful, positive, synchronistic occurrences bringing you beautiful results. But prepare for set-backs and outcomes you may not like. Even with passion and a firm commitment, challenging times may occur; so be a warrior, ready to get up when you've fallen in the heat of battle.

Unfortunately some individuals have difficulty progressing towards their goals while others sail right on, meeting their goals. If you feel motivated, then skip this section.

If you feel a bit stuck, however, then this section may address an issue that hinders your progress. Ignoring your feelings and intuition and the callings of your soul may inhibit the solidification of certain employment possibilities. Lack of basic skills, low self-esteem, addictions, and unresolved childhood issues can be the cause of procrastination and lack of motivation. Poor etiquette, unrealistic objectives, impatience, and inability to be flexible may be the cause of slow progress. Addressing these issues provides an opportunity for emotional and spiritual growth resulting in a new and more confident you. Scan the next few pages and determine if these areas apply to you.

QUALIFICATIONS

If you have acquired an impressive amount of skills with an interesting work history, there is the possibility that employers may find you *over-qualified.* This doesn't mean that you can't get a job; it usually translates to mean that you need to look for positions more suited to your skill level. Individuals in this situation may want to consider working free-lance or as a consultant. They have now acquired a high level of experience, so working as an independent contractor provides for greater flexibility as well as an increased income.

INTIMIDATION

Believe it or not, often times people are not hired for positions because the interviewers feel intimidated by a job applicant. You may be running into this predicament. Candidates who are articulate, polished, attractive, professional, and well qualified cause less confidant people to feel threatened. Normally this type of scenario is very subtle and only felt subconsciously. Interviewers would not admit to feeling intimidated! People are usually just not that honest. Sometimes voice timbre and height can also cause people to feel inadequate, i.e., tall individuals with deep voices. Honestly evaluate yourself. If you offer a great package as a job applicant and you're not being hired, consider that intimidation may be the culprit. If this is the case, relax. With time you will come across a group of people at your level who *want* to interact with someone of your caliber. Do not sell yourself short, but instead hold out for the work situation that feels right to you.

FINDING YOUR HOME

Quite often people are passed over for a position, not because they were not excellent candidates, but instead, they were just not the right fit for the particular organization. Finding the right job is like finding the right marriage partner. The chemistry must match. By this time you hopefully have selected a profession that complements your essence. Now you must also find a place of employment that does the same. You want to feel comfortable and at ease in your work environment. You want to be with like-minded individuals that speak your language. Your job needs to feel like coming home. So, if you haven't been hired, there's a good chance that you just haven't yet crossed paths with your right people and place. Continue interviewing and investigating!

SUPPORT

Emotional understanding and encouragement from friends and family greatly adds to your chances for success in your pursuits. We are all affected by our environment, so it helps to interact with people who embrace your dreams and desire to see you succeed. Negativity brings us down. Disassociate from critical and judgmental individuals; you don't need the agony. One encouraging friend is far better than ten sabotaging so-called friends! If you need to establish a better network of friends, join a group related to your interests, enroll in personal growth courses, volunteer, join a church, or become active in politics. If you make a conscious effort to change the people you interact with, new people will naturally be brought into your life. Be flexible and open, knowing that you will be supported by the Universe.

BASIC SKILLS

Sometimes individuals possess the necessary drive, determination, and passion for their goals, yet they lack the basic skills. Basic reading, writing, verbal communication, and mathematical abilities are needed for most types of careers. If you feel weak in these areas, contact an adult school, community college, community education center or library in your community for information about courses in these basic areas. If you dropped out of high school or did poorly in school, now is the time to learn these necessary subjects.

SELF-ESTEEM

How you perceive yourself greatly affects your ability to succeed in your career. A simple first step to build confidence is to follow the suggestion of well-known motivational speaker, Tom Hopkins: "If you can't make it, fake it!" For additional growth re-read Chapter One, BELIEF, as well as other self-help books. Implement the suggestions offered. Consider joining a support group and/or going to therapy if your confidence level is really bringing you down.

ETIQUETTE & IMAGE

In addition to having good math and English skills, employers want to hire friendly, courteous, polite, energetic people. It is important that you communicate clearly, behave tactfully, follow business etiquette, and groom and dress appropriately. During the last thirty years, society as a whole has seen a decline in standards of behavior, consequently some individuals are not taught these essential skills.

Some individuals will not advance in their profession because they are rude or dull. Other people are obnoxious and arrogant. Problematic behaviors such as being late, talking too much or too little, not listening, lacking common sense, interrupting an interviewer, not smiling, or being listless can cause you to lose job opportunities. Specific behaviors such as shaking hands and making introductions, if done incorrectly, can cost you a job offer. I have met people who looked away from me when speaking, rarely smiled, and had limp handshakes. Individuals with these types of behaviors will have difficulty obtaining employment and advancing in their careers. We are judged by our behavior; therefore, you must present yourself in a professional, upbeat manner. These are the rules of the *life game* we play.

If you feel that you might fall short in these areas, evaluate yourself or ask someone you trust to assess your social skills and dress. Be bold and call the interviewer of the job you didn't receive and ask if they can suggest any changes you could make in order to improve your chances for being hired. If you want further guidance, look for a workshop offered through community education, perhaps on assertiveness or image. Read newspaper columns such as *Miss Manners, Dear Abby,* or *Ann Landers*; or books, such as Letitia Baldrige's *New Complete Guide To Executive Manners,* or *How To Win*

Friends and Influence People by Dale Carnegie. You *can* learn to be competent in your basic etiquette and communication skills.

ADDICTIONS & CHILDHOOD ISSUES

Addictions and unresolved childhood issues can also hinder your ability to carry through your new career plans. Seek help from friends, support groups, seminars, counseling, and books if you suffer from addictions, such as overeating or drinking, depression or irritability, and irresponsibility such as not keeping commitments. *Alcoholics Anonymous* and other affiliated organizations, i.e. *Overeaters Anonymous*, have successfully helped millions of people. Plus these groups are offered at almost no cost. Check your telephone book for groups and meetings in your area. Consider attending a variety of places until you find a group of people that feel comfortable to you. You may want to see your family physician as well. Explore counseling centers and psychologists in your area. For people with personal issues that obstruct their level of optimal achievement, hundreds of resources exist. Leaving these issues unattended will only inhibit your career growth.

A friend of mine, Donna, dealt with overeating and unresolved childhood anger. Through self-discovery, counseling, and a desire to be free from her chains of obsession, Donna eventually let go of the past and moved to a more positive future. She read numerous self-help books, participated in counseling for a couple of years, and implemented the suggestions she received. At times it was painful for Donna to change, but she felt the benefits far outweighed the alternatives. For Donna, the alternative — to live a limited life, angry and overweight, was no longer an option. The right choice was to change. Once you are enlightened, moving forward *is* your only option.

UNREALISTIC OBJECTIVES & IMPATIENCE

Sometimes individuals have a tendency to expect major change immediately. Television shows and advertisements project the perception that results occur immediately. As viewers we see only the successes of fictional characters and personalities. We rarely see the time, effort, and put into for completion. For example, late night news airs sports highlights of touchdowns, slam dunks, and goals made, but we aren't privy to the *years* of weight-lifting, push-ups, sit-ups, running, throwing, hitting, and team practice athletes give in order to achieve such victories. We only see the glorious moment of triumph. When the Academy Awards are presented we view actors in their glitter accepting awards. But, again we don't see the hours they spent researching characters, rehearsing lines, and filming early mornings and late nights. It's fashionable for the media to highlight the shimmer and glimmer of the moment. In many respects our realities our warped by television. To attain major accomplishments, the artist, athlete, director, manager, doctor, and business owner have all dedicated endless hours, weeks, months, and years developing and improving their craft.

When you feel impatient or frustrated about your progress, think realistically: to be skilled in a field is a lifelong pursuit. Most successes are small achievements. Your career is never fully finished; you are always a *work in progress*. As soon as something appears completed, a new angle or project emerges. Creating is continuous, so be patient.

FLEXIBILITY

Your future may unfold differently than you imagine; thus you must cultivate flexibility and adaptability amoung your skills. What you think *should* happen may not. Your desires may not develop in the time or sequence you planned, so instead accept the resources and contacts that come your way. For instance, you may stay at a job longer than anticipated or receive help from someone unexpectedly. Resources and opportunities may appear when you least expect it. When you allow the life process to happen and do not fight it or manipulate it, you feel at ease. Be willing to go with the flow. Accept your feelings and be thankful that you are learning to move in harmony with the world.

THE JOURNEY –
Onward, Comrade

You are now ready to continue on your road to success! Move in the direction of your dreams knowing that your ultimate motivation must come from you. Your drive comes from *within*. No amount of prodding and coaxing from others to complete your goals will create your success. A deep *desire* to see the completion of your goals and experience the thrill of your own energy moves you to take action.

Sometimes, however, you may feel unmotivated and stuck, unable to achieve your goals. Occasionally you truly need a rest, time to rejuvenate your spirits. Monitor your behavior to determine when you need relaxation and when you need motivation. Sometimes a kick-start provides the jump that gets us on a productive path again. If you seek ideas to increase motivation, try some of these suggestions:

- Write your goals on 3 x 5 cards or post-it notes and put them in strategic places around your house to remind you of your commitments.
- Put pictures of the things you want to have, experience, or become in strategic places around your house to remind you of your desires.
- Listen or dance to upbeat, energetic music.
- Exercise on a regular basis.
- Listen or watch motivational audio and video tapes. These can be purchased at bookstores or checked-out from libraries.
- Telephone your voice mail or answering machine and leave yourself an inspirational or reminder message.
- Find a goal setting buddy — someone you trust who is supportive and available to talk with. Make yourselves accountable to each other. A goal setting group is another alternative.
- Give yourself rewards such as a new shirt, or fun outing when, you achieve a goal.

- Review your goals, noticing where you've been and where you're headed.
- Write a *to do* list with realistic times to complete it.
- Adopt a real or fictitious role-model, someone you can emulate.
- Make a date with yourself. Mark on your calendar when you will work on a particular aspect of your goal.
- List all the benefits you will receive from completing your goals.
- Call a friend and ask for a pep-talk.
- Take a break — just do nothing.
- Relax with a bubble bath, massage, nap in the sun.

Experiment with these ideas. Determine if lack of motivation is really a factor in your life. Sometimes we're just over-worked and we need fun and relaxation! Balance is always the key. Work and play in the proportion that's right for you. These motivational tools can help to create a quick boost of energy; but in the end, you must truly desire your goals, wanting with a burning passion to see them in reality. All the external stimulation in the world means nothing unless you have committed internally.

I salute you with honor.
Together we command a mutual
respect; step one two, one two,
towards destiny.

Each day brings adventurous
movement, building, shaping,
creating the path.

Discipline brings momentum,
momentum brings awareness;
Awareness brings connection,
connection leads to enlightenment.

Enjoyment and love surrounds the
doing for experiencing is all we
have in the end.

CONGRATULATIONS -
You're Making It Happen!

I hope you have begun to incorporate into your life the suggestions offered in this book. You are now geared for the lifelong process of career development. Enjoy the process. Your work is a big piece of your life, so savor the moments preparing and experiencing. Once you arrive at your destination, you'll seek a new goal to conquer, a new path to explore.

Your life is like a garden: you cultivate the land, plant seeds, water the growth, spray the pests, all the while nurturing and loving your creations. Repeat the process throughout the seasons. Prepare yourself for your journey, water and nurture your ideas, ward off unwanted creatures and events, and enjoy your creations. Follow the cycle of the seasons. In Winter we hibernate and contemplate the coming year, deciding how we will create our next year. When Spring arrives we *spring* forward with a new approach. Our fresh ideas begin to sprout. Summer brings abundant growth, with bountiful energy; we blossom with the help of the full day's sun. In Fall we've come full circle, *falling* back and letting go of what we don't want in the coming year. In Winter, we once again contemplate and rest for the new year. Move within these natural cycles of Nature and your life evolves easily.

You've begun an exciting journey. Continue your commitment. Patiently establish your career. If you know what you want, step up and begin now! If you're still exploring, continue the process by conducting more interviews, taking exploratory classes, volunteering in your areas of interest and re-reading parts of this book when necessary. Selecting and working in a profession is a spiritual journey, another rite of passage, so give your soul time to naturally release its desires.

Allow yourself to follow the dream that was born within. See the world with a child-like freshness as you explore and complete your goals. Respect your natural instincts and trust yourself by following the path of your destiny.

I wish for you a peaceful soul and a loving heart. May you attain all you desire. Continue your excellent commitment to yourself by creating your own career success.

Always you have been told that work is a curse and labour a misfortune.
But I say to you that when you work you fulfill a part of earth's furthest dream, assigned to you when that dream was born,
And in keeping yourself with labour you are in truth loving life,
And to love life through labour is to be intimate with life's inmost secret.

The Prophet
Kahlil Gibran

• MAGICAL QUEST CREED •

Creating The Career I Want

- I have a life of purpose.
- I am exploring all my options with enthusiasm.
- I am committed to living the life I have imagined.
- I have taken charge of my life.
- I am on my way to continued success.

_____ *is a CAREER CREATOR.*

I wish for You a fantastic future filled with commitment. excellence. happiness. and love.

_____

Bibliography

A Guide For The Advanced Soul, Susan Hayward. Avalon Beach, Australia: In-Tune Books, 1984.

The Artist's Way: A Spiritual Path to Higher Creativity, Julia Cameron. New York: Jeremy P. Tarcher Putnam Books, 1992

Begin It Now, Susan Hayward. Avalon Beach, Australia: In-Tune Books, 1987.

Chicken Soup For The Soul: 101 Stories To Open The Heart And Rekindle The Spirit, Jack Canfield and Mark Victor Hansen. Deerfield: Florida, Health Communications, Inc. 1993.

Coming Alive From Nine To Five: The Career Search Handbook, Betty Neville Michelozzi. Palo Alto, CA: Mayfield Publishing Company, 1984.

Creating Affluence: Wealth Consciousness In The Field Of All Possibilities, Deepak Chopra, M.D. Navato, CA: New World Library, 1992.

Creative Visualization, Shakti Gawain. Navato, CA: New World Library, 1979.

The Damn Good Resume Guide, Yana Parker. Berkeley, CA: Ten Speed Press, 1989.

Live Your Dreams, Les Brown. Les Brown Unlimited, New York: William Morrow & Co., 1992.

The New Webster's Library of Practical Information, compiled by Donald O. Bolander. Lexicon Publications, Inc., 1987.

Please Understand Me: Character & Temperament Types, David Keirsey and Marilyn Bates. Del Mar, CA: Prometheus Nemesis Book Company, 1984.

The Prophet, Kahlil Gibran. New York: Alfred. A. Knopf, 1985.

Reflections In The Light, Shakti Gawain. Navato, CA: New World Library, 1988.

The Resume Catalog: 200 Damn Good Examples, Yana Parker. Berkeley, CA: Ten Speed Press, 1998

Think And Grow Rich, Napoleon Hill. New York: Fawcett Crest Books, 1960.

The Treasury Of Quotes, Jim Rohn. Irving, TX: Jim Rohn International, 1993.

You'll See It When You Believe It, Dr. Wayne W. Dyer. New York: Avon Books, 1989.

Women Who Run With The Wolves, Clarissa Pinkola Estes, Ph.D. New York: Ballantine Books, 1995.

NOTES

Magical Quest
Six Steps to Career Success

To order *Magical Quest* complete the following information:

Name:_____

Address:_____

City:_____ State_____ Zip _____

Telephone:_____

email address:_____

Magical Quest: quantity_____@ $18.00 per book   = _____
(Discounts on quantities of 10 or more, please inquire.)

Sales Tax: add 8.25% for products shipped in CA   = _____

Shipping: $4.00 for first copy, $2.00 for each additional copy = _____

TOTAL: make check or money order to Tarin Frances   = _____

Send this form and payment to:

Sirene Impressions
3712 East First
Long Beach, CA 90803
USA
Telephone: (562) 438-0545
email address: tarinfrances@earthlink.net

Send Us Your Thoughts!

My staff and I would love to hear from you. Let us know your thoughts and feelings about the book and your career travels! Use this page to drop us a note; mail to the address below.

With love and peace,

Sirene Impressions
3712 East First Street
Long Beach, CA 90803
USA
email - tarinfrances@earthlink.net

Magical Quest
Six Steps to Career Success

To order *Magical Quest* complete the following information:

Name:_____

Address:_____

City:_____ State_____ Zip _____

Telephone:_____

email address:_____

Magical Quest: quantity_____@ $18.00 per book   = _____
(Discounts on quantities of 10 or more, please inquire.)

Sales Tax: add 8.25% for products shipped in CA   = _____

Shipping: $4.00 for first copy, $2.00 for each additional copy = _____

TOTAL: make check or money order to Tarin Frances   = _____

Send this form and payment to:

Sirene Impressions
3712 East First
Long Beach, CA 90803
USA
Telephone: (562) 438-0545
email address: tarinfrances@earthlink.net

Send Us Your Thoughts!

My staff and I would love to hear from you. Let us know your thoughts and feelings about the book and your career travels! Use this page to drop us a note; mail to the address below.

With love and peace,

Sirene Impressions
3712 East First Street
Long Beach, CA 90803
USA
email - tarinfrances@earthlink.net

NOTES

NOTES

NOTES

NOTES

NOTES

NOTES

NOTES

NOTES

NOTES

NOTES

NOTES

NOTES